INK FOR PRINTMAKING

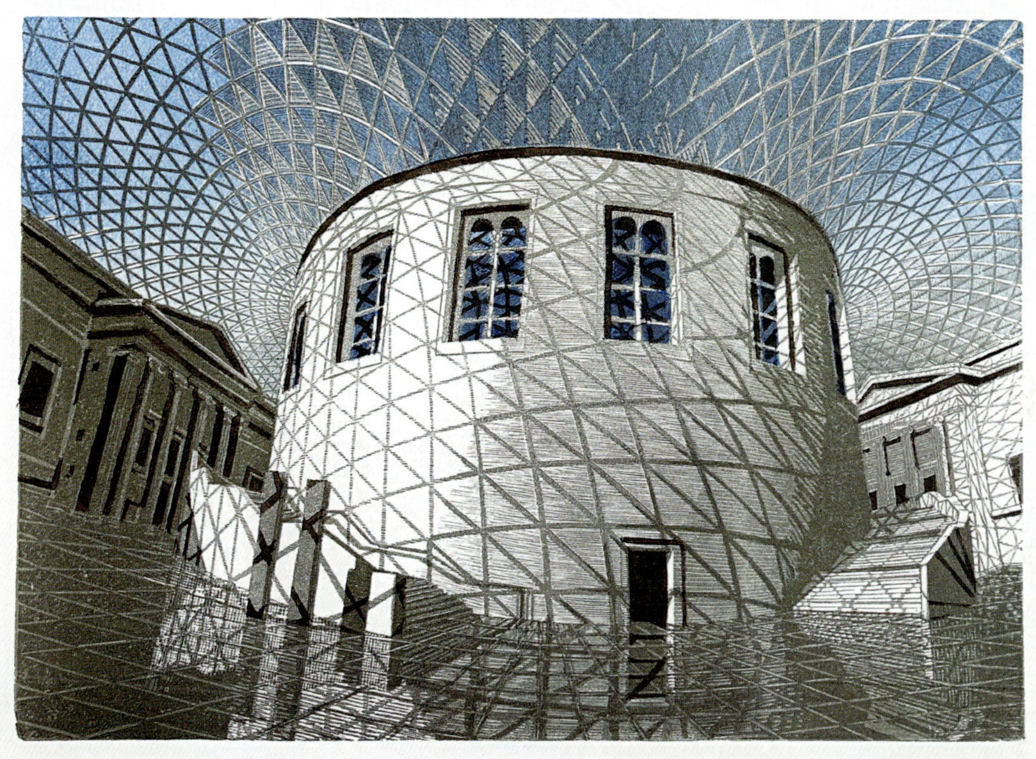

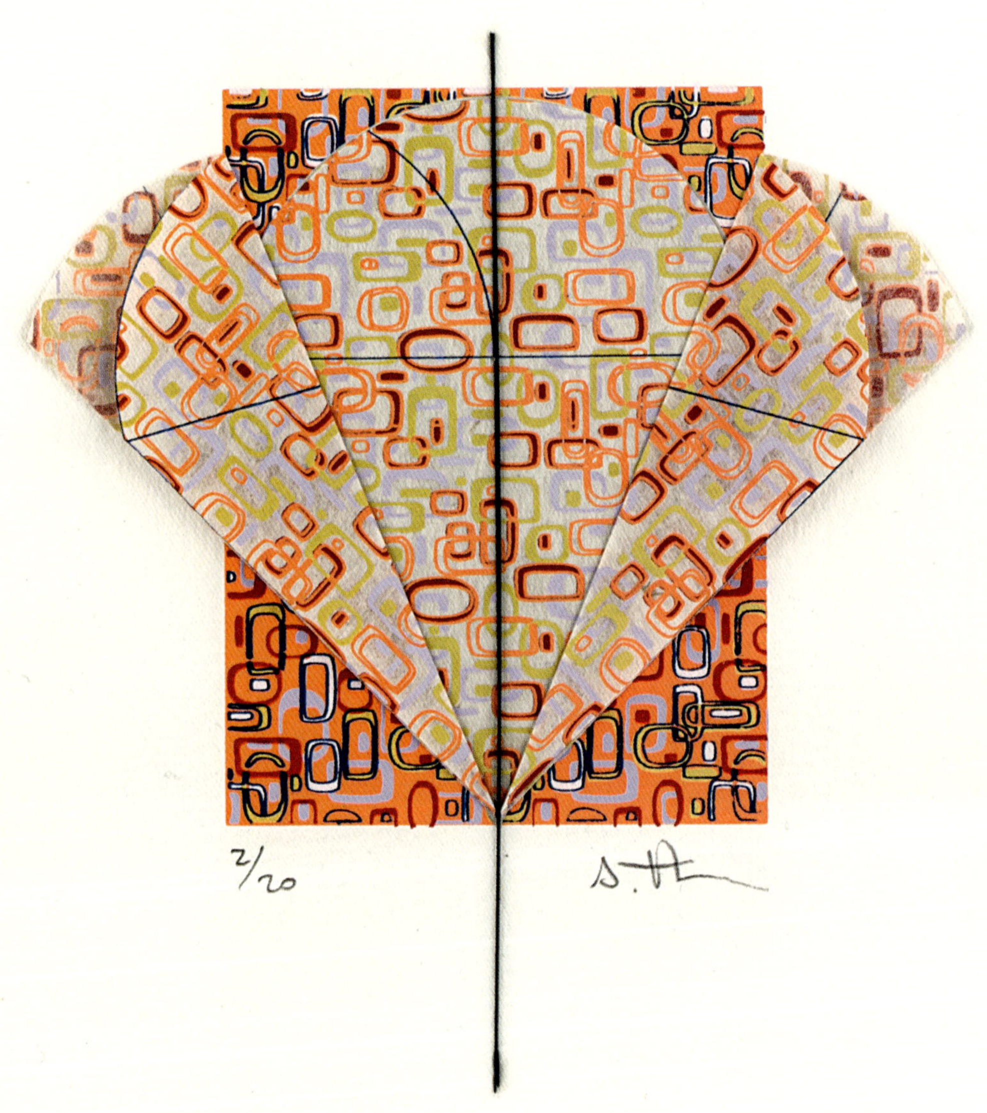

2/20

INK FOR PRINTMAKING

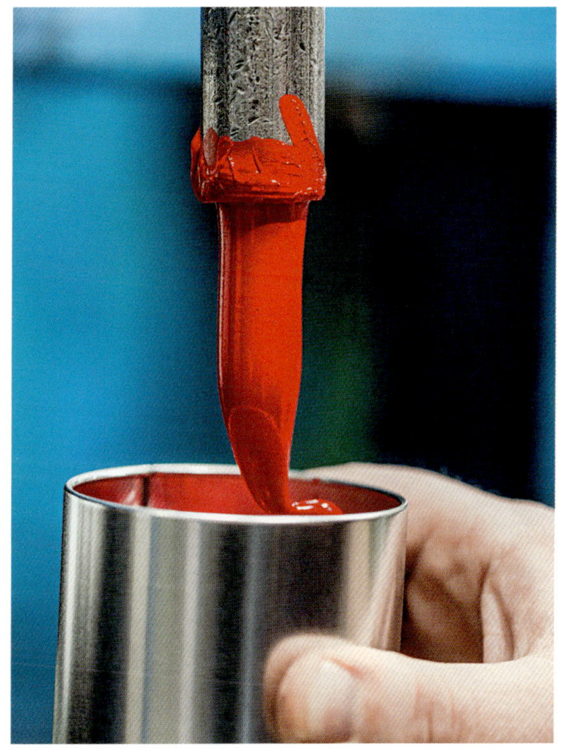

THE ART, CRAFT AND CHEMISTRY OF INK

STEPHEN HOSKINS AND MICHAEL CRAINE

HERBERT PRESS
LONDON · OXFORD · NEW YORK · NEW DELHI · SYDNEY

HERBERT PRESS
Bloomsbury Publishing Plc
50 Bedford Square, London, WC1B 3DP, UK
Bloomsbury Publishing Ireland Limited,
29 Earlsfort Terrace, Dublin 2, D02 AY28, Ireland

BLOOMSBURY, HERBERT PRESS and the Herbert Press logo are trademarks of
Bloomsbury Publishing Plc

First published in Great Britain 2025

A catalogue record for this book is available from the British Library

Library of Congress Cataloguing-in-Publication data has been applied for

ISBN: 978-1-7899-4202-6; eBook: 978-1-7899-4203-3

2 4 6 8 10 9 7 5 3 1

Page layout design by Jerry Goldie Graphic Design
Printed and bound in Dubai

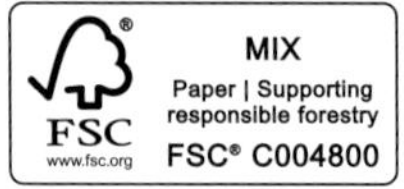

To find out more about our authors and books visit www.bloomsbury.com and sign up for our newsletters

For product safety related questions contact productsafety@bloomsbury.com

Front cover
Top: **Henrik Simonsen** *Yellow light,* **2016. Screen print, 90 x 80 cm.**
Photo: Sally Gimpson © Henrik Simonsen
Bottom: **Red, yellow and blue pigment.**
Photo: Jo Hounsome
Photography © Cranfield Colours

Back cover
Hegman or fineness-of-grind (FOG) gauge.
Photo: Jo Hounsome
Photography © Cranfield Colours

Page 1
Anne Desmet *British Museum – Blue Sky*, **2023. Wood engraving (on lemonwood block) with linocut and stencil printing, 17.4 x 24.8 cm.**
Photo: Anne Desmet © Anne Desmet

Page 2
Stephen Hoskins *70's Wallpaper*, **2020. Screen print, handmade paper and carbon fibre rod, 28 x 38 cm.**
Photo: S. Hoskins © S. Hoskins

Page 3
Tubing etching ink.
Photo: Jo Hounsome
Photography © Cranfield Colours

CONTENTS

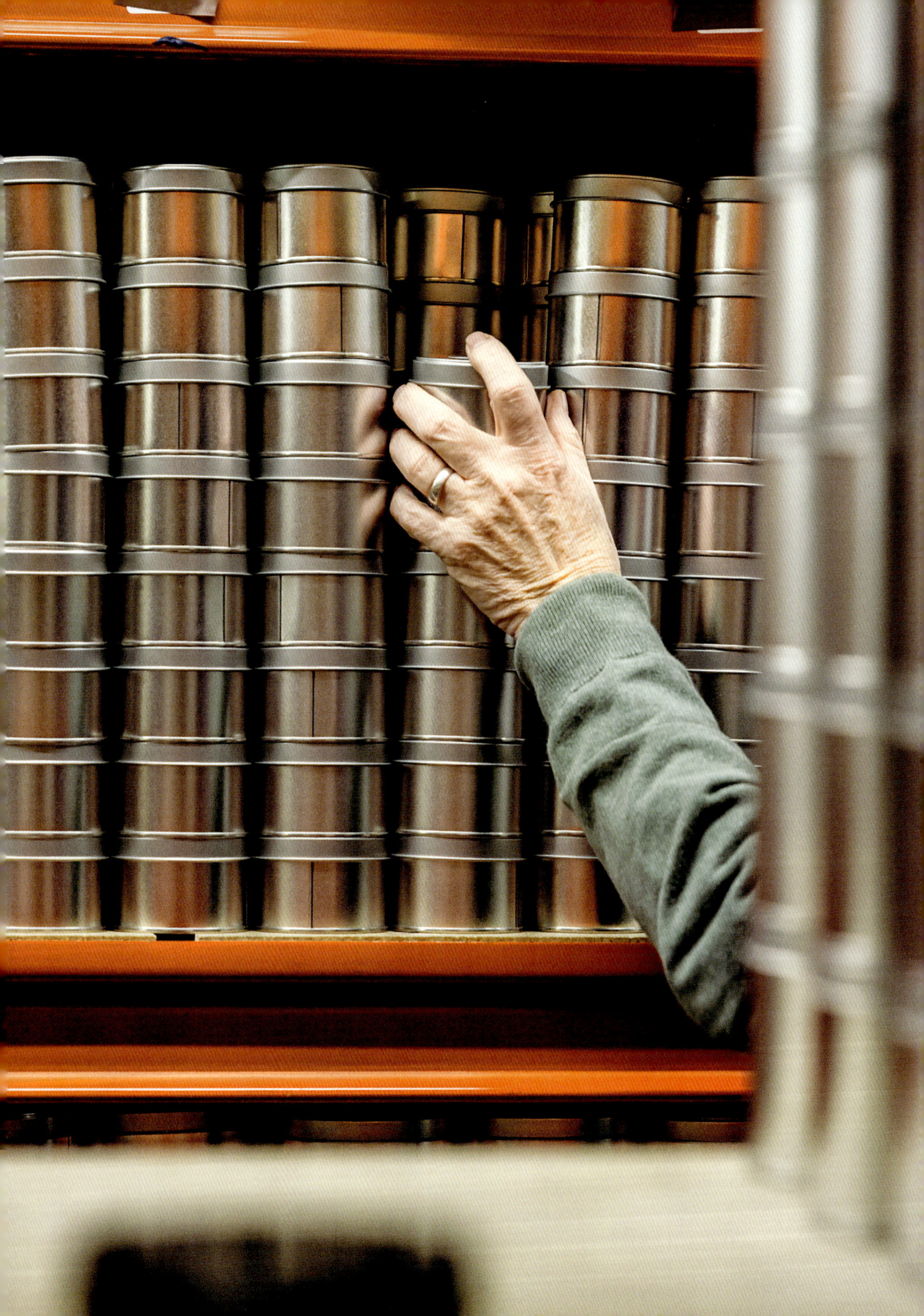

INTRODUCTION

Stephen Hoskins' original book *Inks* was published in 2004 and written during 2002–3, when published material on printmaking was primarily the preserve of those who had access to presses, dedicated materials, and formal training or tutelage from an experienced printmaker or editioning studio. At that time, the young internet's global reach was 682 million people: less than 10 per cent of the population. As of July 2024, there are 5.45 billion internet users worldwide, which amounts to 66 per cent of the global population; in the UK, it is closer to 98 per cent, and in the USA, 97 per cent. This reach has democratised the practice of printmaking.

This democratisation has led to the emergence of an entirely new and expanding breed of printmakers who produce prints of high quality on low-cost tabletop presses or even with a spoon or Japanese baren. This, in turn, has increased demand for open-access printmaking and editioning studios. It has also facilitated the creation of large communities of like-minded printmaking practitioners. The internet is both an educational tool and a platform for self-help and problem solving; what it does not do is offer a comprehensive overview of how printmaking ink is made, an accessible and concise history of ink development, or guidance and information on its manufacture and use. This volume aims to address those issues.

Twenty years ago, artists tended to have favourite colours or types of ink across a range of brands without necessarily favouring any particular one. Yet their choices of ink influenced the image to be printed. During Stephen Hoskins' original research, he was heartened by discussions about the relation of process to concept, in a period when craft process was something that critics found unfashionable and often dismissed as a lesser activity and not an integral part of the creation of a work of art.

In the intervening years, the process of making ink has regained respect, and with it an awareness that inks are central to the art itself. Printmakers, through blogs and social media channels, are far more vocal about their preferences. This is good for sharing and overcoming problems, but can be dangerous when erroneous advice or theories are put forward with little or no regulation or solid background research to support them.

◀ **Tins of ink ready for labelling.** Photo: Jo Hounsome Photography © Cranfield Colours

While speaking to the creators and makers of art back in 2003, it was clear that knowing how to achieve results was of crucial interest, and this remains so. We were and are therefore particularly grateful to all the artists and studios who sent documentation of the ink they used. Among these was the exemplary practice of institutions such as Tamarind Institute in Albuquerque, New Mexico and USF Graphicstudio in Florida, which keeps records of processes employed alongside the normal socio-historic documentation that is undertaken by art critics and historians.

We hope that in time this will become the norm accepted by all museums and collectors. To understand the artist's true intention, the means of making should be viewed alongside a work's conceptual and social context. The *why* and the *how* are essential aspects in advancing knowledge and abilities in our field. Because people create fine prints, much has been written about *why*, but little has been written about contemporary progress in *how* to create beautiful print results. This book has been written to redress this balance in a small way.

Why do printmakers need to know what is in their ink, apart from knowing it can affect their health and the environment? Because it is a great deal easier to make good art if you understand the nature of the materials you are using.

Printmaking is at heart based upon technical process; although printmaking no longer bears any close relation to the high-tech, large-scale commercial printing process, at some points they are still connected. This can be illustrated easily by referring to prints' historical contexts, as all printmaking techniques were once industrial processes. Ink and its manufacture still bridge the divide between industry and art.

A quick search using keywords on the internet reveals a wealth of information, but we know of no other contemporary book that focuses solely on ink for printmakers. The primary texts concerned with the history of ink and printing date from the early and mid twentieth century, and deal in copperplate or simple relief and lithographic inks; one was written by Wiborg in 1926, the other by Bloy in 1967. A historical link between the production of ink for commercial and artists' use comes in that Michael Craine's grandfather designed the manufacturing plant for the Ault & Wiborg ink factory in 1940s London.

No history of printmakers can be written without reference to the second book, *A History of Printing Ink, Balls and Rollers, 1440–1850*. In fact, the only printmaking book that deals with ink to any extent, apart from Abraham Bosse's book on etching from 1655, is the *Tamarind Book of Lithography*, which covers only ink for lithography. Anthony Gross gives a more contemporary description of how to make etching ink in his 1970 book on etching. There are also

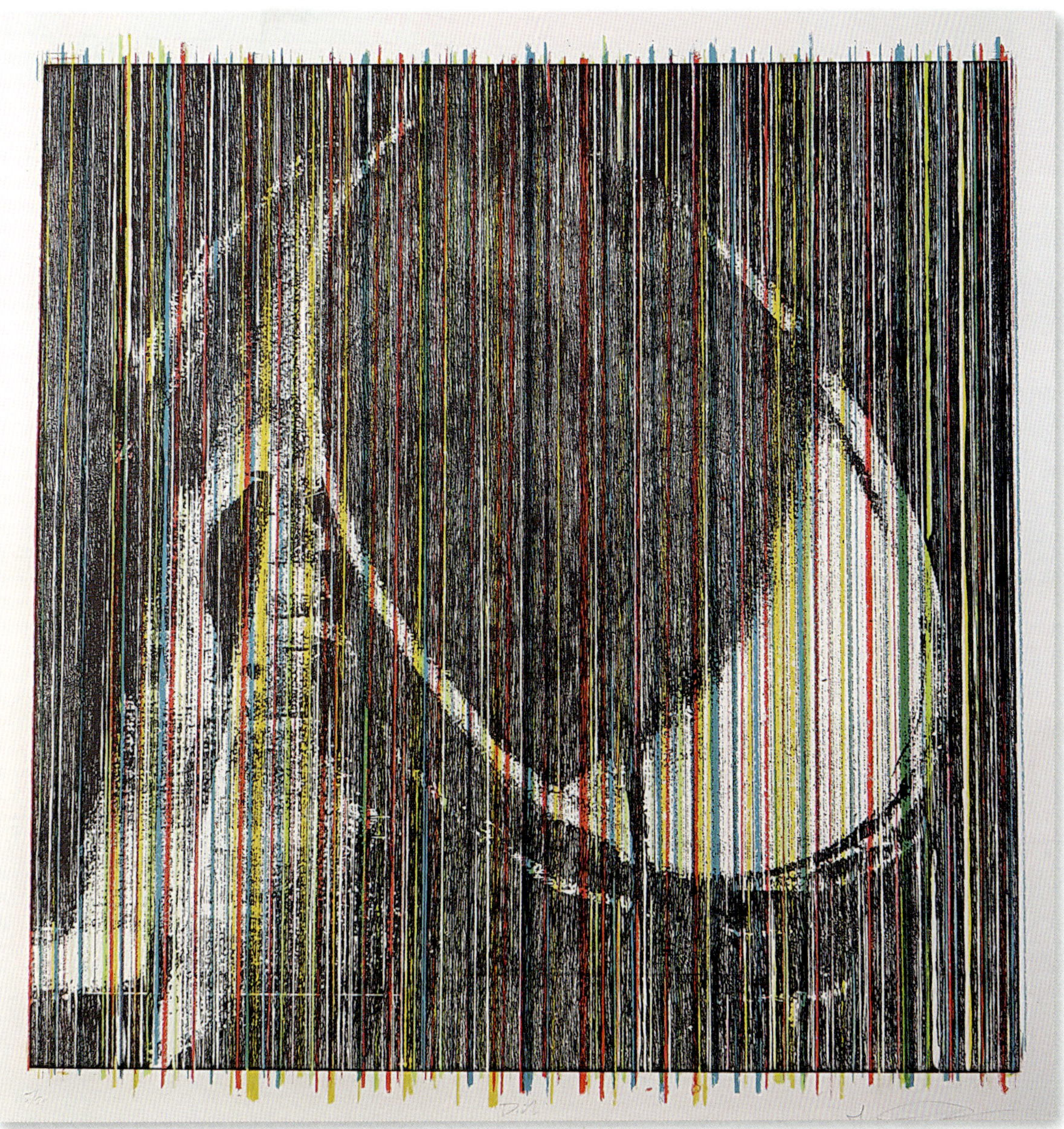

several short discussions in other major printmaking books, usually limited to describing only a particular brand or discipline. However, the processes of constructing ink for etching, relief and lithography are very similar, and it makes sense to have all the information in one book.

This study gives an overview of the development of the classic printmaking processes. It supplies the principles that not only allow us to understand the ink aspects for printing but also to create the adaptations in ink, which will allow the artist to fine-tune their skills in developing their print. It also provides insight into the changes that have taken place over the last 20 years – the acceptance of inkjet, digital, laser cutting and Risograph as integral parts of the printmaking canon – in addition to the continuing rise of relief printing and letterpress, particularly *mokuhanga,* as a means of reducing the overall environmental footprint of the concerned printmaker.

While this book deals with a specific artistic niche, it provides much needed answers to important questions about the process of inkmaking, and the properties of the ink itself. We will not always answer every question in detail, but we will indicate directions in which those answers may be found.

For example, there is much confusion over the distinction between what is an environmentally safe ink and what is safe for the user. There is, equally, much confusion as to the properties of a lightfast ink and which inks are, therefore, lightfast, what this means for printmakers, and whether ink or paper is in itself 'archival', or if it is a product that can contribute to the archival properties of the finished print.

Extending the ability of modern print includes understanding the differing needs and properties of, say, a commercial ink developed for high-speed lithography and inks specifically developed for the printmaker.

This book talks, therefore, about the construction of ink for different printing processes and what the constituents are primarily made from. It also contains a historical framework to provide context for the information about ink and printing. We then cover the description of the principles of ink manufacture and its behaviour on the press, and its final result in terms of permanency and decay of the image. We conclude with a listing organised to help printers navigate these principles and their own professional practice. These chapters on process try to describe the specific properties required and available from an ink. The tension between requirement and availability generates the need to know how to adjust or alter the basic product for a particular task. A comprehensive listing of manufacturers and suppliers has been included, together with a glossary of technical terms and their printmaking translations.

Despite co-author Michael Craine's role as managing director of Cranfield Colours, and because of Stephen Hoskins' role as an academic researcher, we have strived to be impartial and not to promote any particular brand of ink. The choice of ink remains a subjective decision related to the requirements of the individual artist, the method used to print, and the paper surface to be printed on. We do, however, firmly believe that tailor-made printmaking ink will invariably suit an artist better than a commercial-process ink. Therefore, recommending one particular brand above another is not relevant. The views about particular brands of ink are those expressed by the artists and studios interviewed for this book and, although they may help you make an informed choice, bear in mind that their choices are made to suit their own particular circumstances and subjective judgements.

▶ A batch of ink after mixing and before milling. Photo: Jo Hounsome Photography © Cranfield Colours

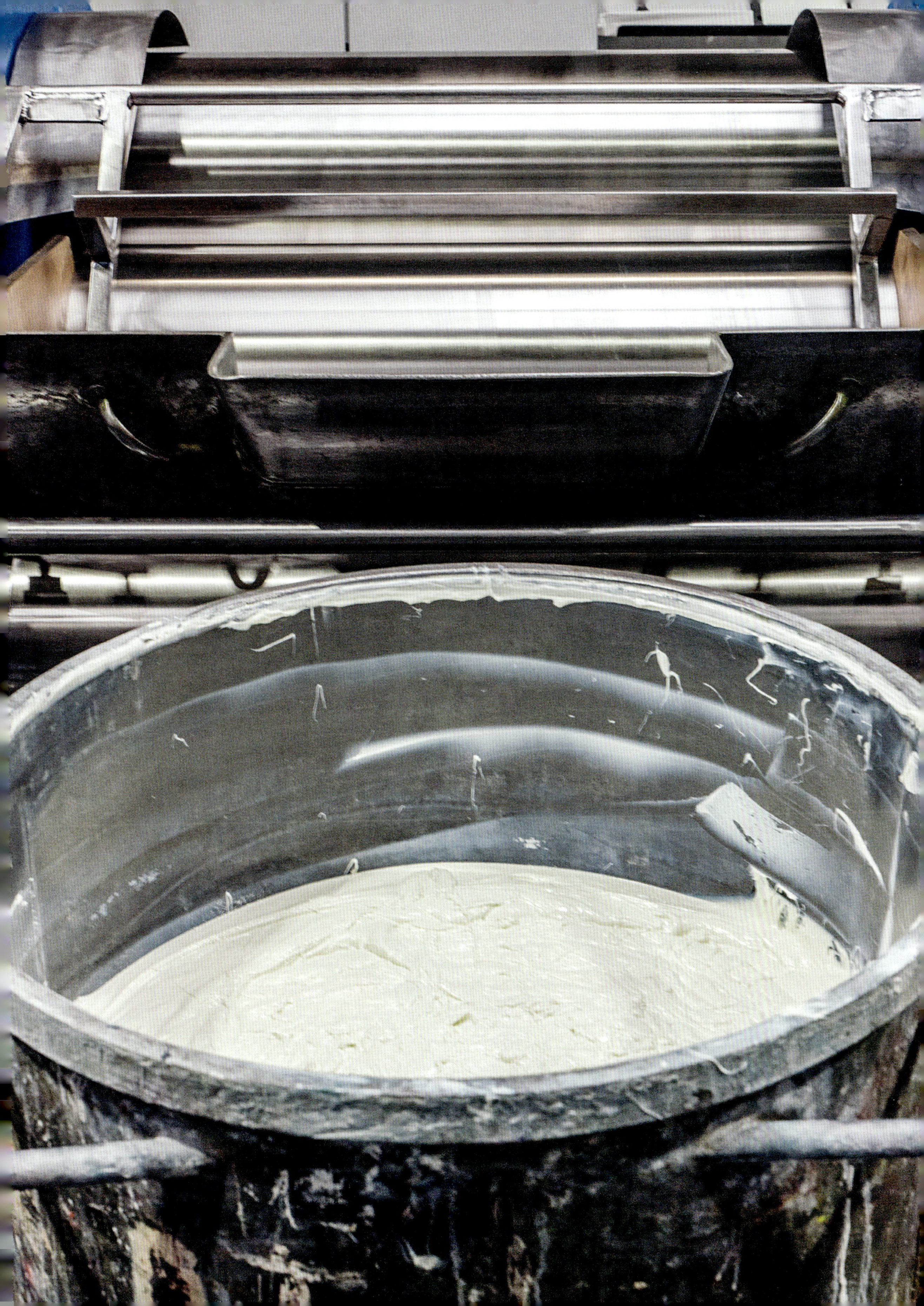

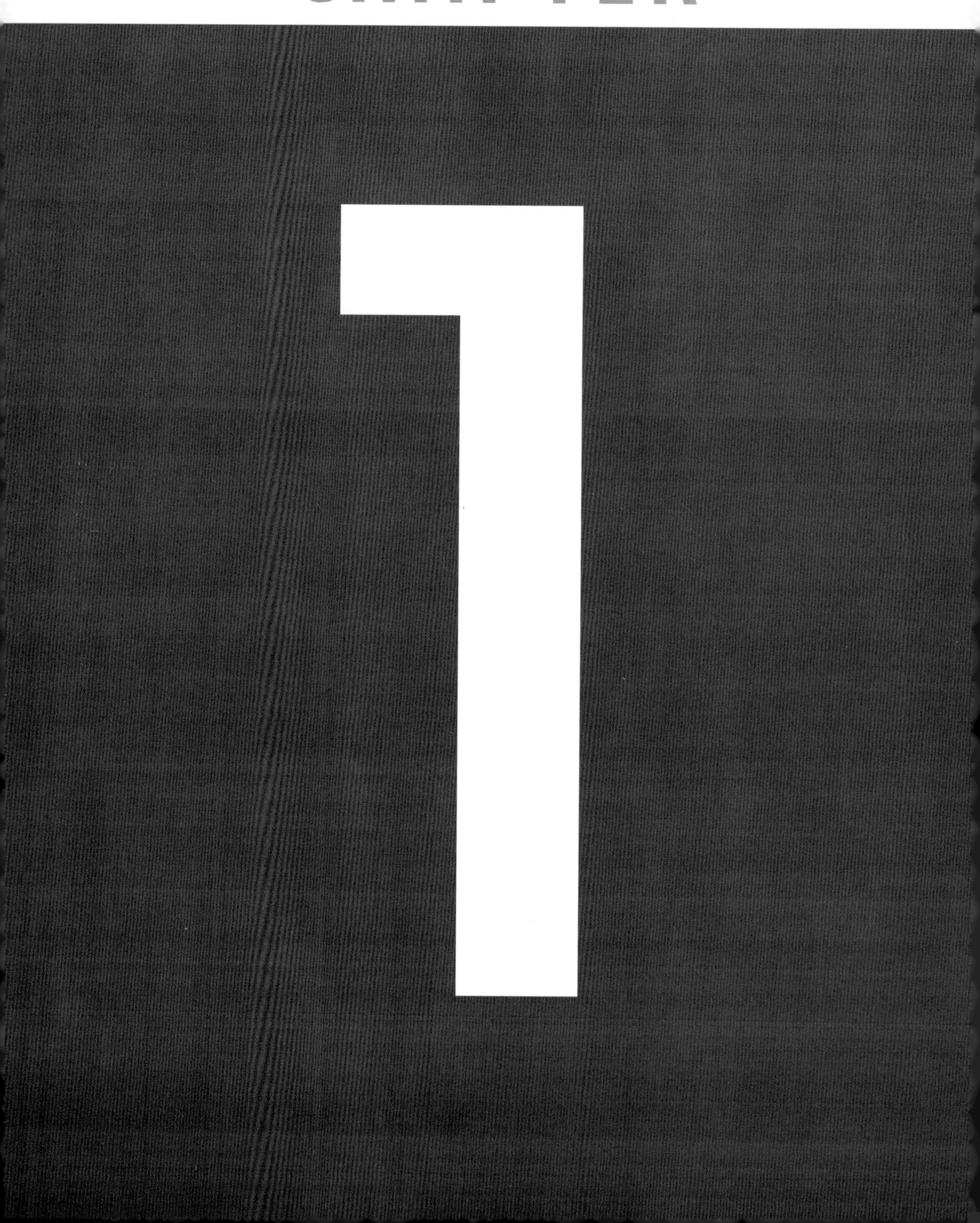
CHAPTER
1

HISTORY

THE DEVELOPMENT OF INKS

The history of printing is determined by three fundamental material developments: the creation of ink, the development of paper and the use of a printing matrix. The development of ink and paper occurred separately to the invention of the printing matrix, which came much later. Carter and Goodrich's seminal text from 1923, *Invention of Printing in China and Its Spread Westward*,[1] states that the history of ink is obscure, but there are indications that a writing ink may have been used on a bamboo book that predates paper – the *Zhushu Jinian* from 299 BCE.

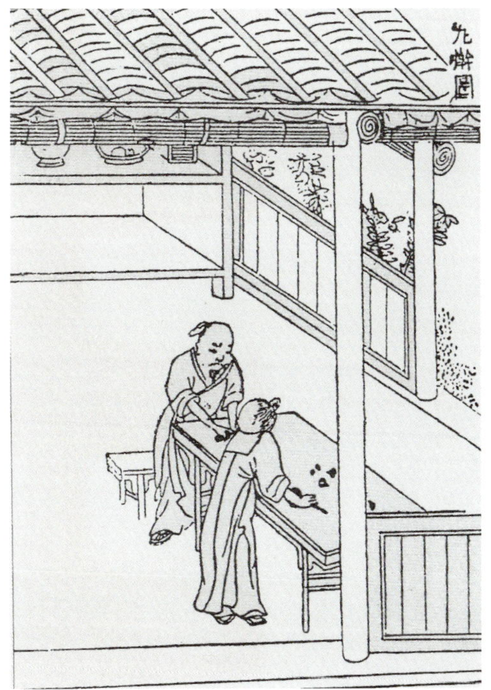

▼ **Chinese ink manufacture in the 14th century: rolling sticks of ink.** Image from 1882 publication by Maurice Jametel.

Carter and Goodrich cite popular opinion that the development of a writing and printing ink was ascribed to a Wei Tan, who died in AD 251. This ink consisted of lampblack mixed with a gum solution to make a paste, which was then dried into blocks or sticks; the stick was rubbed with water on a concave stone just before use. This method, which is still in use, produces excellent ink for printing woodblocks and for writing, but is at its best when used with absorbent paper, which soaks the ink up so that clear traces can be seen on the back of the printed paper.

The second material element is paper, the creation of which, according to Carter, is often ascribed to the eunuch Cài Lún in AD 105. Carter was sceptical that this date was correct, and evidence now disputes that attribution. Yi Xumei and Lu Xiuwen describe how, '[i]n 1986, a paper map was excavated from a mausoleum of the Han Dynasty at Fangmatan, Tianshui, Gansu. Archaeological study has indicated that it is the map of the Qin Kingdom of the

Warring States Period. On this map, mountains, water and roads are drawn with ink. The paper is of khaki, the remaining part of which is 5.6 cm long and 2.6 cm wide. This map can be dated to periods of the Wen (187–179 B.C.) and Jin (156–141 B.C.).'[2]

Woodblocks were first used during the Sui Dynasty (AD 581–618) and became popular in the Tang Dynasty (AD 618–707). Many records and artefacts survive from this time. The earliest extant examples of woodblock printing are Buddhist writings, found in Turpan, Xinjiang and in Gyeongju, Korea. A scroll of the *Pure Light Dharani Sutra*, printed between AD 706 and 751, was found in a stone stupa (pagoda) in Gyeongju.[3] This sutra was printed with 12 woodblocks and glued together to form a scroll 630 cm long. It was printed on Korean paper produced from mulberry bark. Black writing ink, first developed in China, has changed very little over the centuries but in modern times, the introduction of coloured sticks has expanded the range of writing inks. Both are still obtainable in blocks and sticks, just as they were 2,000 years ago.

Although the Chinese had a method of movable wooden type for printing books, it was the Koreans in the twelfth century who first invented movable metal type. The earliest extant example of a work printed using movable metal types is the *Jikji*, printed at the old Heungdeoksa temple in Cheongju city in July 1377. *Jikji* was printed in two volumes; the first volume has not yet been found, but a copy of the second is kept in the National Library of France. The Koreans were printing books in volume by the time of Gutenberg in the fourteenth century,[4] but Gutenberg's greatest innovation was combining available, usable skills into a single printing system: winepress technology was adapted for print, and the gunsmith's precision-casting ability was used to create type; finally, and specifically relevant to this book, the recent ink improvement for printing saints' pictures and playing cards was adapted and became essential for all printing.[5]

Although some authors claim that Gutenberg invented oil-based ink, the commercial picture printers had been using this technique since the early 1400s. According to Colin Clair, 'the earliest dated European form of xylographic or woodblock prints are religious souvenirs known as "helgen". The earliest recorded helgen is a portrait of the Virgin dated 1418 in the Royal Library in Brussels'.[6] A Florentine inventory from 1430 lists woodblocks for printing cards and images of saints 22 years before Gutenberg first printed.[7] The invention of oil-based paint lies much earlier, as evidenced by the Buddhist wall paintings at Bamiyan in Afghanistan. The paintings date from the seventh to the ninth centuries, and contain the earliest extant examples of the use of oil paint; the binding medium was either walnut or poppy oil. *The Wall Paintings*

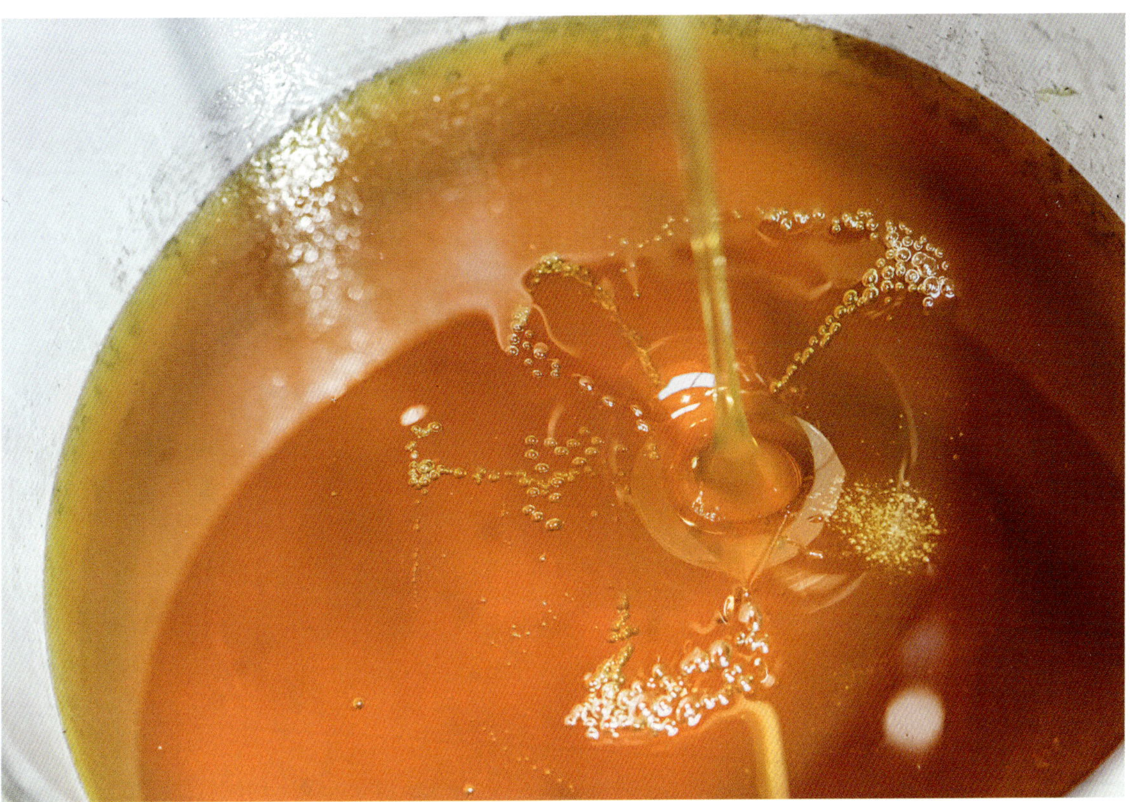

of Bamiyan, Afghanistan extensively documents the use of oil paints.[8]

Gutenberg's significant contribution (without underestimating his contribution to type founding and casting) was the use of an oil-bound ink in printing metal type. Its introduction was caused by his use of movable metal type and, of course, the invention of the printing press. A water-soluble ink will not easily print from metal as the ink is repelled from metal's naturally greasy surface. Therefore, it made more sense to use ink bound in oil to avoid rejection, and so that the ink would adhere to the metal surface. This type of ink has the added advantage of being waterproof and therefore not susceptible to mould: an important consideration in damp Northern European climates. Gutenberg did not invent oil-based colour; the first steps in using oil-bound paint by European artists were happening at the same time. According to Vasari in *Lives of the Artists*, Jan van Eyck invented oil paint around 1410,[9] although this has long been disputed. Van Eyck was one of the earliest Northern European painters to use the technique, as demonstrated by the painting of *The Arnolfini Portrait* from 1434. The actual ingredients of Gutenberg's ink have been the subject of much speculation, although there is no doubt over the quality of his ink and printing.

THE EARLY RELATIONSHIP BETWEEN PAPER AND INK

Paper from this era also plays a significant role in the development of oil-based ink. Unlike the thin, delicate paper from the Far East, which could be rubbed onto the printing block without tearing, European writing paper was much thicker and rougher, with a heavy-size coating. To obtain a good print, the paper has first to be damped, allowing the paper fibre to soften and swell. The printing matrix and paper are then put into a screw press, where the type can be pressed into the soft, damp paper under pressure. A water-based ink would bleed in these circumstances; the oil-based ink gives a crisp, clean impression.

The oil has remained a constant throughout the history of artists' ink in Europe. Linseed oil is still the primary ingredient; the only discernible change is in the method of processing. Historically, linseed was literally burnt. This highly dangerous process consisted of heating the oil in a lidded copper cauldron placed on a tripod over a fire until it boiled – Moxon's *Mechanick Exercises* from 1684 illustrates such a cauldron.[10] As the fumes came off the boiling oil, they were ignited with a lighted piece of paper attached to a long stick and allowed to burn. This might happen seven or eight times in a boiling. The length of time the oil burnt determined the viscosity, and therefore strength, of the oil. A short period of burning resulted in the equivalent of a light copperplate oil. A long period resulted in strong oil, more akin to a strong copperplate oil or a heavy litho varnish. This process does not fundamentally change the chemical composition of the oil; it just renders it more viscous.

There are many apocryphal tales stemming from the history of this process, and it is no surprise that varnish makers were traditionally banished beyond the city walls due to the high volatility and potentially explosive properties of boiling linseed oil. Many early recipes list the use of onions or bread to alter the characteristics of the oil.[11] It is now assumed that these additions did very little to alter the chemical nature of the ink; they were probably either indicators of temperature, or helped to clear scum and impurities in the oil from its surface as it boiled. The apocryphal tales suggest the oil-soaked bread was given to the apprentices as a preventive against tuberculosis.

Oil-based typographic ink as used by Gutenberg did not change significantly over the next 300 years, apart from the addition of rosin to aid stiffness and to stop the ink spreading when printed on the paper, and litharge, or oxide of lead, which was used as a drying agent. Typographic printing from cast lead type (letterpress) was to dominate commercial printing for the next 500 years.

For printmaking, with its wide range of techniques, it is necessary to consider ink in more detail. Each of the major printmaking processes has developed its own variation, which in turn has set the reference points for contemporary inks available on the market.

THE DEVELOPMENT OF RELIEF PRINTING AND ITS DEMAND FOR INK CHARACTERISTICS

The earliest woodblocks in the West were used for textile printing. It is thought that textile printing may have originated in India around 3000 BCE, although no textiles or blocks have survived. Strabo (63 BCE–AD 20) documents Indian printed textiles, and Pliny the Elder (AD 23–79) describe what sounds like the painting of textiles before dyeing with various mordants to tint the fabric various colours. The earliest extant printed example is a child's tunic from Akhmim in Upper Egypt.[12] It dates from the fourth century AD and is white linen, block-printed in blue with a diamond-shaped pattern. Two early wooden blocks for printing remain in existence.

The earliest woodcuts on paper in the West date from between about 1402 and about 1425.

The John Rylands Research Institute and Library at the University of Manchester has in its collection a woodcut of St Christopher, dated 1423.[13] The majority of these early prints are characterised by bold cuts, where the wood has been cut away to leave a strong black line, which was then hand-coloured. By the second half of the century, the prints became more complex. Albrecht Dürer was the unsurpassed master of the woodcut in the late fifteenth century. His cuts are so detailed it is almost impossible to believe they were cut from a plank of wood. The nature of woodcuts – that they were printed from blocks of wood – saw them

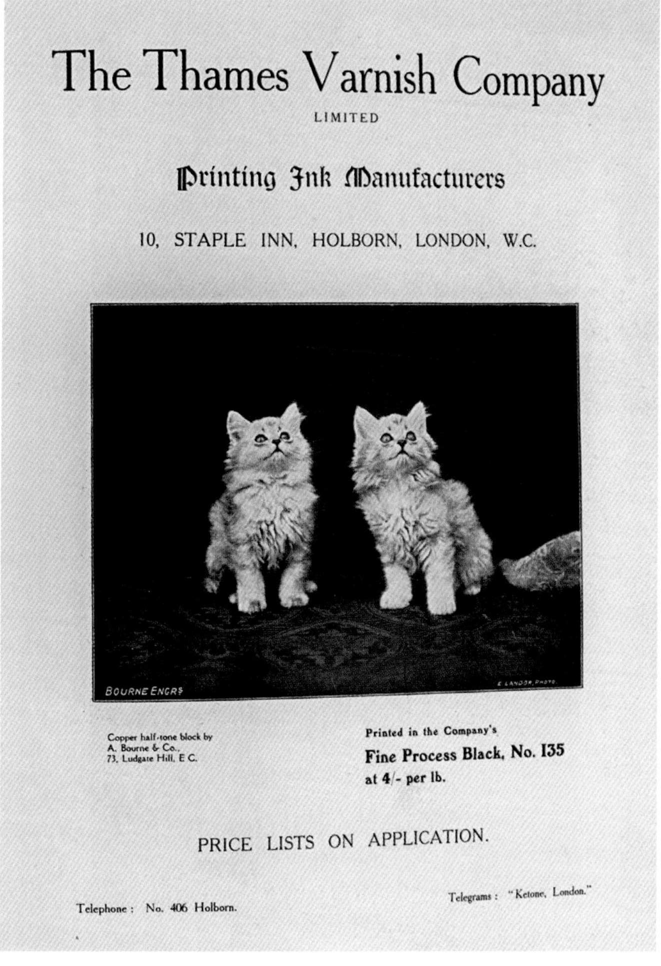

▼ **Thames Varnish Company advertisement from the *Penrose Annual*, 1905.** Photo: Jo Hounsome Photography

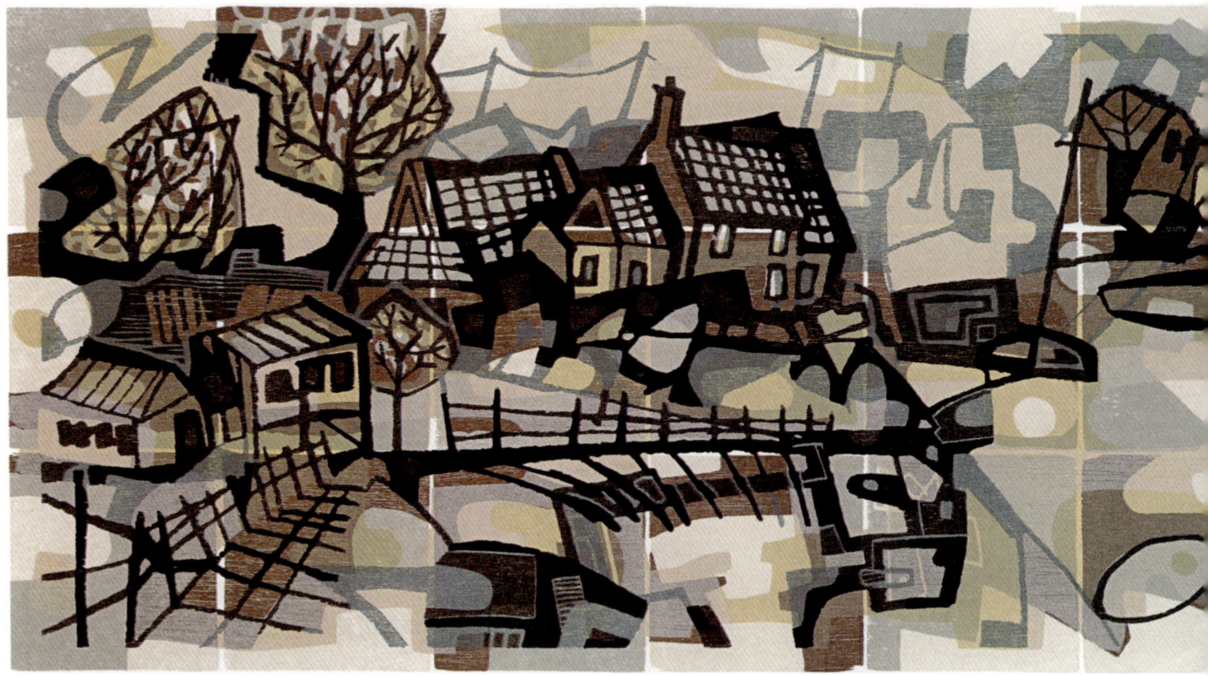

▲ **Neil Bousfield *Corner Cottage*, 2024. Woodcut, 16 x 32 cm.** Photo: Neil Bousfield © Neil Bousfield

progress from being a single picture to serving as illustrations in the text. Blocks could be cut type-high and locked into the chase to be inked and printed with the metal type.

In the eighteenth and nineteenth centuries, the practice of engraving the end-grain rather than the plank allowed an increasing sophistication of printed line. Thomas Bewick was the early master of this technique in England, and during the nineteenth century wood engraving became the primary means of commercial text illustration; in the late 1870s, the Dalziel Brothers employed up to 36 engravers at one time to meet demand.[14] After the introduction of photo-etching zinc plates in the early twentieth century, wood engraving as a commercial process died out. It was much easier to make an etched zinc photoplate in either halftone or line and then mount it on a block to type-high than to spend days engraving a small block of end-grain wood. Size was no longer a restriction.

In the 1920s, wood engraving underwent a revival, and was used by the likes of Clare Leighton, Joan Hassall, Gwen Raverat, Agnes Miller Parker and Gertrude Hermes. In recent years wood engraving has again enjoyed great popularity.

In the twentieth century, with the introduction of the linocut and the general broader scope of printing now more commonly known as relief printing, the ink deposit seems to have become much heavier. Hoskins wrote in 2003 that

many contemporary prints were characterised by an almost physical surface quality of ink that can be seen in the work of artists such as Sandy Sykes and Stephen Mumberson. This change in ink deposit is an indication of the split that occurred around the 1920s between commercial art prints and limited edition fine-art prints. It is at this point that the manufacture of printmaking inks for artists began to diverge from that of commercial ink. This is partly because the artist demands an ink with very different drying, tack and adhesion properties, and one that will not fade or cause metameric properties when mixed. The nature of the thicker ink deposit was perhaps a phenomenon more prevalent during the end of the last century.

In recent times, perhaps influenced by the rise in letterpress and *mokuhanga*, thinner ink films seem to be more of the norm. One other phenomenon that has grown rapidly over the last 20 to 30 years is the rise of the artist's book and the closer relationship between illustration and printmaking. All these factors have contributed to the changing ways that artists use and view their ink.

MOKUHANGA

Over the last 20 years, there has been a resurgence of the Japanese *mokuhanga* technique for wood and lino block printing. This is a derivation of the original Chinese woodblock printing technique, and uses water-based inks. One reason for its revival may well be an assumption that it is more environmentally friendly than using oil-based inks, in addition to those properties of water-based inks appreciated by Western *mokuhanga* artists. Woodblock printing in China is still primarily carried out with water-based sumi ink.

Traditionally, sumi ink is made from a carbon black mixed with a hide glue. Animal hide is soaked in water to produce a 'stock', which is then treated with lime to break down the hides. The hides are then neutralised with a weak acid solution, and heated in water to around 70°C. The glue liquor is then drained off. More water is added, and the process repeated at increasing temperatures. The glue liquid is then dried and chipped into pellets, which are reheated and mixed with either carbon or coloured pigment to form the blocks of sumi ink.

LETTERPRESS

Letterpress as a commercial process almost died out during the 1980s. During the 1970s, it was still possible to undertake an apprenticeship in monotype setting or in linotype casting, but by the mid 1980s this had all disappeared. Phototype setting had taken over and the dominant cheap printing process

was lithography. This, in turn, died out with the introduction of desktop publishing in the early 1990s and the rise of the photocopier and the laser printer. Letterpress than began a revival after the turn of the twenty-first century as a reaction against desktop and digital publishing. Letterpress has now become an artistic practice in its own right. There were and still are subsets, including the fine-print book publishers, the artist's book makers, the letterpress studios printing for a love of letterpress and the artist printmakers who use letterpress.

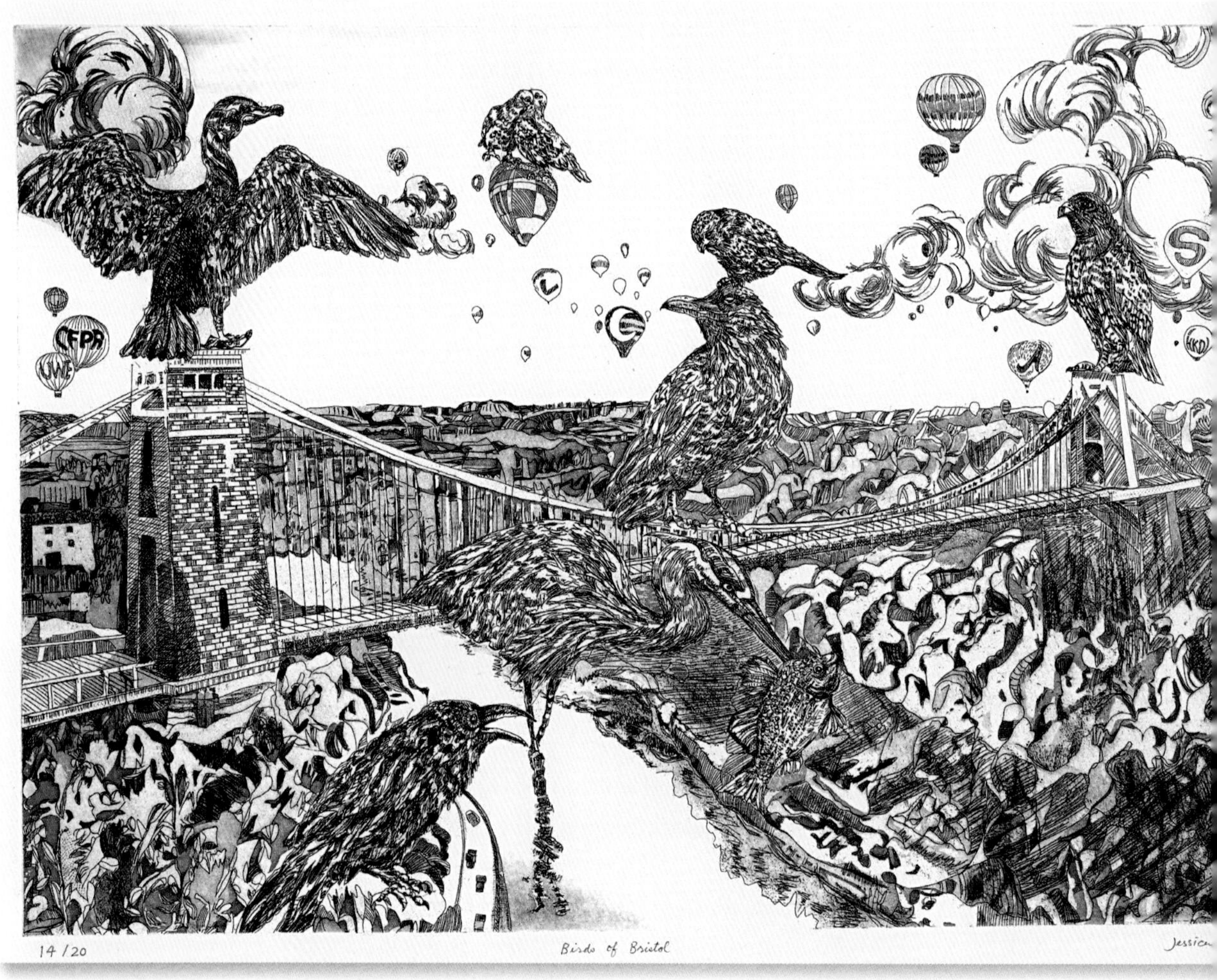

▲ Jessica Ho *Birds of Bristol,* 2019. **Etching, 56 x 76 cm.** Photo: CFPR © CFPR, UWE Bristol

THE INTAGLIO PROCESSES: ENGRAVING, ETCHING, MEZZOTINT AND AQUATINT

Working at this time was perhaps one of the greatest figures to have influence over the German engraving tradition: Schongauer, known as the 'Master of Playing Cards', and described by Alan Shestack as '[t]he first personality in the history of engraving'.[15] His name is related to a series of engraved playing cards, sets of which exist in the Bibliothèque Nationale in Paris, and the Dresden Print Cabinet. The prints are characterised by a mixture of short cuts and punched dots. Schongauer proved to be a major influence over Dürer and his contemporaries in the late fifteenth century, both in technique and style.

In Florence, engravers, with the exception of Pollaiuolo, were all known as artists of second or third rank. The north of Italy, on the other hand, can boast one of her great painters, and, in fact, one of the greatest masters of what was then modern art, Andrea Mantegna, who is known to have been one of the early engravers. Born at Vicenza in 1431 and trained in the classical school of Squarcione at Padua, he settled about 1459 in Mantua, remaining there until his death in 1506. Arthur Hind says of Mantegna's prints:

> 'the outline is deep and strong, but the return lines of shading (laid at an acute angle between the parallels) are so lightly scratched in the copper as to have lasted out very few printings. Early impressions of Mantegna, with the somewhat clouded and mysterious tonality given by the lighter lines, are of extreme rarity, but later impressions, where the outlines alone show distinctly, are by no means infrequently met in the sale room.'[16]

The inks for intaglio printing, like the inks used during the early development of all other printing processes, were always very simple. In 1645, Abraham Bosse published the first-known example of an etching ink recipe,[17] which listed boiled nut oil and Frankfurt black (also known as vine black, which is made by burning dried wine lees). Since then, etching and intaglio inks have changed very little in principle. A greater range of linseed viscosity is used, dependent upon the requirements of the artist and the technique used for a particular plate. For example, a weaker, less viscous ink is used if a strong plate tone is required, and a stronger, more viscous ink is used if a clean, crisp line is desired. Many artists still make their own black ink to this day, using a carbon black pigment and linseed oil.

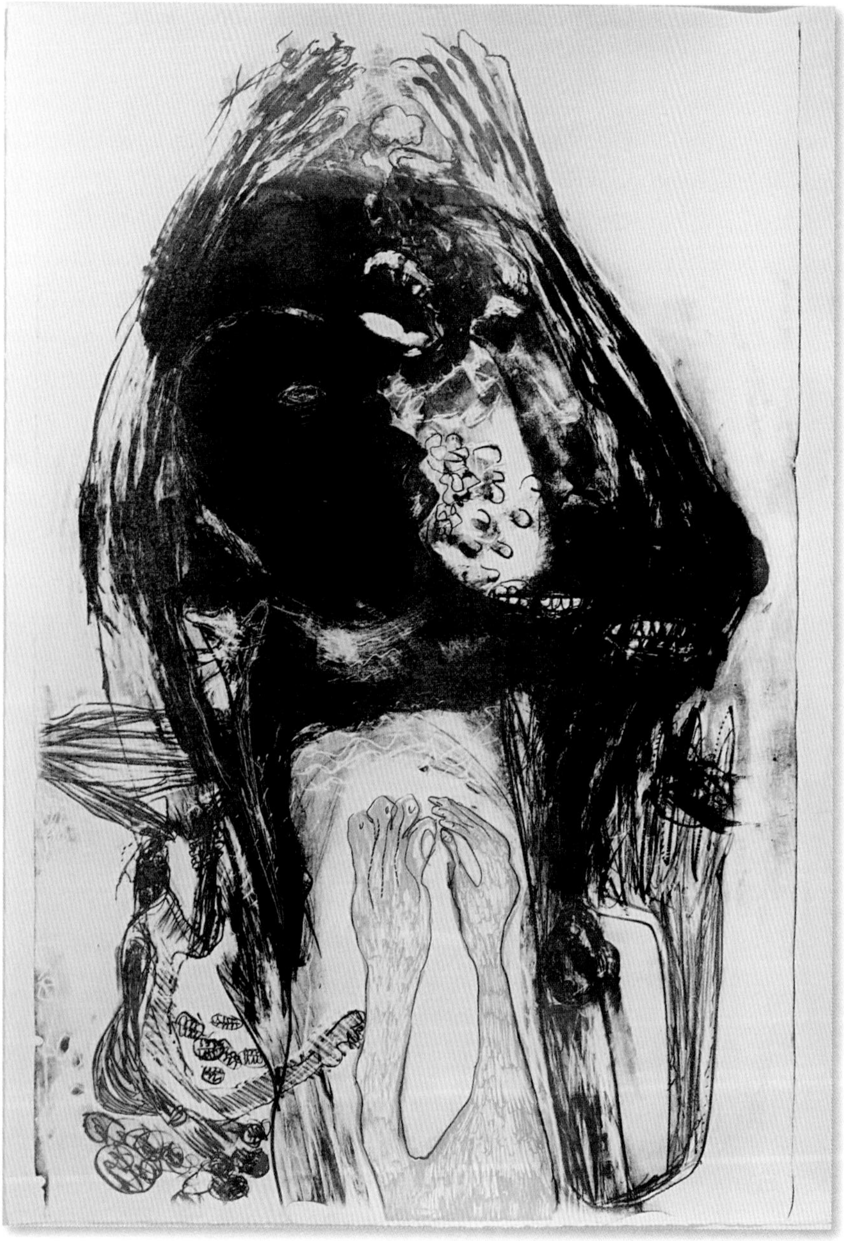

◄ **Pélagie Gbaguidi**
Hibernus#1, **2022.**
Stone lithograph and
silkscreen, 107 x 76 cm.
Photo: Frans Masereel
Centrum © Frans Masereel
Centrum

LITHOGRAPHIC DEVELOPMENTS AND CHANGES IN INK

The invention of lithography in 1798 by Alois Senefelder has perhaps the most romantic documented history of all the printmaking processes. By writing his laundry list on a piece of limestone with a greasy crayon, Senefelder changed the course of printing history and created a totally different principle for making prints. Lithography is a planographic process, where the ink sits on the surface of the stone or plate and can be applied selectively without altering the matrix. This was the first process where the ink was not placed either by a cut or a groove. With the new technique came the addition of further ink ingredients. At first the inks changed very little. Senefelder's recipe of 1818 contains just linseed oil and lampblack; in the same year, Dijon's François-Ambroise Mairet lists the addition of fatty soap and white wax in his book *Notice Sur la Lithography*.[18] These ingredients are presumably added to increase the ink's resistance to water. In 1889, Lorilleux, the French ink manufacturer, noted the addition of wax and a small amount of spirits of turpentine used by German lithographers.[19] He also noted that this practice was undertaken by people who still make their own ink, so by this point it must have been common to purchase ready-made ink. The wax was presumably added to reduce the possibility of scuffing the surface of the print when dry.

Until the mid twentieth century, letterpress was the dominant creative and technological force. Lithography grew slowly throughout the late nineteenth and twentieth centuries, becoming the prime means of colour printing.[20] In the late 1960s, with the introduction of high-quality photo plates and copper plates for long runs, lithography emerged as the main printing process. When the newspaper industry changed its working practices and presses in the late 1970s and early 1980s, the use of letterpress almost died out; it was mainly the perceptiveness of artist printers that kept letterpress qualities alive through the private press and their appreciation of the tactile and visual quality of the impressed page and the elegance of monotype setting. Stone lithography re-emerged slightly earlier, thanks to the efforts of printers such as Crommelynck and Mourlot in Paris, June Wayne and Kenneth Tyler in the USA and Stanley Jones in the UK. Strangely, in the early years of desktop publishing, commercial lithographic printing thrived.

But now, in the early twenty-first century, with the advent of social media, screen-based advertising, short-run print and print-on-demand, lithography is the dominant commercial print media for long run and big editions of books. The dominance of the small commercial lithographic shop on the high street is over, and digital print processes such as Indigo and high-quality laser printing have taken over; these techniques make it possible to produce individual versions within a long print run. For example, photobooks are usually printed by Indigo, a hybrid of lithography and laser printing.

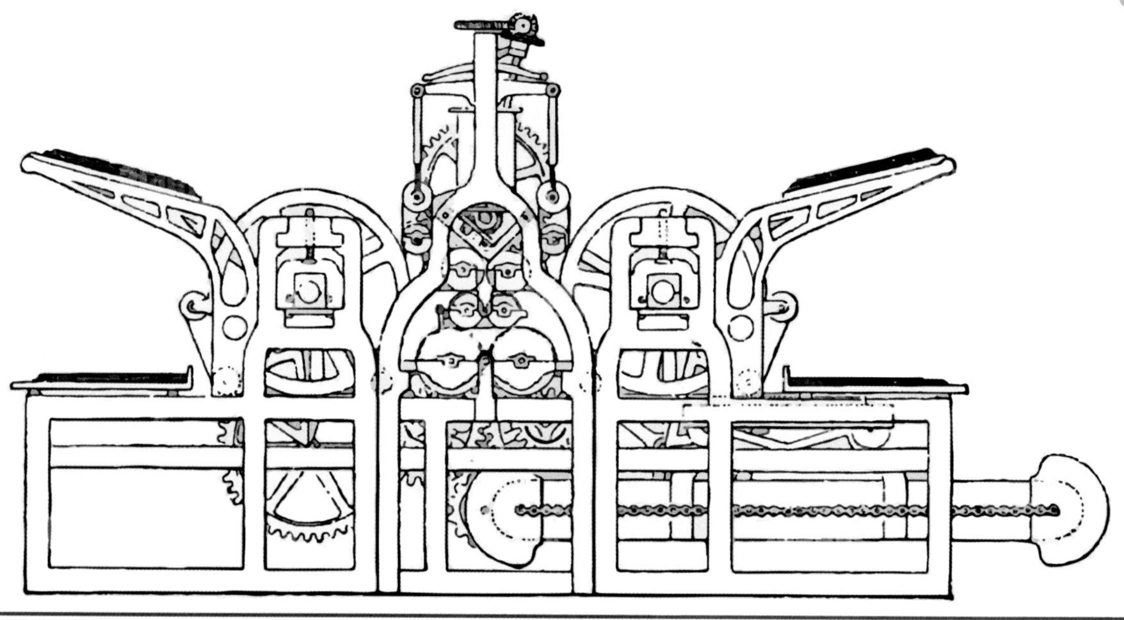

FLEXOGRAPHIC PRINTING

Originally, flexo – also known as photopolymer or solar plate – was called aniline printing. It is fundamentally a photosensitive relief-printing process, primarily used in the printing of packaging, although as the quality of flexo has improved, so the range of items it prints has increased. Some assessments put the proportion of the print industry that uses flexography as high as 15 per cent of the total print market.

Aniline printing dates back to the end of the nineteenth century, with the first press being built by Bibby, Baron and Sons in the USA in 1890. It gained popularity in the late 1920s, and used rubber rollers with a relief-printing surface flexible enough to be used on a wide range of substrates. The process gained a reputation for poor-quality printing and unhealthy ink, but the quality gradually improved; it was renamed 'flexography' in 1952 to more accurately reflect the diversity of substrates it could print, and in an attempt to overcome aniline printing's poor reputation.[21]

Flexography really began to take off with the introduction of photopolymer plates in varying degrees of shore hardness and depth of polymer. Currently, flexo prints everything from labels for shampoo and washing-up liquid bottles to the giant cardboard boxes that your fridge or television are delivered in, and from food packaging to printed ceramics. Flexographic plates were originally designed to be exposed flat and then wrapped around a cylinder to be printed. These days, the vast majority of commercial flexo is conducted

▲ **A Koenig & Bauer perfecting press at Bensley's printing works, London.** Source: Arthur Powell, *A Short History of the Art of Printing in England, 1877.*

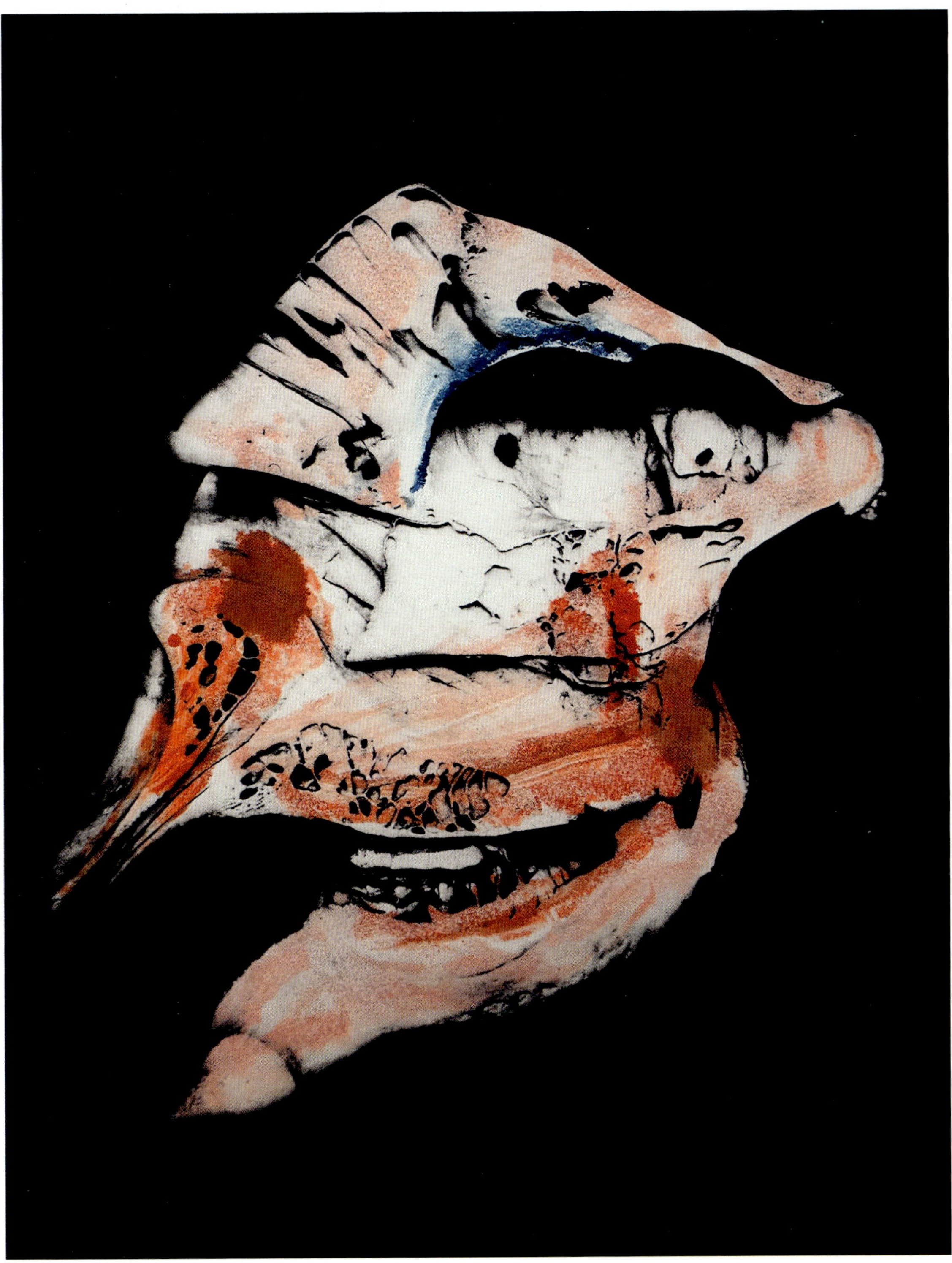

▲ **Laura Clarke Oaten** *Punch*, **2024. Polymer photogravure and monoprint, 55 x 44 cm.**
Photo: Laura Clarke Oaten © Laura Clarke Oaten

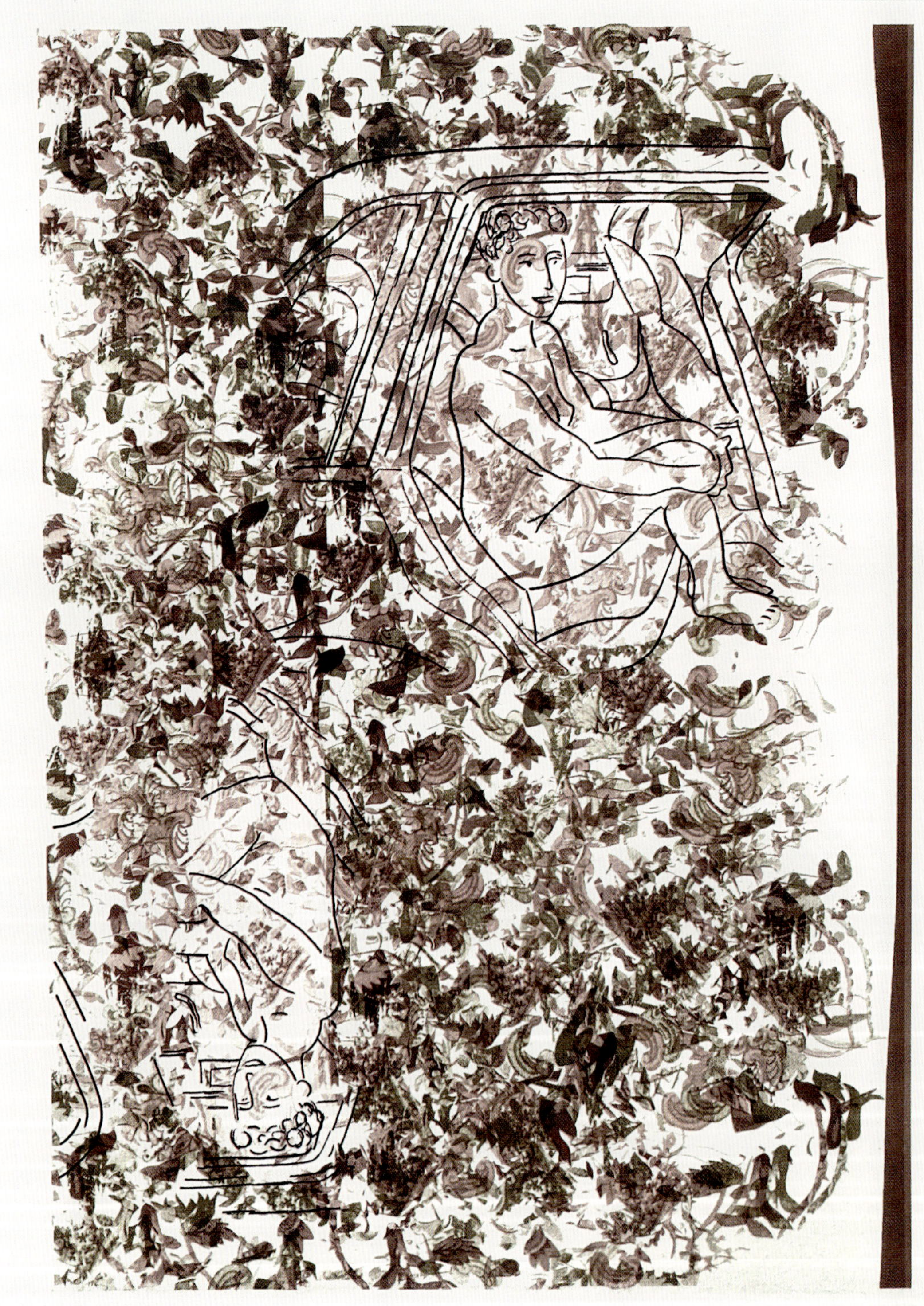

using a preformed cylinder that is exposed, developed and slid straight onto the machine rollers for printing.

Over the last 20 years, the process has gained increasing importance to printmakers. It is now extensively used as a replacement to photogravure (as an intaglio process) and uses a metal-backed plate designed to be wrapped around a magnetic steel cylinder, or a clear plastic-backed version designed to be glued to the cylinder. While there are specialist commercial inks for flexo that are usually water-based, these are designed for high-speed printing and are of little use to the artist printmaker, who tends to use either printmaking relief or etching ink, depending on whether the plate is being used for letter-press or intaglio printing.

THE PHOTOMECHANICAL PROCESSES: COLLOTYPE, WOODBURYTYPE AND PHOTOGRAVURE

In 1822, a new process for printing emerged when Joseph Nicéphore Niépce produced the first photographic image and spent the next 10 years trying to etch the result onto copperplate, thus laying the foundation for photomechanical printing. This idea was pursued by others as well: in the early 1850s, Henry Fox Talbot perfected a halftone technique using gauze and resin dust.

Nicéphore's cousin Abel Niépce de Saint-Victor perfected the process in 1854[22] and it is now known as 'photogravure' or 'heliogravure'. In 1855, Alphonse Poitevin filed the patent for the collotype process, also known as *'phototypie'* or *'Lichtdruck'*. Both these near-continuous-tone photomechanical processes rely on the action of light to harden a coating of gelatine sensitised with potassium or ammonium dichromate.

Gelatine sensitised with ammonium dichromate will harden as it receives light. In the case of photogravure, the gelatine is a coated layer on a sheet of absorbent paper, and when a continuous-tone negative is placed on top and the gelatine is exposed to light, the gelatine hardens in relation to how much light it has received. When the gelatine sheet is washed in water, the soft parts of the gelatine wash away and the harder parts remain fixed to the paper in varying depths, dependent on the light received. The gelatine layer is then transferred to a sheet of copper and a fine aquatint is applied. The plate is then immersed in six successive ferric chloride baths, each weaker than the last. The water in the ferric chloride weakens the gelatine, causing the plate to bite in smooth tonal steps.

Collotype relies on a similar thin layer of gelatine on a glass plate. After exposure and washing, the gelatine, when re-wetted, absorbs water in relation

◀ **Charlotte Hodes** *Untitled*, **2003. Collotype, 47 x 32 cm.** Photo: Paul Thirkell © CFPR, UWE, Bristol

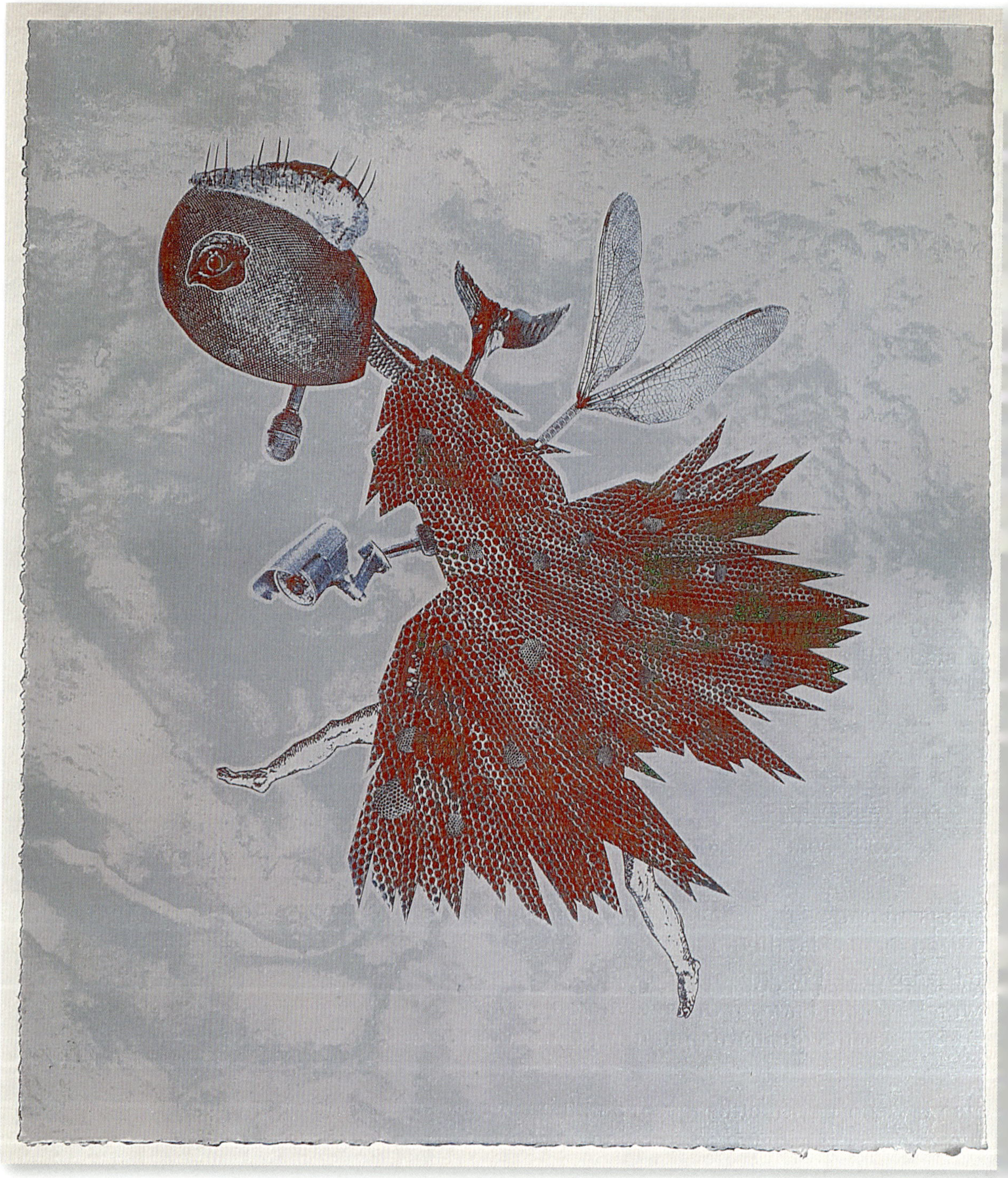

▲ **Justin Diggle** *Drone Puppetry*, **2022. Laser-engraved screen print, 56 x 76 cm.**
Photo: Justin Diggle © Justin Diggle

to the amount of light received in the exposure. Collotype may reject ink in the same manner as lithography, but is a more delicate and sensitive process, capable of rendering the finest grey tones.

In 1865, Walter Woodbury patented the Woodburytype process, the first and only truly continuous-tone photomechanical print process ever invented. Woodburytype relies on a thick slab of light-sensitive gelatine to form the basis of the printing matrix. Although the ink for this process is perhaps something of a side issue, it still deserves its place in any description of printing history because it uses liquid heated gelatine pigmented with a carbon black to replace the traditional oil-bound ink.

The dust-grain photogravure process, epitomised by the work of Paul Strand and Steiglitz in the early twentieth century, is capable of developing the most delicate of near-continuous-tone photographic etched plates; it was to develop into rotogravure – the high-speed, high-quality commercial print process. This process still dominates large sectors of the industry where high-quality print is desired in very large volumes. Notable contemporary examples are the UK postage stamps printed by Harrison & Sons of High Wycombe until June 2003, and now printed elsewhere by De La Rue. Other everyday items printed by commercial gravure are food wrappers, such as for Twix and Mars bars, using up to 12 colours.

SCREEN-PRINTING: THE LAST OF THE CLASSIC PRINTMAKING METHODS

The screen-print process as we know it is relatively new, having been invented at some point during the first decade of the twentieth century.

Its origins are disputed, with some attributing it to the Knights of St John who, in the fourteenth century, painted pitch onto gauze stretched over barrel hoops to print banners, and others to the delicate Japanese stencils held together with fine strands of hair, that were used from the seventeenth century onwards.[23] However, each of these is far removed from the actual process, which today uses a frame with a mesh stretched over it to form a screen, a squeegee and a stencil. Even if you accept this definition, there is still much confusion relating to the origins of the process. To quote Pat Gilmour in her catalogue to the *Mechanised Image* exhibition of 1978:

> 'Despite the fact that it is the only graphic medium to emerge this
> century, it is as difficult to piece together the early history of screen-
> printing as to reconstruct 15th-century relief printing from the
> incunabula of the woodcut.'[24]

The defining moments for the birth of screen print as we know it occurred either at the end of the nineteenth century or at the beginning of the twentieth. However, there is no doubt that it was firmly established by 1916, when the patent application of the Selectasine Company confirmed screen-printing's existence prior to the issue of the patent. A survey of all the relevant patents from 1880 to 1916, however, reveals a patent from 1887 issued to Charles Nelson Jones of Michigan which has most of the attributes of the screen-printing process. Additionally, in 1907, Samuel Simon of Manchester, England, was granted a patent that had many elements in common with the 1916 Selectasine patent.

Guido Lengwiler's *A History of Screen Printing* was published in 2013, and this definitive volume clearly places the extant origins of screen-printing to the screen-printed pennants (small flags used on ships for signalling, also used by American sports fans to support their teams) from the Philadelphia region of the USA, circa 1906.

In the early days of screen print, commercial paint was used; by the 1930s, efforts to improve print quality and speed saw the development of commercial screen-print inks that were initially based on the paint previously used. So screen-print ink developed from a paint into an ink, creating a new principle for printing based on strong pigment mixed from an opaque base or vehicle. This is unlike lithographic ink, which was mixed in a transparent vehicle.

The process for the graphic arts, and therefore artists, took a major turn in the 1960s with the development of thin film inks. Up until this time, the ink deposit on the paper had been relatively thick and fairly crude in detail compared to the other print processes. The 1960s and 1970s were a high-water mark for artists' screen-printing. Using new ink methods and stencil materials rapidly expanded the possibilities and scope of the process for artists and commercial printers, as exemplified by the work of Warhol in America and Chris Prater of Kelpra Studio in the UK.

In the early 1980s, greater awareness of health and safety, linked to environmental issues, became prevalent amongst printmakers. This led to a reappraisal of the heavy solvent used in the manufacture of screen-print ink, and many artists turned to water-based acrylic ink for screen-printing.

At the University of the West of England during the 1990s, we ourselves did much to promote the cause of healthier conditions for the user; we tested all the available products and developed new courses and healthy ceramic screen-printed transfer systems.

Here is probably a good place to talk about the history and development of artists' acrylic paint, which fundamentally forms the basis of the acrylic inks

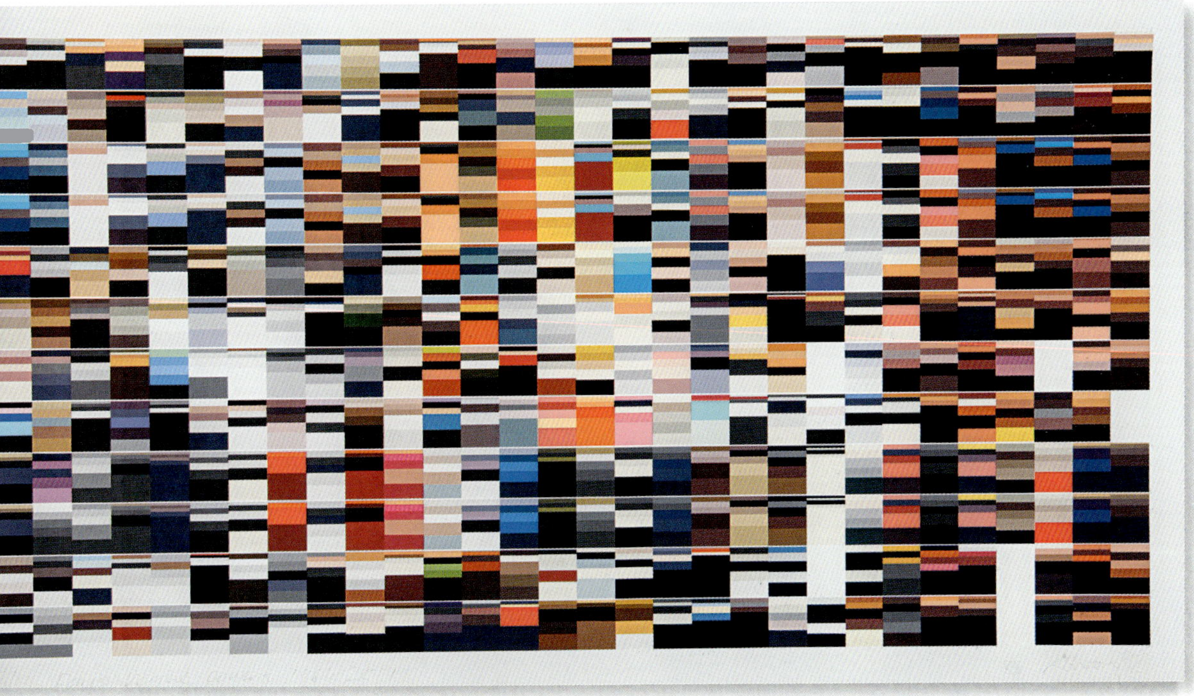

▲ Arthur Buxton *Paris Vogue Covers 1981–2011*, **2012. Pigmented inkjet print, 56 x 76 cm.** Photo: Paul Laidler © CFPR, UWE, Bristol

we now use in screen-printing, and are also available as relief-print inks and intaglio ink. There is currently much discussion between both practising print-makers[25] and acrylic ink and paint manufactuers[26] about the environmental impact of acrylic paint, and whether microparticles are worse for the environment than volatile organic compounds (VOCs). The best source of information on a general history of their development is an article in *Tate Papers no.2*, 'Conservation Concerns for Acrylic Emulsion Paints: A Literature Review' by Elizabeth Jablonski, Tom Learner, James Hayes and Mark Golden:

'Henry Levison, a chemist-turned-paint maker, founded the company Permanent Pigments in 1933, which produced the first line of waterborne acrylic emulsion paints called Liquitex® in 1954. He often supplied artists in exchange for soliciting their advice, occasionally hiring them as consultants or staff. The development of Liquitex® came not long after the introduction of the first artists' acrylic paint, Magna®, by the paint makers Leonard Bocour and Samuel Golden in 1947. Magna® acrylic paints were solution paints and quite distinct from waterborne emulsion paints. In practical terms, Magna® dried quickly by evaporation of an organic solvent; it remained resoluble in many hydrocarbon solvents as well as further layers of paint and could be blended with oil paint. In contrast, the drying process of

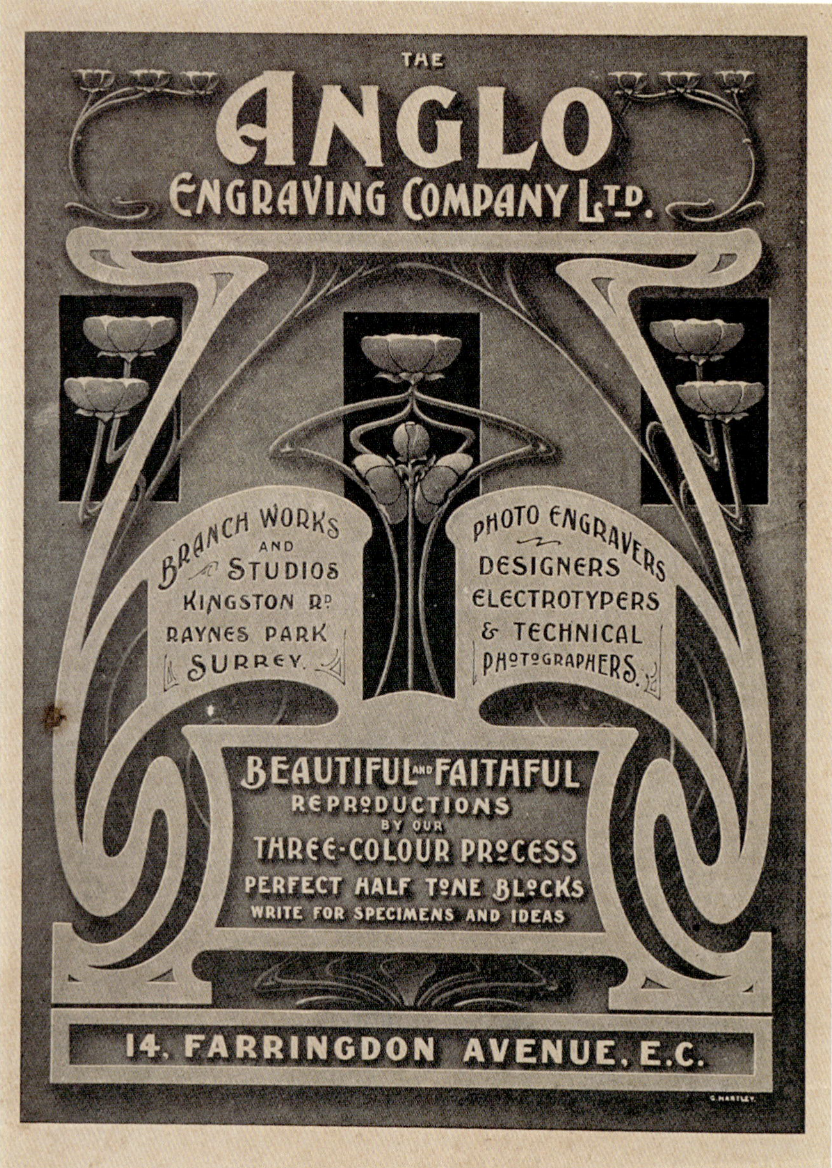

◄ Anglo Engraving Company Ltd advertisment from the *Penrose Annual* 1905. Photo: Jo Hounsome Photography.

emulsion paints involves a complicated coalescence of emulsified polymer spheres after an initial evaporation of water. These paints become insoluble in water – and further layers of emulsion paint – after they have dried.

Confusingly, many terms are used to refer to waterborne acrylic paints, such as acrylic emulsions, latex, and polymer colours. In fact, technically, they are dispersions rather than 'emulsions', because they are composed of tiny beads of solid, amorphous polymer suspended in water. The fact that these paints could be diluted and thinned with water, instead of mineral spirits, made them – and continues to make them – very appealing to artists.'[27]

Both Liquitex and Golden are still available as paint, and both companies produce a screen-print base medium to which the paint can be directly added to make a screen-printing ink. Other manufacturers such as Daler-Rowney make screen-printing bases. Companies such as TW Graphics and Speedball make acrylic-based screen-printing inks that are based around acrylic paint formulations.

INKJET, RISOGRAPH AND DIGITAL PRINTING

Digital technology currently dominates not only the commercial print world, but has also made major inroads by influencing printmakers who use new technology. Yet this technology we have embraced is actually not quite as new as we might believe. Xerography, or electrostatic printing, the technology for laser printers and photocopiers, was invented by Chester Carlson as early as 1938.[28] The first colour scanner was invented by Ronald Kirsch at the National Bureau of Standards in the USA;[29] the first computerised commercial scanner – the Magnascan 450 – was produced in 1969 by Crosfield;[30] and in 1969, A.B. Dick introduced the first commercial inkjet printer – the Videojet.[31] All these technologies were introduced commercially when letterpress was still the dominant commercial printing technology.

After the desktop revolution in the late 1980s and early 1990s, quality achievement in commercial inkjet printing started to influence artists, and we have seen a move backwards from commercial printing into the realm of fine print in the last decade of the twentieth century. This is not a unique example; as previously explained, both lithography and letterpress have been reclaimed from their commercial roots to become a primary artistic tool. Screen-printing is in the late stages of this process, where the art practice is slowly separating as a process from commercial expediency, and in time, as with lithography, the two will be almost unrecognisable to each other.

The commercial and technical achievements of inkjet printing have influenced a few, and some famous artists such as Richard Hamilton and Wolfgang Tillmans in the UK were early adopters of the technology. However, the breakthrough for today's artist printer came in the early years of the 2000s with the availability of new low-cost, high-resolution, wide-format inkjet printers.

The Risograph, a variation of the mimeograph, was invented in 1958 by the Riso Kagaku Corporation, and continues to be refined.[32] Artists started to use the process from the early 2000s onwards. Hoskins first encountered the Riso for creating stencils for enamel on metal printing in around 2006. Currently, it is a very popular process used by many illustrators, graphic artists and print-makers. The current technology uses a rice bran-based oil in its inks in order to be more environmentally friendly.

COLOUR AND DEVELOPMENT OF CONTEMPORARY MANUFACTURE FOR PRINTMAKING INKS

Colour printing occurred alongside developments in printing with black. Colour was used in woodcut printing from an early stage, as evidenced by the early Chinese block printers. In the north, colour was used in a sparing and subtle manner; the southern Chinese block printers used more exuberant colours. Although, in the West, Gutenberg used colour, it was always to copy the colour codes that scribes had used since Roman times. In fact, early Western printing often only included single-colour illustrative outlines, which were later coloured in by hand to individualise each book. This tradition goes back to the earlier incunabula, or block books, to the producers of playing cards and, to a lesser extent, the printers of religious ephemera which were on sale to pilgrims all over Europe. One of the earliest known examples of a book printed in two colours using engraved woodblocks was the *Mainz Psalter* printed by Fust and Schoeffer in 1457.[33]

The invention of mezzotint (attributed to Ludwig von Siegen in 1642) enabled Jacob Christoph Le Blon to invent, in 1720, multiple-colour printing from three single plates – red, yellow and blue respectively[34] – the forerunner of today's CMYK (see p.199) print technology.

At this point, although a gradual change was taking place whereby printers were beginning to purchase their inks from manufacturers, ink was often still made by the individual printer, and this would continue to be the case for another hundred years.

From the 1800s, pigment and dye manufacture played a major role in the history of ink. Colin Bloy's *A History of Printing Ink, Balls and Rollers, 1440–1850* finishes in 1850 for a good reason. Major changes to ink began to occur from the mid nineteenth century onwards, because two factors came into play that changed the face of printing. The first is the advent of coal-tar dyes such as aniline purple, first invented by William Henry Perkin in 1856. This was initially known as Tyrian purple, but by 1859 it was referred to as mauve. Perkin's

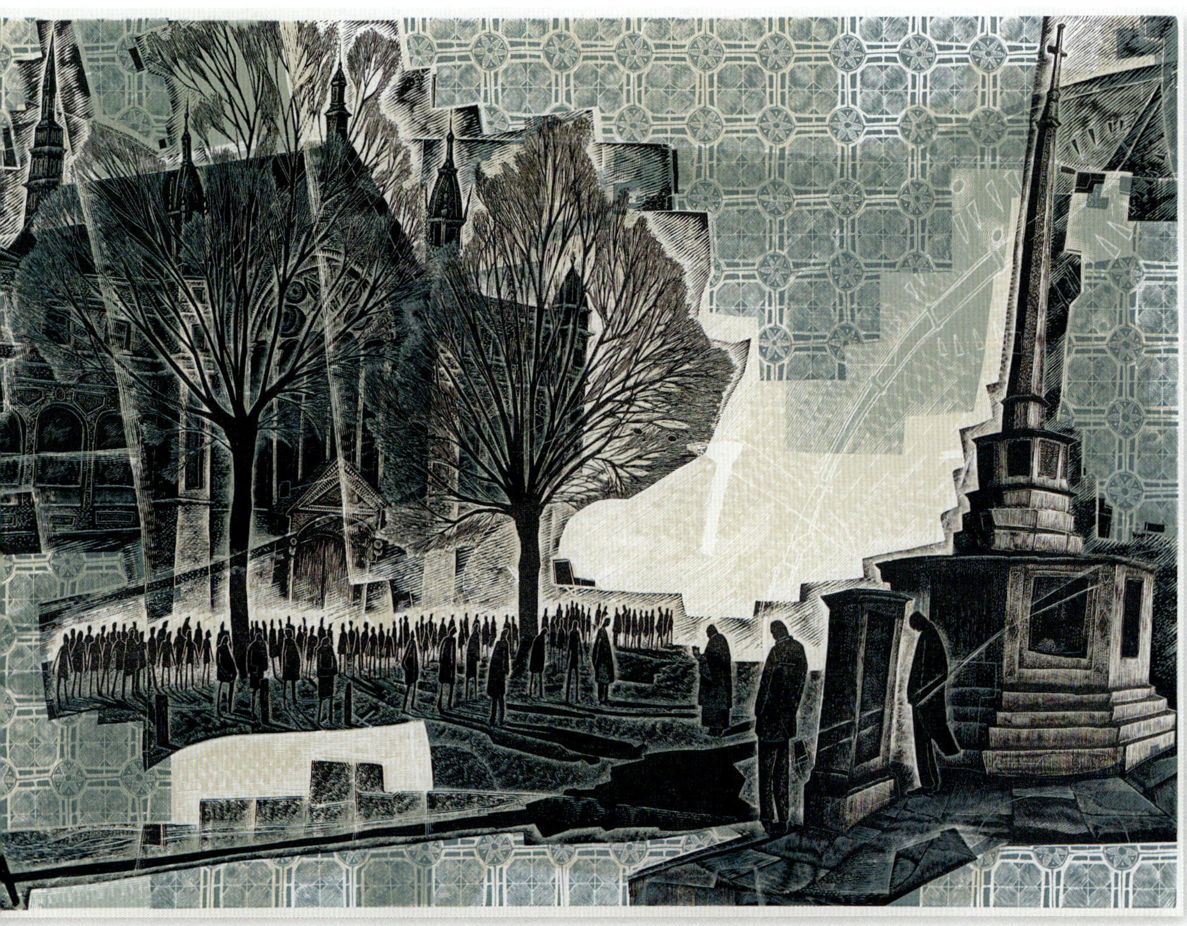

▲ Neil Bousfield *Leslie Paton: Memory and Places,* 2019. **Multiple block relief engraving, 24.5 x 34.5 cm.** Photo: Neil Bousfield © Neil Bousfield

discovery paved the way for modern colour chemistry and parallel chemical developments in the pharmaceutical industry. By 1873, when Perkin sold his dye company, the foundations of the European chemical industry were already in place.[35] His rivals were the companies that later became Bayer, Hoechst, BASF and Ciba-Geigy.

The second factor to accelerate ink development was greater speed in printing. The introduction of mechanisation had made way for stronger presses and more control of the image. But the introduction of steam-powered presses enabled such speeds that ink characteristics had to change. By 1816, Friedrich Koenig had introduced the cylinder press to *The Times*; the press was capable of generating 1,500–2,000 print impressions per hour. Koenig & Bauer still manufacture presses.

With the introduction of stop cylinder presses such as the Wharfedale and the Hoe in the 1850s, print speeds moved up to 3,000 impressions per hour.[28] Not only were large numbers of sheets being printed but, consequently, the inking

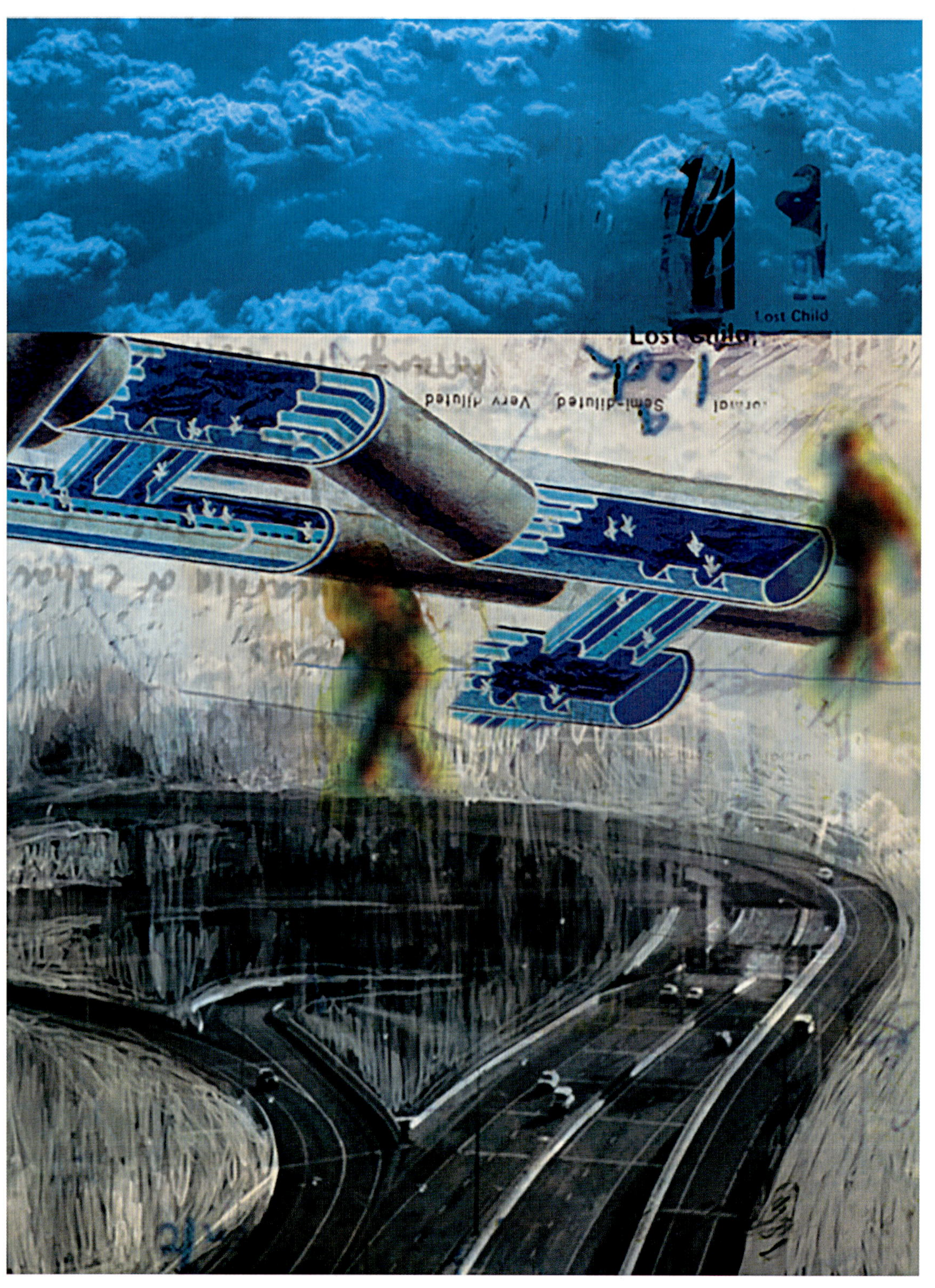
Lost Child
Lost Child

rollers were turning much faster; to enable this to happen the construction of ink for these presses also had to change. Factors such as shear, tack, film weight and, particularly, drying time became related to the more specialised machine that you were printing on.

The interesting period for the printmaker is that point in the early twentieth century when ink manufacture split. Commercial ink was manufactured for the high-speed presses, and for a while the older-style specialist inks were manufactured alongside the new products. By the 1970s, all these manufacturers (such as Mander-Kidd, Johnston & Cumbers, Coates Brothers, Fishburn, Ault & Wiborg, and Shackell Edwards) had given up making the specialist ink and were concentrating on high-speed volume production. At this point, several new players entered the market and some traditional ink makers, such as Charbonnel, became primarily producers of ink for artists.

Ink for the commercial industry has become more and more specialised, to the extent that the ink manufacturers for very large printing firms now make and deliver ink by the tanker load, rather than by the tin. This leaves only the small, very specialised ink maker with the ability to make ink from available pigment in small batches. Such specialist manufacturers are more than rare – they are almost extinct. Their true numbers are hard to discover, as ink can be made by one manufacturer for several distributors to market under their own labels. In 2004, there were only around 15 worldwide, and since then the problem has become even more acute; specialist ink manufacturers of ink for etching, relief and hand lithography can now probably be counted on the fingers of one hand. These manufacturers need the support of printmakers to continue making the products printmakers need. The ink buyer needs to remembered this. The cheap, mass-produced alternatives may suit the pocket in the short term, but if the availability of special ink that is really needed dwindles due to lack of demand, it will ultimately only be the printmaker who is to blame.

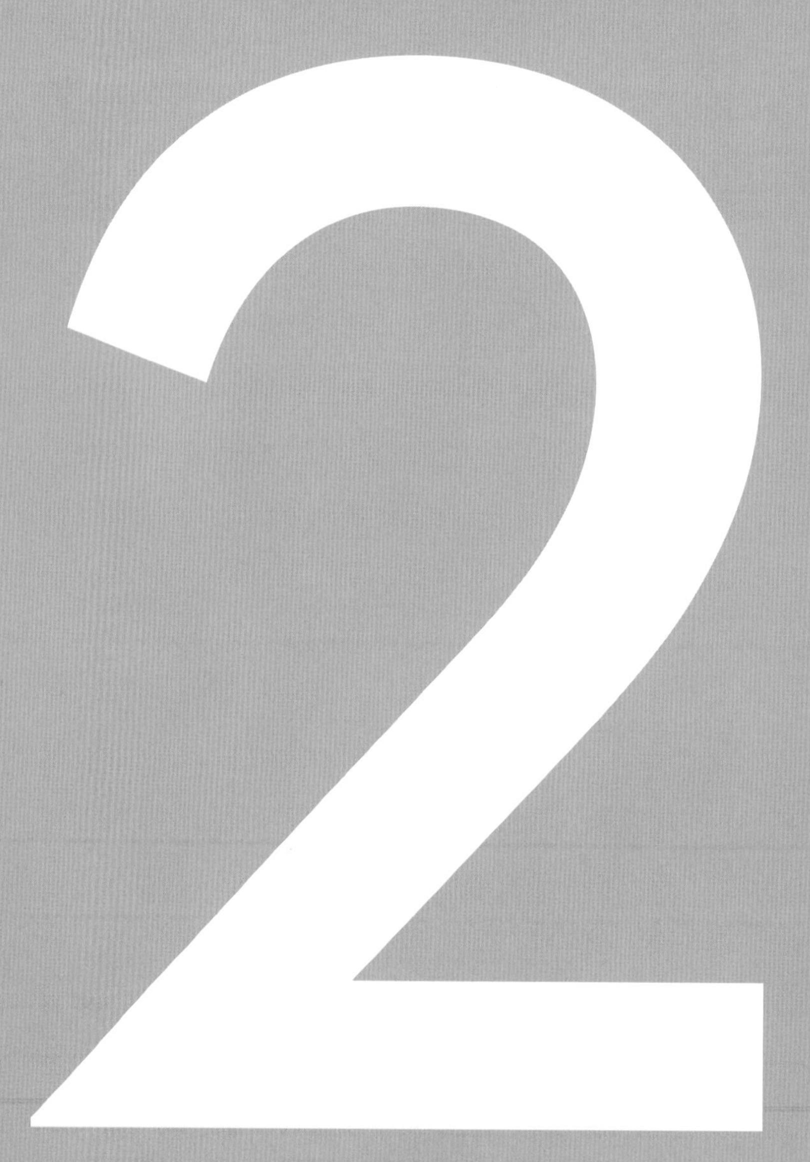

CHAPTER

2

WHAT IS AN INK AND HOW IS IT MANUFACTURED?

'Ink' is a broader descriptive term that covers more than just the common paste- or gel-like formulations used in printmaking. It is perhaps helpful to start by excluding those images that are not produced using ink, such as photographic silver halide images and those produced by heat on dedicated thermal paper. The term 'ink' encompasses a wide array of formulations, from dry toners used in photocopiers, inkjet technologies to liquid inks applied by pen and brush. We will restrict our attention to printmaking inks, whether they be oil-, alcohol-, acrylic- or water-based. Their defining factor has less to do with their formulation than their application to a substrate from a printing plate of some description.

A set of consistent concepts and terms is essential when handling and experimenting with ink, particularly if you want to extend the range of your work. Ink in its simplest form is a means of transferring colour in a specific shape or area onto a substrate (usually paper), and of bonding that colour to the surface of the paper. This requires the colour to be in the form of pigment or dyestuff with a vehicle (in our case primarily oil) to bind and stick the colour to the surface; this is usually referred to as a medium, varnish or vehicle. Ink may also contain: driers or antioxidants to aid or slow the drying of the ink in bulk; waxes to prevent the print from marking; and other additives to make an ink suitable for a particular discipline or to change properties such as hardness, friability or gloss. An example would be the addition of certain driers that fulfil a catalytic role in the drying process when a lithograph takes in moisture during the lithographic process.

For an artist's use, an ink needs to have as few additives as possible. The less that is added to an ink, the easier it is to control its function and to understand what might be needed to adjust it for the particular purpose required. An example of a simple ink using just pigment and vehicle without contemporary additives can be found in Abraham Bosse's 1645 recipe[36] for an etching ink that uses just Frankfurt black and boiled nut oil as a vehicle.

'How to make the printers Inke

The printers black used for our plates is call'd in French noir d'Allemayne, and by our Drugists Keen-rus; it comes from Francford, and is sold by the Salters; That which is excellent is of velvet colour and somewhat resembling it, friable between the fingers like the finest chalke, or flower: and of the properties it is fits to take notice, for there is a counterfeit sort made of lees of wine burnt, which is nothing so faire, but harsh and injurious to the plates.

But first, you must take a good quantity of the purest nut-oyle, and put it into a large Iron-pot, to which is fitted a cover which must lye exactly close, Fill it within 4 or 5 inches then apply the cover: Thus set it or hang in a good fire, letting it boyle, least it endanger the house, and therefore your eye must be continually on it, to keepe it in motion and stirr it about with some Iron Ladle or spatula; so as being now very hott, it make take fire gently of it selfe. Or be easily inflamed with the blaze of a paper, as wine is burnt: When thus it has taken fire, remove it from the Trevet, to a corner of the chimny perpetually stirring it, yet so as the burning may continue above halfe an hower: and this to make the weaker sort: after it has thus burnt, clapping the cover on the pot it will be extinguished, providing it be very close, other wise you must cast a cloath upon it, which will immediately suffocate the flame. Then let it coole a little, before you poure it into the vessel, in which you intend to keep it.

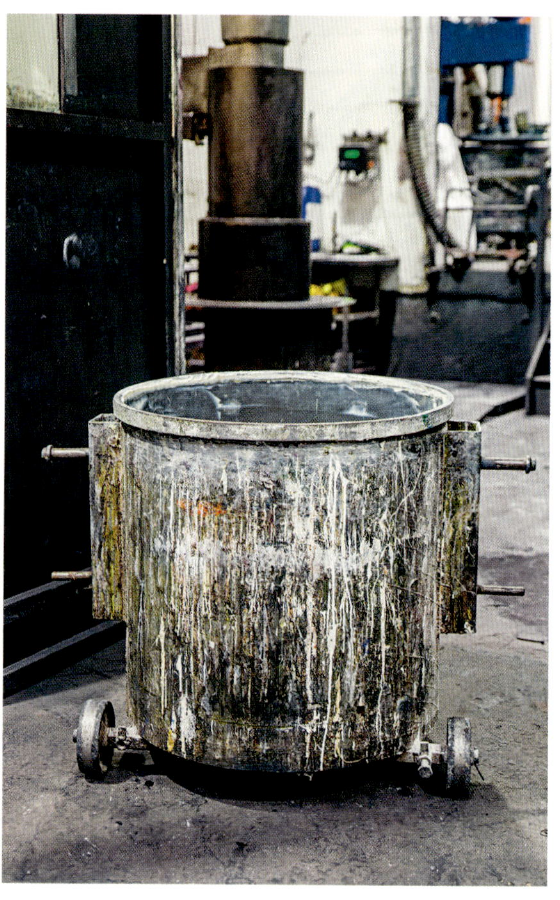

▲ **Ink mixing bowl.**
Photo: Jo Hounsome Photography © Cranfield Colours

> When this is don, fill the pott againe with more raw nut-oyle,
> as you did before: To make a stronger sort boyling it in the same
> manner, with this onlye difference, that it is to be suffered to burne
> a great deal longer, moving and stirring it till it become very thick
> and glewy, filling and drawing into threads like a syrupe, which you
> may essay from tyme to tyme, by letting a few drops coole upon the
> plate. There are some who boyle an onion, or a crust of bread in the
> oyle, to render it (as they thinke) the less greasie.
>
> If the fire (as frequently) have too violently seized upon it, cast in
> halfe a pint of fresh oyle: but to prevent all danger, you may boyle
> it abroad in the open aire, if the weather be calme and seasonable.
> The Oyle thus prepared, you must grind the blacke upon a Painters
> marble with a good large muller; Thus take about halfe a pound at
> a tyme and bruise it on the stone, then put to it about halfe a pint
> of your weakest oyle, (being that which you first boyled) or in a
> quantity according to that of your black; for some colour will drink
> up more than other, and it were better to put to little than to much,
> and therefore in grinding, use discretion; for the drier it be ground,
> the better: having thus coarsely ground it, range and heape it up at
> one of the corners of the marble, or some other convenient thing
> which may hold it; then take it in smaller portions, and grinde it
> over againe by degrees till it be exceedingly fine, and range this
> also towards another coine of your stone; spread it againe upon the
> marble and add to it of your strongest oyle about as much as you
> judge may fill a hens egg; Grind and incorporate these very well,
> and reserve it for your use in some earthen pott glaz'd, covering
> and securing it from dust and ordure; and thus you have the Inke
> prepared for your plates.'

The account gives us a fair indication that ink making was a foul-smelling, and therefore open-air, event. Due to the well-chronicled risk of explosion and the fact that many of the black pigments were derived from burning animal bones, ink making was consigned to the edge of a town. As the need for ink increased, the printers (often linked with religious orders in Western Europe) sub-contracted its manufacture to commercial ink makers. As the best ink makers grew in skill and competence, they began to make for more printers. The first record dedicated ink maker was Guillame de Launay of Paris in 1522.[37]

Abraham Bosse's recipe still influences good etching inks today, although linseed oil rather than nut oil is now primarily used. It makes a single-pigment ink with good permanence that would be easy to print, and is just as effective today as it was in 1645. This can be borne out by Anthony Gross's 1971[38] recipe, which used:

> Raw linseed oil
> Heavy copperplate oil
> Imitation Frankfurt black

Or his professional printers' recipe of the same date:[39]

> One-third French Black
> Two-thirds Frankfurt Black
> 50% medium copperplate oil
> 50% light copperplate oil

An example of a contemporary etching ink is likely to contain the following ingredients:

> Etching Ink – Hansa Yellow
> 30% Hansa Yellow Pigment
> 20% Extender pigment (calcium carbonate)
> 35% Linseed stand oil (40 poise) (poise = measurement of viscosity)
> 15% Light stand oil (5 poise)

WHAT ARE THE CONSTITUENT PARTS OF AN INK?

The easiest way to describe what goes into an ink in generic terms is to list the primary ingredients and give a brief explanation of their function.

VEHICLE

The term 'vehicle' indicates its own function – the passenger is the pigment. Defined another way, the vehicle is both the carrier and the glue for the colour. In water-based relief inks and screen-printing ink, the vehicle is generally an acrylic polymer. In water-based inkjet ink, the vehicle is water.

The primary vehicle for oil-based printmaking inks is linseed (flax) oil, which was originally boiled and then set on fire to create a burnt oil. These days, boiled linseed is created by heating the oil in a pressure vessel; the resultant oil is now usually referred to as a 'stand' oil, and retains all the properties of the original burnt oils.

Historically, nut oils were used in certain ink formulations, not least because they are generally lighter in colour. However, various issues caused them to fall from common use. The linseed (or flax) oil industry became and remains comparatively large, efficient and reliable. There are at least nine distinct types of linseed-derived oil available, and the size of the industry means that ink and paint makers can have confidence that they will receive a sustainable supply of oil of known provenance. Today's ink manufacturers use linseed oils that are filtered of contaminants, or 'mucilage', and are a light- to mid-straw colour.

The walnut oil industry is smaller, and the oils are generally treated and chemically engineered to exhibit properties more suitable for wood finishing than for fine-art printmaking. These products may have been insufficiently purified for use in a print that will, not unreasonably, be expected to last for many decades and beyond. As is the case for many nut-based oils, walnut oil has an increased tendency to go rancid when exposed to air. It is part of the natural drying process, but may be partly to blame for walnut oil's fall from favour.

Alkyd oils, or 'resins', are 'modified' linseed oils known as 'drying' oils. They have several advantages over the more natural, unmodified source oil, in that they have usually been treated to improve friability (cracking or inflexibility), or to enhance gloss, pigment wetting and flow. The term 'alkyd' is a combination of the words 'alcohol' and 'acid' – the two elements used in the modification process.

'Varnish' tends to be used as a generic term for the vehicle, and can mean many things depending on the age of the book you are reading or the printmaking process you are dealing with. Varnish historically referred to burnt linseed oil; today, the nearest replacement for a burnt oil is a heat-polymerised oil known as a 'stand oil'. In lithography, it refers to the oil added to the ink to adjust its printing properties. This has also now been replaced by a series of stand oils.

For most printmaking uses, a series of oils has always been available, ranging in viscosity from weak to very strong. Ink makers may use several oils or varnishes of differing viscosities within a single ink; the average viscosity of the two or three varnishes used in a multiple-varnish ink will give a very different result to an ink using one varnish. This is because the physical properties of the oil, such as tack, adhesion, wetting properties and drying, are all appreciably altered by the viscosity and the amount of polymerisation or pressure that the oil has been subjected to.

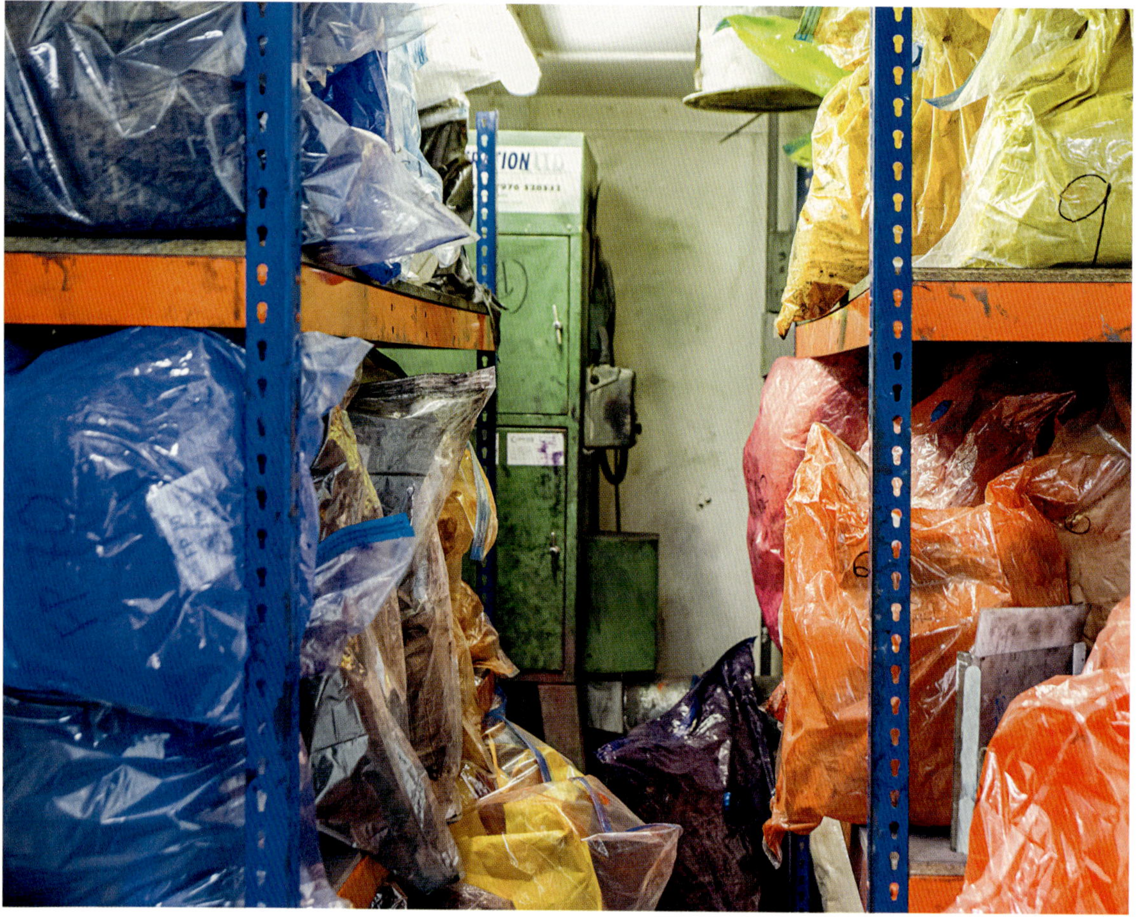

PIGMENT

The Color Pigment Manufacturers Association defines pigment as:

> '… colored, black, white or fluorescent particulate organic and inorganic solids which usually are insoluble and essentially physically and chemically unaffected by the vehicle or substrate in which they are incorporated. They alter appearance by selective absorption and/or by scattering light. Pigments are usually dispersed in a vehicle for application. Pigments retain a crystal or particulate structure throughout the coloration process.'[40]

Carbon black, also known as 'gas' black, is produced by the incomplete combustion of natural gas, which produces very fine particles of soot. The size of the particles produced explains why it has so steadily kept its place as a pigment of choice for many lithographic inks. Because the particle is small, it

▲ **Dry pigment in storage.** Photo: Jo Hounsome Photography © Cranfield Colours is relatively easy to grind and the individual pigment particles are less likely to be saturated by the damping required in the lithographic process, which could otherwise lead to emulsification or scumming. It is the small particle size that makes carbon black less popular in other disciplines; for example, the resultant ink can stain a woodblock.

Lampblack, or vegetable black pigments are produced by burning the source material (these days commonly hydrocarbons) in an atmosphere that has a limited amount of oxygen. Those old enough to have owned or seen a paraffin light will picture the smoky flame and subsequent soot, formed when the wick was untrimmed and the flame was too large for the area within the glass. The same principle applies in this manufacturing process, and the soot, once settled, is collected and sieved. The soot particles are larger than in a simple carbon black.

Bone black is produced by burning animal bones in an environment with limited oxygen. The resulting charred bones are finely crushed and graded by particle size. In terms of density, the strength of a bone black is understated and the pigment can give a delicate result.

Understanding the physical structure of a pigment is important, as is the fact that they should not be confused with dyes. This is an important demarcation. Generally, dyestuffs are soluble, whereas pigments are solid particles that are simply dispersed or suspended in the varnish, rather than dissolved.

Pigment materials for inks were often produced by the pharmaceutical industry, and the origins of the pharmaceutical industry lie in nineteenth-century dye manufacturing.

Apart from some genuine earth pigments beloved by printmakers (and less so by ink makers), colour pigments currently used in the printing industry and for most artists' paints are predominantly synthetic, and pigment manufacture constitutes a very small part of the chemical industry. It may at first seem strange that artists' pigments have strayed so far from their natural origins; however, naturally occurring pigments are not generally consistent in either their particle size or their colour, and do not provide the consistency that ink manufacturers and artists require. Today's society demands colour constancy; therefore, the answer is for the pigment to be synthetic.

Colour for pigments is classified by two common systems. Performance or chemical standards for industrial materials and components are set by the American Society for Testing and Materials (ASTM), and a more comprehensive system for both pigments and dyes comes from the Colour Index™. First published in 1925, and now published online by the Society of Dyers and Colourists and the American Association of Textile Chemists and Colorists, the Colour Index™ is the international reference database on colourants, their nomenclature, constitution, main applications and suppliers.

Colourants are listed according to the system of Colour Index™ generic names and constitution numbers. It has 27,000 listed colours under 13,000 Colour Index™ Generic Names, of which 600 are pigments.

However, for the artist, the American system is documented alongside popular colour names in *The Artist's Handbook of Materials and Techniques*, by Ralph Mayer, which is now updated by the Ralph Mayer Learning Centre at Yale School of Art. It also lists the spectral characteristics and a commentary on the potential hazardous nature of each individual pigment. Therefore, we refer you to this excellent volume, which relieves us of the burden of replicating data that can be easily found elsewhere.

Pigments are commonly referred to as either 'organic' or 'inorganic'. In past times this made sense, as pigments were classified in relation to their origin. The term 'organic compound' no longer means materials derived from natural vegetable or mineral sources, but refers to compounds of carbon; 'inorganic compounds' no longer refers only to synthetic materials. The label 'inorganic pigments' covers almost all pigments that do not contain carbon in their structure. There are certain exceptions to this such as cyanides (Prussian blue being an example), which are classified as inorganic even though they contain carbon.

Inorganic pigments (mineral)

- Native earths: ochre, raw umber, etc.
- Calcined (reduced by heat to powder) native earths: burnt umber, burnt sienna, etc.
- Inorganic synthetic: cadmium yellow, zinc oxide, etc.

Organic pigments

- Vegetable: gamboge, indigo, madder, etc.
- Animal: cochineal, Indian yellow, etc.
- Synthetic organic pigment

These days, most pigments are manufactured, so the traditional classifications bear little relation to a pigment's origin. In addition, the list does not deal with lake pigments, which are precipitated from dyes. Lakes are essentially coloured particles where the colourant (often a dyestuff) clings to a neutral carrier base, into which the pigment is both chemically and physically absorbed.

Base material and colourant

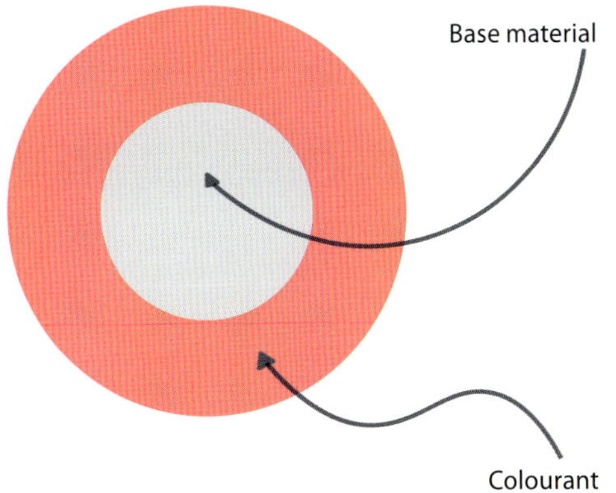

The white inorganic pigments used in printmaking inks may be strict pigments such as titanium dioxide and zinc oxide, or they may be 'extenders' like alumina hydrate. The former contribute to the opacity or covering power of the ink, while extenders are intentionally relatively transparent. This is due to the different refractive indices of the pigment and vehicle. Extenders are widely used to reduce the colour strength of pigments that would otherwise be unbalanced in their strength when compared with other inks within a range. This can be done without introducing unwanted opacity.

Some pigments have fallen from use over the last 50 years for reasons of availability, price or toxicity. The known health hazards associated with certain heavy metal pigments, including lead and chrome pigments, have seen them disappear from all but restoration printmaking work. Other pigments have simply fallen out of fashion as tastes change, or they are sourced from areas of political unrest and instability that have become impossible to reach.

The 'pigments' used in metallic inks are minute flakes of a copper and tin alloy for gold and bronze inks, or aluminium powders for a silver effect.

Fluorescent pigments, commonly bold red, yellow, orange, blue or green, can absorb invisible UV light and, having slowed down the frequency of the wavelength, emit the colour on a spectrum visible to humans. This means that florescent colours appear brighter and more brilliant than conventional pigments. Often, UV light is responsible for this brilliance, although other florescent pigments are stimulated by daylight alone. They are generally not used in fine-art printmaking, partly because they are a recent innovation but, more importantly, when printed at the thin film weights achieved by relief, etching and lithographic printmaking, their lightfast values are not seen as sufficiently high for works of art of archival quality. Fluorescent inks are, however, popular in screen-printing, although there is little published data on their lightfast properties.

DYES

Dyes are molecules of colour dissolved in the vehicle, as opposed to pigment particles which, when in an ink, are in suspension. Dyes are generally less stable and less lightfast than their pigment counterparts, and therefore tend not to be used in artists' ink manufacture, except in lakes. However, in general terms, due to chemical composition, a dye-based product will normally be more intense in colour than its pigmented equivalent.

In the last few years, with the advent of specialist wide-format printing, purpose-made ink has been developed to be more lightfast than previously obtainable. The spotlight in ink research has been turned upon the differences between chemical dyes and pigments in the context of artists' use. The early problems of dye-based inkjet ink are diminishing rapidly, having been solved by inkjet manufacturers developing pigmented-ink sets; this proves the general tenet that pigmented ink tends to be more lightfast than dye. However, due to the nanoparticles in an inkjet pigment ink, it is often difficult to distinguish between a pigment and a dye.

HOW IS INK FOR ARTISTS MADE TODAY AND WHAT ARE THE DIFFERENCES FROM HIGH-VOLUME COMMERCIAL INK MANUFACTURE?

Identifying the main companies who make ink especially for the printmaker is a useful exercise in discovering the range, prices and qualities available to contemporary printmakers. The prime manufacturers of ink are: Cranfield and Hawthorn Printmakers in Britain, Charbonnel, manufactured by Colart, in France, and Speedball and Gamblin in the USA. In addition, there are various distributors of etching and relief inks with their own branded products made to their own specifications. Alongside these producers, who are manufacturing predominantly for the traditional printmaking disciplines, HP, Canon, Epson and others produce, with the same level of care, digital inks for archival photography and use by artists.

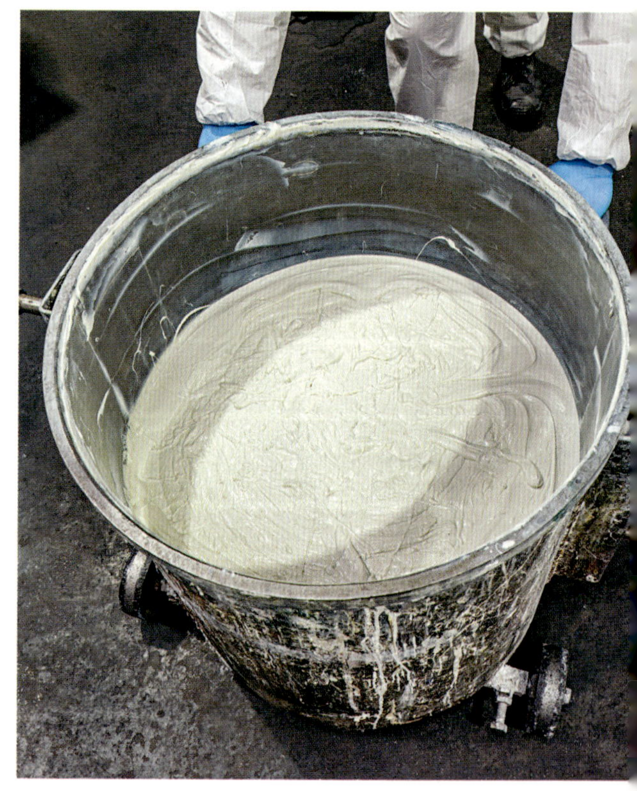

▼ **White ink waiting to be milled.** Photo: Jo Hounsome Photography © Cranfield Colours

INK MANUFACTURE

The sixteenth century saw the commercialisation of print and the development of ink makers in Britain. Unfortunately, making ink to a budget in poor conditions resulted in an inferior product. Oils were often insufficiently boiled, and diluted with

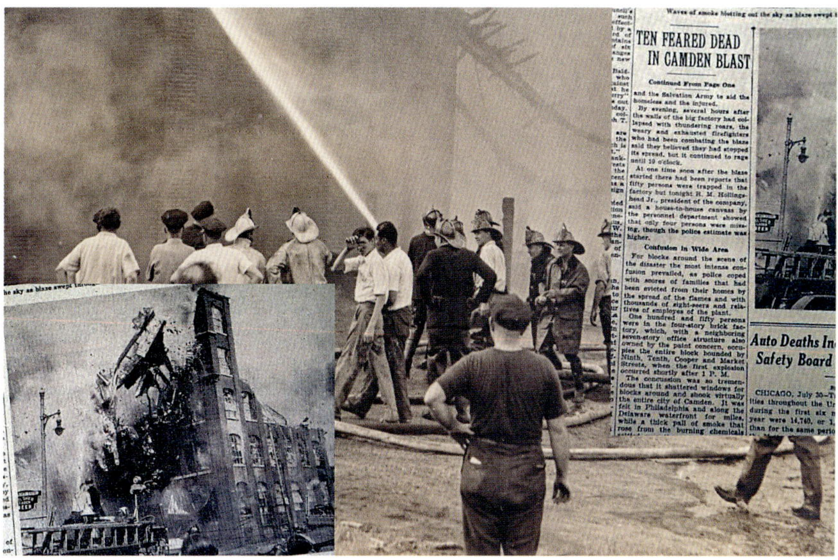

huge quantities of pine rosin, pitch and, for reasons of economy, tallow fat from abattoirs. The pigments selected were also poorly prepared and yielded variable results. By the mid eighteenth century, with increased automation, bulk production and the loss of the care and skill provided by artisans working to a small scale, the quality of inks had regressed. Rogers and Fowle established the earliest known American printing ink factory in 1742 in frustration and disappointment at the poor-quality inks coming from England and France at the time.

By the mid 1850s, advances in pigment manufacture and the demand for better-quality inks to reproduce what could now be captured by the advances in the new science of photography, the industry had both the materials and volume to attract investment. Ink production remained a dirty business: there was the smell, as large quantities of wood, household waste and animal carcasses were burnt to create soot for pigmentation; there would also have been the heat from varnish boilers, the ever present problem of dust, and the constant risk of explosion. It was, therefore, still an industry consigned to the edges. In London, even up until the 1970s, the majority of the British ink companies were situated within an area of five square miles in the East End area of Stratford, around Sugar House Lane and Mile End Road.

Historically, ink making was a dangerous business. There is a risk of explosion associated with any dust and, up until the 1950s, the pigment mixing shop was equally as dangerous as the mill hall. Across the factory environment there was little machine guarding; many staff suffered chemical poisoning or injury, and a number of ink and paint factories went up in flames. Mixing blades were unguarded, and heavy metal pigments were used in poorly ventilated areas with no extraction. As was the case with many industries, power was supplied to the mills via leather belts running from a central drive shaft, which was often unguarded and presented a constant risk of injury. In the days before protective equipment and hazard assessment and management, the risks were many and varied.

This was an international problem; a *New York Times* report[41] from the 1940s covered a blast (caused by either pigment or solvent) that claimed the lives of at least 10 people.

Despite the dangers, both the ink and paint trade were seen as having a certain status within the industrial world in the eighteenth and nineteenth centuries. The products manufactured were at the forefront of modern chemistry and spanned both commercial applications and artistic endeavour. There was a high degree of cooperation between competing companies, not least because staff moved around the industry in search of promotion. Family lines would continue within colour houses, with several generations working within the same company, while cousins, aunts and uncles worked in companies nearby.

Co-author Michael Craine traces his family's involvement in ink through a company started in 1863. While the street that Johnston & Cumbers occupied is now beneath the 2012 Olympic Village, many of the terms and traditions live on despite the industry's dispersal away from London. Cranfield's stiffest varnish is still referred to as 'rat catcher'. It was not only used by the ink trade but also at the docks where, once poured onto the dockside, it provided an efficient if rather inhumane method of catching vermin from visiting ships or the River Thames. Tradition still continues at Cranfield with the ink makers' cricket match on Christmas Eve, which dates back to the days when many ink companies rubbed shoulders in London's East End: Parsons, Fletcher & Co, Max Frondshdorf, Gilbeys, Capitol, Ensor Inks, Shackell Edwards, Coates, Lorilleux & Bolton, and Fishburn all being names that have disappeared from the area. It was not only ink that was made on the banks of the Thames: pigment manufacturers like Blythe Burrell Colours were situated where The O2 arena is today, only a few miles away from where Leon Frenkel boiled oil under the noses of the inhabitants of East London well into the 1990s.

Printmaking ink manufacturers were historically smaller independent companies, often family run with around 10–20 employees. Some remain so to this day but the majority were swallowed up by the petrochemical industry between the 1970s and the 1990s. Even the production of black pigment moved from small independent producers to an adjunct of the oil industry.

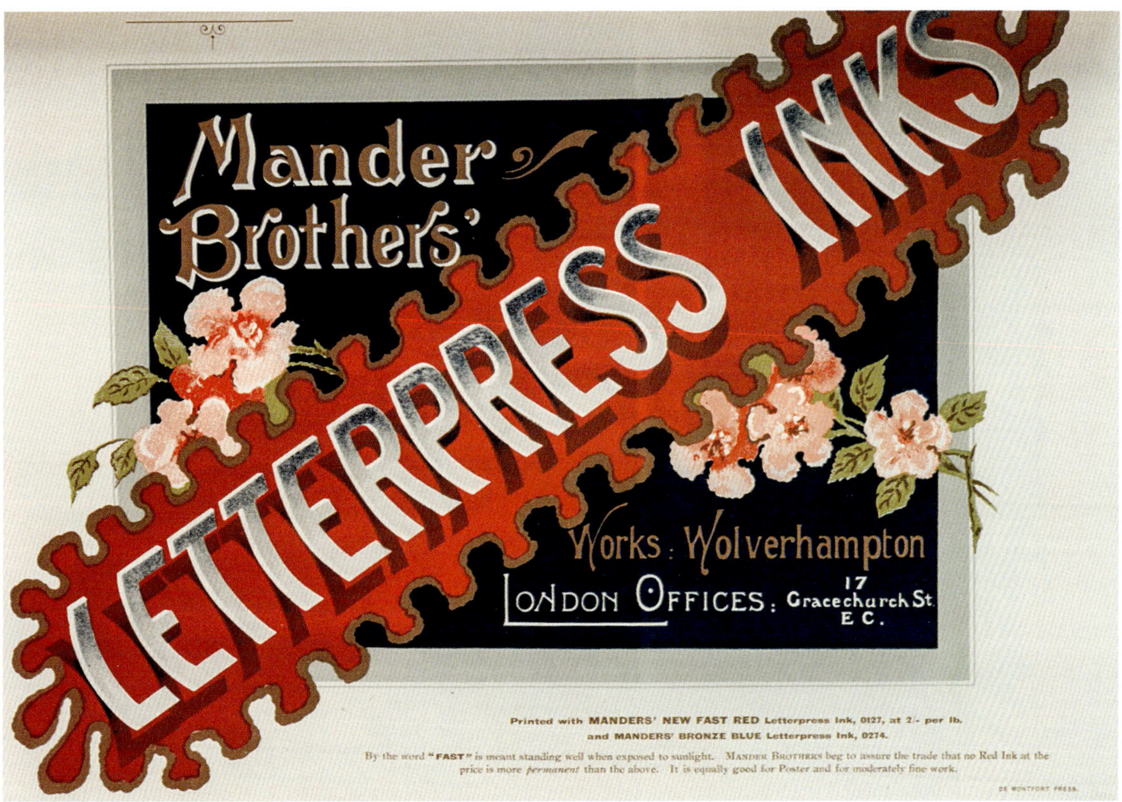

▲ **Mander Brothers' ink advert from** *The British Printer*, **March 1894.** Photo: Jo Hounsome Photography

Further pressures were placed on the ink industry with the increased popularity of speedier lithographic presses, at the expense of letterpress. Many independent ink producers were simply unable to evolve and reformulate in time.

Some small companies continue to manufacture ink from pigment using traditional oils such as linseed as their primary vehicle. Most commercial ink manufacture is undertaken by large corporations who manufacture ink by multiples of tons. The commercial manufacturer will either buy the pigment premixed in a vehicle to a colour specification or manufacture the premix on another site.

The specialist manufacture of printmaking ink is characterised by its production process of mixing, milling and matching.

Printmaking ink manufacturers will buy their raw powdered pigment directly from a pigment manufacturer, if they are buying larger quantities, or from one of the diminishing number of third-party suppliers for smaller quantities. The pigment is then tested against previous batches, weighed, and mixed with a vehicle such as linseed oil. These days the linseed used is often a heat-polymerised oil also known as copperplate oil or stand oil. It is a naturally occurring triglyceride vegetable oil derived from the seed of the flax plant *Linum usitatissimum*, which has been refined and polymerised. Contemporary production methods ensure control of chemical and physical properties. Closed-kettle processing has replaced the traditional burnt linseed oil for two reasons. First, closed-kettle heat-polymerised oil is consistent and has very predictable qualities. The second reason is that, given contemporary health and safety legislation, the potential for setting fire to a boiling cauldron of ink would not score highly in any insurance assessment. The oil and the pigment plus any other ingredients necessary, such as wax and extenders, are then taken forward for mixing.

Ink makers will sometimes talk about the 'thirst' of a pigment, by which they mean its oil absorbency. An absorbent pigment will take more oil into its structure, producing a thicker paste; a less thirsty pigment will behave more like a non-absorbent ball bearing and the finished product will be of lower, perhaps too low, viscosity. It is for this reason that the ink chemist retains the final say on the ratio of pigment to varnish both in general terms and (especially with variable earth pigments) on a batch-to-batch basis.

It is worth noting that pigments vary in colour strength, oil absorption, structure, particle size and shape, ease of dispersion, opacity, density, hardness, etc., and that all these properties affect the final character of the ink produced. For example, given the same binder, some pigments will accelerate the drying process, and some produce long, sticky inks, while others tend to make shorter, buttery inks. Each formula therefore reflects the general principles of ink for-mulation and the particular qualities inherent in the chosen pigment. Thus, in a very real sense, the pigment imposes its unique character on any ink it is in. But it is also important to remember that the manufacturing process influences the final character of the ink. For example, the high colour strength needed in lithographic inks is achieved in part by high pigment loading and in part by grinding at higher shear pressures than are necessary for an etching ink. Most formulas therefore provide only a limited part of the picture, unless they are accompanied by details of manufacture, an understanding of the raw materials being used and awareness of the intended end use. It is almost impossible to recreate an ink from a recipe alone.

The obvious defining factor of a pigment is, of course, its colour, but the experienced ink chemist and mill operator will recognise other attributes. Those who have been manufacturing ink for a long time will know the pre-dominant colours being made on a given day simply by the odour in the mill hall: ultramarine blue will have a pungent sulphurous smell, and earth colours will smell of an engineering workshop or a rainy day after a dry spell!

▶ **High-speed dispersion mixer blade.** Photo: Jo Hounsome Photography © Cranfield Colours

▶▶ **High-speed dispersion mixing.**

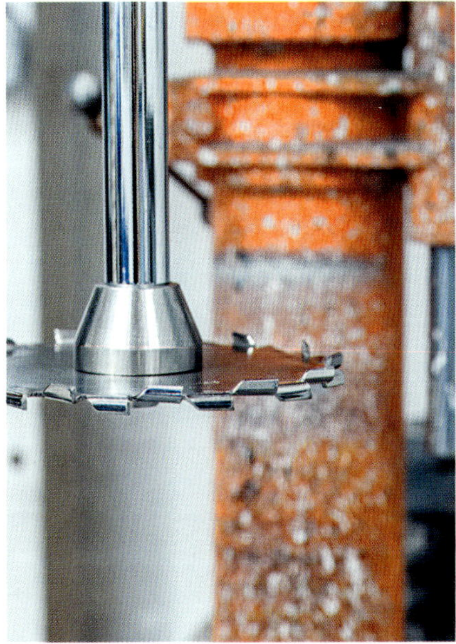

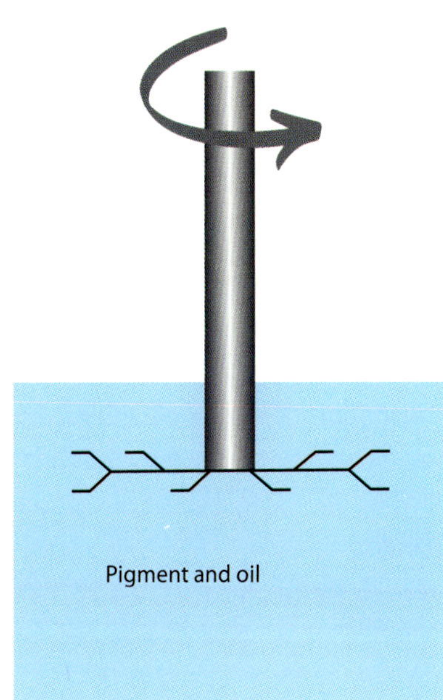

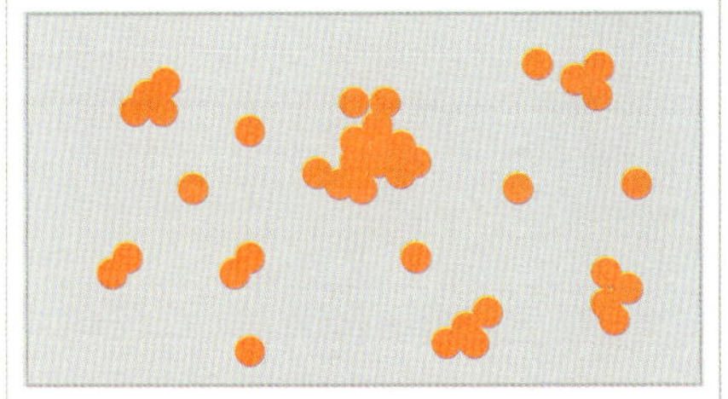

▲▲ **Aagglomerated particles.**

▲ **Well-mixed particles with an even coating of oil.**

Mixing

Mixing is done in an enclosed high-speed dispersion mixer. The reason for mixing is to coat each of the particles of pigment evenly with the vehicle, in this case linseed oil. Mixing, and the mechanical agitation of pigment and varnish, ensures that no dry pigment remains and air is replaced with oil (pigment wetting). Mixing also starts to break up the larger groups of pigment particles known as agglomerates.

One of the primary concerns for any ink manufacturer mixing ink from pigment is agglomeration, or flocculation. This simply refers to particles clumping together in lumps and not allowing the vehicle to coat their surfaces evenly. Avoiding this problem is important for achieving the best colour fidelity for maximum efficiency, and therefore the least cost to the manufacturer and customer. Poorly ground inks with agglomerates give rise to a number of destructive (as well as unpleasant) ink phenomena. The more each particle is separated and coated with the vehicle, the better the reflectance of light and the stronger the colour. Such qualities are, of course, crucial for developing the highest quality result desired by artist printmakers, but awareness and appreciation of ink quality allows for ease of work on the press.

There is also a danger of this particular problem with the fine particles in lithographic ink, if flocculation occurs following the manufacture of the ink.

This is a long-term problem, as the phenomenon increases over time when an ink has not been properly ground. When the printmaker comes to use such an ink on the litho stone, problems can arise if water reaches the dry particles of ink that have not been coated by oil; the water fount solution and the ink can combine or emulsify. We then have a mixture of ink, some with particles coated with water, some with particles coated with oil. The two sets of ink can bond together, forming an emulsion that is attractive to both oil and water. This emulsion then acts in a similar manner to soap, causing the oil and water components of the process to mix together, the printing plate to scum up and the essential mutually repellent qualities of ink and water to be lost.

Milling

Once mixed, the ink goes forward for milling. Milling fulfils two functions: the first is to compensate for possible problems with small pockets of the ink that might not be fully mixed. By submitting the ink to a second, different process, milling ensures that each particle is 'wetted', or evenly coated with the vehicle, and that there are no agglomerate lumps or dry parts in the ink. The second is to grind the ink, breaking up and reducing the clusters (agglomerates) of pigment to the desired particle size. In lithographic ink, as a rule this should be as small as possible (5 microns) in order to obtain the maximum colour strength. Etching ink is an exception to this rule; if the particle size is too fine then the ink can be difficult to wipe from the plate. Fortunately, handmade etching ink can never be ground too finely, but does run the risk of flocculation.

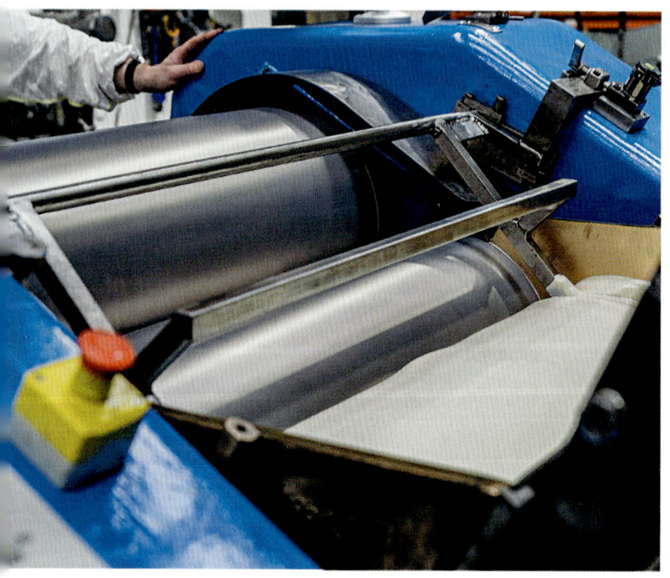

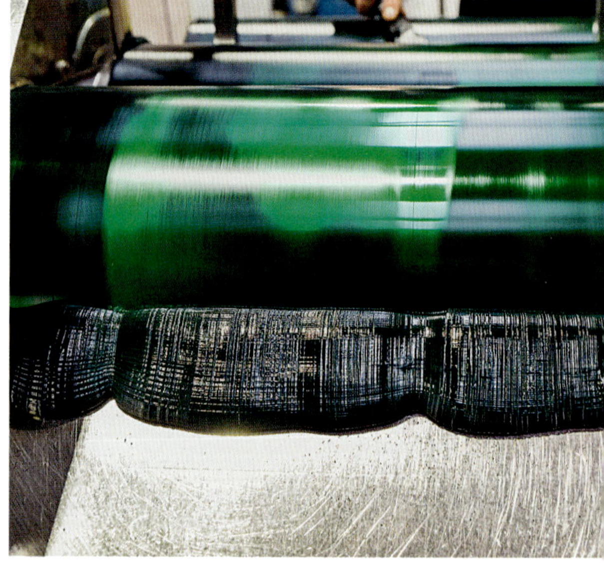

▼◀ **Triple roll mill.** Photo: Jo Hounsome Photography © Cranfield Colours

▼ **A triple roll mill milling colour.** Photo: Jo Hounsome Photography © Cranfield Colours

Fig 1: Triple roll mill: direction of grind

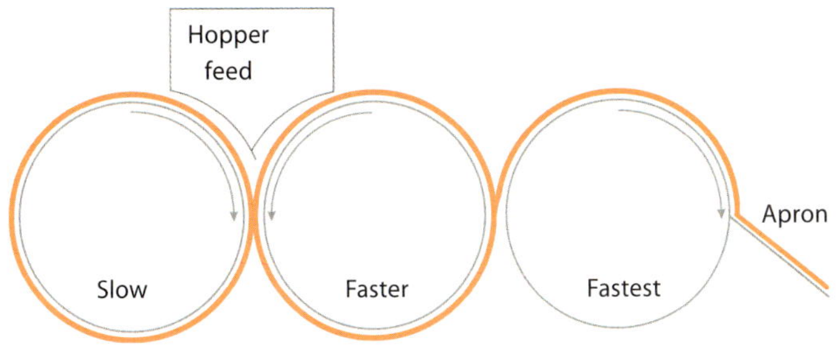

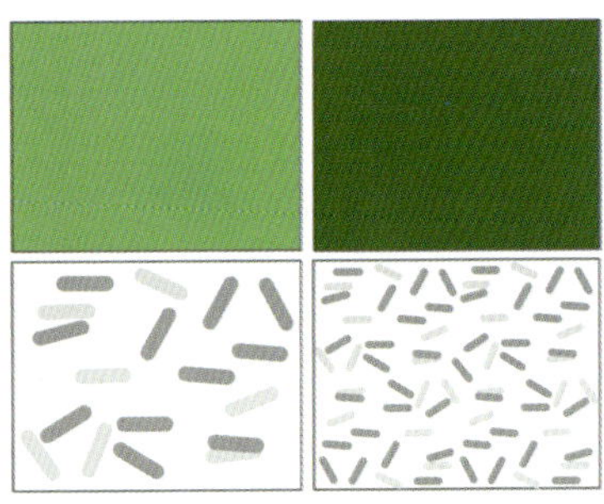

Particle size: A finer grind results in a smaller particle size, and therefore a darker ink.

Milling works by shearing action and is normally undertaken on a triple roll mill (see Fig 1). The mill consists of three hollow cylindrical steel rollers of equal size, through which cold water is run to keep the temperature down while in operation. The three centrifugally cast precision-engineered rollers are geared to run at different speeds, with the contacting rollers moving in opposite directions. Thus, the back roller rotates forwards, the centre roller rotates backwards at a faster speed, and the front roller rotates forwards at the fastest speed. It is this action that simultaneously stretches and compresses the ink as it passes through the rollers, thus breaking apart pigment agglomerates.

Mixed ink is placed in the mill between the back and centre rollers and collected from a plate held at 45° against the front roller. The gap between each roller is controllable, as is the speed of each one. The hollow cylinders are water-cooled on the inside, and it is these three factors (pressure, speed and temperature) that determines the fineness of grind and the pigment dispersion within the ink. Milling will continue until the correct particle size is achieved.

Particle size

Particle size is important as it affects strength, hue, rheology (flow characteristics – see p.201), stability, transparency and opacity. In some cases, particle size is more important in printmaking ink than in commercial ink. For commercial ink, the aim is to obtain the smallest particle. There are two reasons for this: the first is that the smaller the particle, the stronger the colour, which particularly applies to transparent ink; the second is that a stronger colour reduces the cost.

All the above applies to lithographic ink. In relief ink, however, a much thicker film weight is being carried because opacity is more important. In an etching ink, the ink must be easy to wipe, so, depending on colour, a larger particle can be helpful because it will wipe off the surface of the plate more easily but stay stuck in the line more readily.

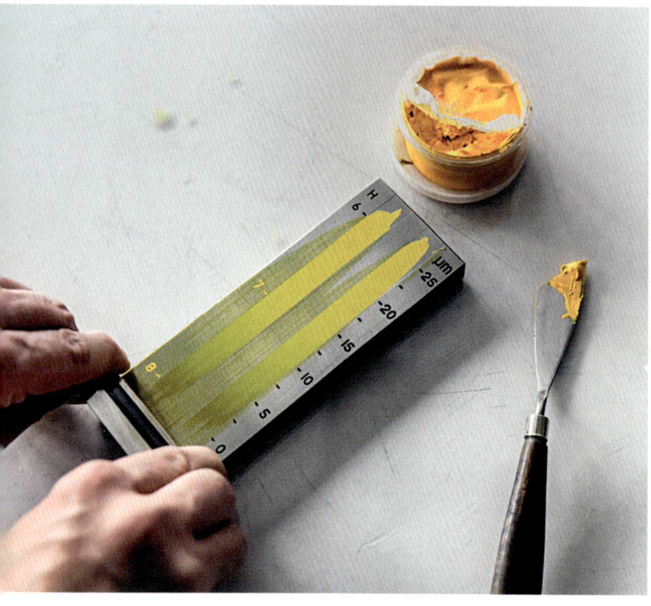

Fig 2: Principle of FOG gauge

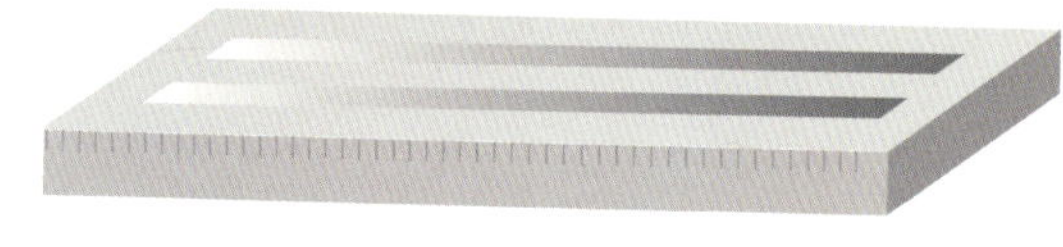

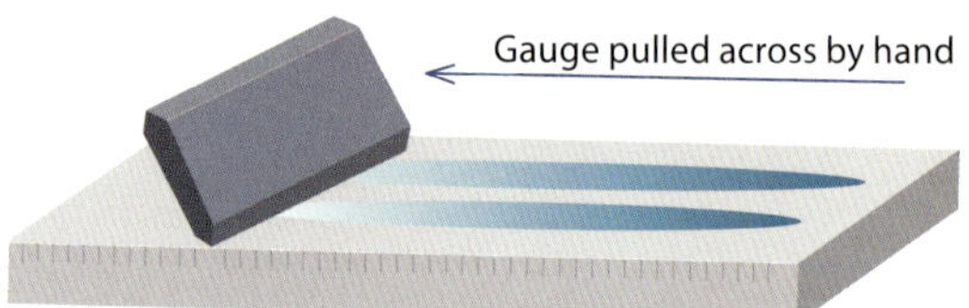

◀ **Hegman or fineness-of-grind (FOG) gauge.** Photo: Jo Hounsome Photography © Cranfield Colours

The particle size and degree of dispersion of an ink are measured with a simple device known as a FOG or Hegman gauge. The gauge has a pair of shallow channels set into a stainless steel block. Each channel is about 1 cm wide and slopes up to surface level from a depth of about 1 mm. A small blob of ink is placed in the deep end of the gauge and this is then drawn towards the shallow end with a stainless steel squeegee. The ink shows visible scratches at a point where the particle is too large to pass under the squeegee and is instead pulled further up the slope, and a measurement is taken from a calibrated scale at the side of the gauge at the break in the ink. The size of the particle is then calibrated in microns (see Fig 2)

Matching

There are a number of accepted methods and standards for testing methods for printing inks. Fundamentally, testing falls into three general categories:

1. Shade, strength and colour properties including lightfast values;
2. Physical properties, primarily viscosity, tack and fineness of grind;
3. Drying times.

Some tests are carried out on the wet ink during or after manufacture, while others (such as lightfast testing) can only be carried out on the dried ink film, as on a print.

1. Testing of shade, strength and colour properties including lightfast values

The first test is the comparison of shade and strength, and to some extent gloss. This is best done visually in the first instance using the quick and (under the right conditions) sensitive method of the drawdown test.

A suitable substrate is pre-printed with a solid black bar across the test sheet, 2–3 cm wide. Two small drops of the inks being compared are placed at the top of the test sheet. Generally, one will be the batch being made and the other will be taken from the 'standard' – the original approved formulation against which all subsequent batches are measured. This needs replacing from time to time, but by using as few standards as possible, a drift away from the colour and quality of subsequent batches can be avoided. The drops are positioned about 2 cm apart and the ink technician will make sure that both have similar flow properties to prevent unequal film thicknesses. The drops are drawn down the test sheet under even pressure using a smooth, slightly flexible, even-edged metal scraper blade. The two inks will run together, but a boundary will be maintained between them that serves as a line of comparison.

It's a real skill and pleasing to watch, as with a flick of the wrist, the technician will momentarily release the pressure to form a narrow, thick film mass. The hue and strength of the two inks can be compared when drawn down over the white paper, and differences in opacity are evident when drawn over the printed black bar. Further differences can be spotted by the trained eye in the thick film at the end of the drawdown, for example where a transparent ink will often appear darker or 'hollow'.

This test is important for the manufacturer as a control test between one ink and another and as a comparison of shade and colour. For the printmaker, a drawdown is equally important, but it is best done on a sample of the actual printmaking paper you are using (Somerset, Arches, Fabriano, Hahnemühle, etc.). In addition to checking how a colour will print out, it is often useful to tap out a sample with your finger to get a thicker and thinner film, which may be more representative of how the colour will print for you in your studio set-up.

2. Testing of physical properties, primarily viscosity, tack and fineness of grind

The measurement of rheology requires complex mathematical calculations, but it is of huge practical consequence for the printmaker. The viscosity and tack of oil-based inks required by the various printmaking disciplines are different, and variations will impact the print quality.

Viscosity refers to the ability of ink to flow; the more viscous an ink, the greater its resistance to flow. For example, glass is an extremely viscous liquid that will eventually flow. There are examples of very old windows where the glass is thin at the top and thick at the bottom because, although we generally view glass as an inert solid, it has a viscosity that decreases as it rises in temperature, thus making it more fluid as it gets hotter. Water, on the other hand, has a very low viscosity.

Manufacturers of ink commonly measure viscosity for printing ink varnishes with a falling bar viscometer. This is a simple device consisting of an internally water-cooled metal collar plate with a hole in the centre. A round bar of the same diameter is placed into the hole with a blob of varnish on the end to act as a lubricant. The bar has weights attached to the top, and its rate of descent through the hole is measured across two points. The weight is then increased, and the bar's drop rate is measured again. A series of measurements are compared against a chart to work out the viscosity of the varnish in poise (See Fig 3).

Other viscometers work by placing a sample of ink between two plates. The top plate turns and, dependent of the viscosity of the fluid being tested, a force is exerted on the second plate which can be translated into a quantifiable unit of viscosity. Very low viscosities of oil and other fluids can be measured using a series of Zahn cups, where a known quantity of fluid is timed as it drains through a precisely engineered hole in the base of a cup or ladle.

The Churchill tackmeter is used for describing both the stickiness of an ink and its tendency to mist or fly off a roller.

The majority of printmaking inks will be thixotropic; in simple terms, this means that when stirred, warmed or agitated, the ink will become

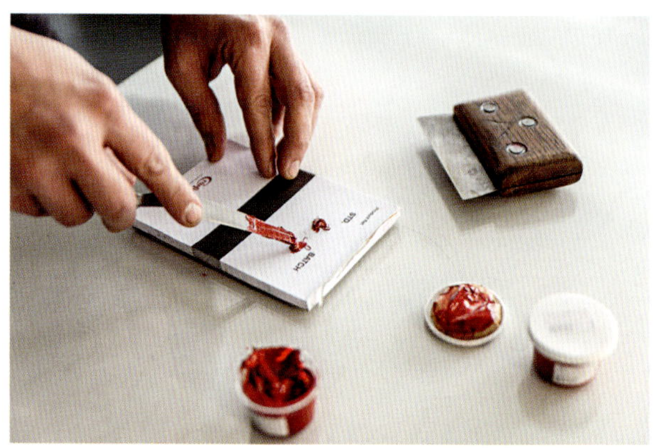

Placing ink on the paper for making a drawdown.

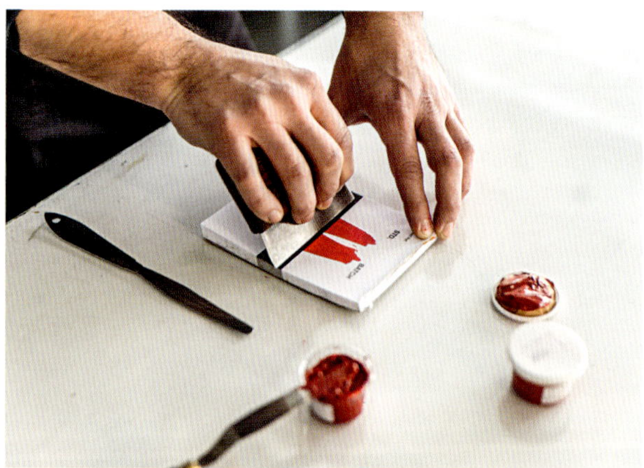

Drawing the ink over the sheet with a steel blade.

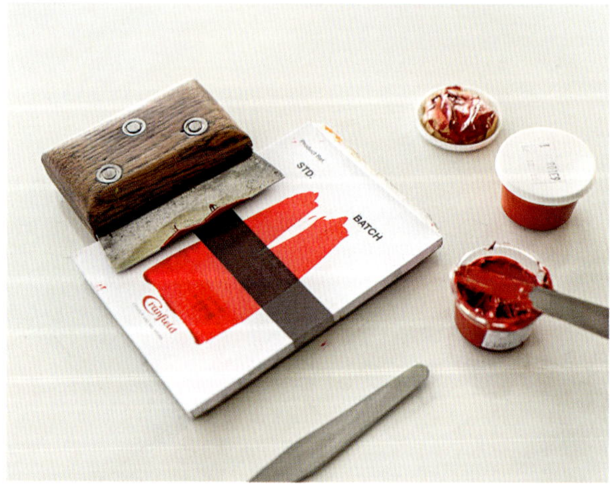

The finished drawdown.
Photos: Jo Hounsome Photography © Cranfield Colours

Fig 3: Principle of the falling bar viscometer

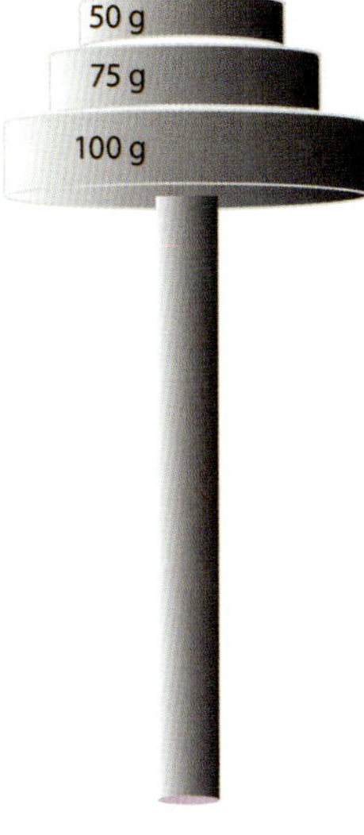

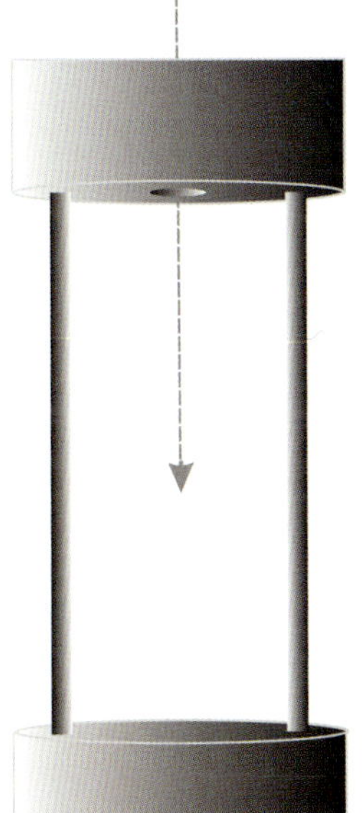

▶ **Falling bar viscometer.**
Photo: Jo Hounsome
Photography © Cranfield
Colours

more fluid. When you get ink out of a tin, always work it with a palette knife on a slab first before rolling it out, to get a measure of its consistency. As you work the ink, you will find its consistency changes because you are imparting more heat to it and therefore loosening the oil. Gauging the thixotropic characteristics of an ink at the time of manufacture is generally down to the skill and experience of the ink maker in assessing how the ink regains its structure after it has been agitated by a palette knife on a glass slab.

A range of further tests include testing the rub resistance or adhesion of the ink to a suitable substrate. The adhesion of ink to paper surface is an important factor within ink manufacture. For successful printing, an ink must adhere to the substrate for the lifespan of the product, whether it's on paper, board, film, foil, plastic, metal, glass or rubber. The vehicle system is the element most responsible for an ink's adhesive properties, although colourants can have an effect depending upon their chemical compatibility with the vehicle and the ratio of pigment to vehicle.

As with drying, adhesion can occur in several ways. On absorbent substrates, vehicle penetration is key. On non-absorbent surfaces the vehicle resin's ability to form a continuous film and its chemical affinity with the substrate are most important. Ink solvents provide the wetting and flow-out of ink to give the continuous film necessary for good adhesion. Selection of raw materials and formulation of the appropriate vehicle is essential to proper adhesion.

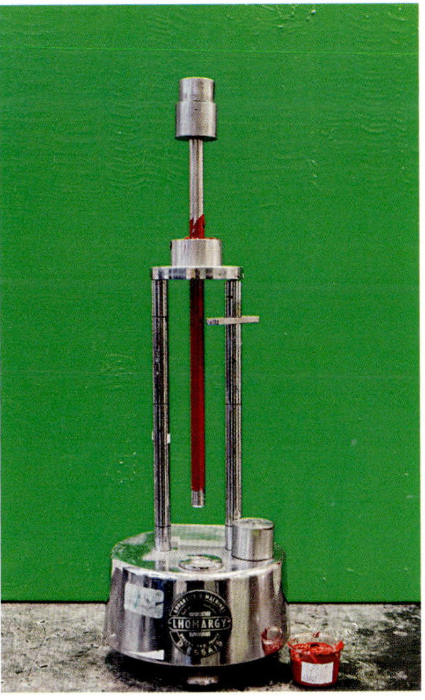

The lightfast testing of inks tends to be an ongoing evaluation of raw materials as they arrive, or when formulations are added or altered. Because of the lengths of time involved in each test, it is not something that is done while the ink waits to be passed in the laboratory. Commonly, a lightfast testing machine will contain an air-cooled xenon light source that will condense many weeks of Florida sunshine into a matter of hours. Using the Blue Wool method of evaluating the rate and extent of fading, each ink can be given an accurate Blue Wool number between 1 and 8 (with 8 being the highest score possible).

3. Testing of drying times

Methods and devices exist for testing drying times for both the ink on a non-absorbent surface – glass – and in a more applied 'real life' paper example. The drying characteristics of an ink are critical for several reasons, the most obvious being that a print cannot be handled or used until the ink has dried and developed a surface film, also known as film integrity. The way an ink dries can be an important factor for the printmaker. Drying also affects the speed with which a print can be overprinted.

In most cases, the first phase of ink drying is setting; immediately upon being applied to the paper, the vehicle or liquid portion of the ink begins either to evaporate or to penetrate the stock, causing the ink to thicken. Setting is followed by actual drying via one or more possible mechanisms, e.g., absorption, oxidation, evaporation or polymerisation. The specific mechanism is determined by the relationships between the printing process itself, the ink vehicle system and the substrate.

Inks that are applied to an absorbent substrate, such as newsprint paper or an uncoated artists' paper, dry by absorption. The fluid portion of the ink penetrates the substrate, leaving an ink film on the surface. Depending upon the printing process, this ink film may undergo additional drying procedures.

In oxidation, components in the ink's oils chemically combine with oxygen in the atmosphere to form a semi-solid or solid ink film. This often occurs in combination with absorption. Oxidation can be accelerated by the use of driers in the ink formulation or by the application to the print of heat or infrared radiation (dependent on the type of vehicle).

Since non-porous substrates such as plastic films and glass cannot absorb ink vehicles, they require inks that dry either through evaporation or by polymerisation. In the former, vehicle solvents evaporate, leaving resins and other materials behind to bind the pigments to the substrate. Evaporation from the inks must be rapid enough for complete drying, but not so rapid as to cause instability while the inks are rolled out on the slab or are still on the rollers of a press.

Some further tests are only initiated when significant changes to the formulation are required. One such is the method for testing taint and odour. This consists of a jar containing a broken bar of chocolate as a control, and one that contains both the broken chocolate and paper printed with the ink in question as the test. Because chocolate absorbs odours easily and the contrast is marked, the experienced nose will be able to check whether the odour is familiar and acceptable, or if it is unpleasant, rancid or overpowering.

Water-based formulations

The terms 'vehicle' and 'colourant' can equally be used in the family of inks commonly, and perhaps inaccurately, described as water- based. A better name would be 'water-containing': the vehicle may be aqueous copolymers or a water-miscible oil, but the general principles of manufacture remain broadly similar to the historic methods of oil-based formulation. The comparative ease with which water-based inks can be cleaned makes them suitable for production on bead or ball mills, which are cheaper to run than three roll mills. Manufacturers will be reticent to divulge the exact methods of production, but ball mills are popular towards the lower-quality end of both paint and ink manufacture.

A ball mill consists of a hollow cylinder that ranges in size from the volume of a bucket to that of a small car. This barrel chamber rotates about its axis, which may be either horizontal or at a slight angle and is partially filled with chemically inert balls. These grinding balls may be made of chrome steel, stainless steel, a ceramic, or rubber. The inner surface of the cylindrical shell is normally lined with an abrasion-resistant material such as manganese steel or rubber.

The general idea behind the ball mill is an ancient one, but it was not until the industrial revolution and the invention of steam power that an effective ball milling machine could be built. It is the action of the balls falling over one another through the ink as the cylinder turns that provides the force required to separate and disperse the pigment particles. Generally, ball mills would be unsuitable for viscous formulations, but for water-based products, they provide a cost-effective means of production.

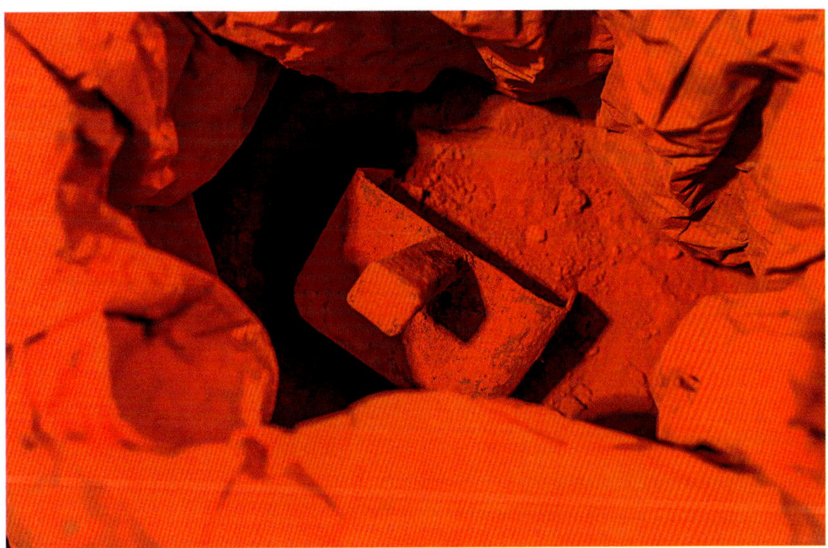

▶ **Red pigment.** Photo: Jo Hounsome Photography © Cranfield Colours

Water-based formulations are in many respects more of a chemical construction than oil-based equivalents. Besides the pigment and the copolymer vehicle, additives are required to stop bacterial growth in the container (biocides) and mould on the print (fungicides). The viscosity of water-based inks is seldom the result of the natural absorbency of the pigment, but must be controlled by the addition of thickening agents. Formulations may be further complicated with wetting agents and additives to keep the pigment in suspension and to stop it from settling out and sinking to the bottom of the container. Other additives may be required to control the pH, which is hugely influential during the manufacturing process.

The great advantage of simple water-based formulations is undoubtedly the speed with which they dry. The corresponding disadvantage is that the printed film can be more easily re-wetted in moist conditions and is more vulnerable to marking even once dry. Because water-based inks can more easily travel along the hollow centre (lumen) of paper fibres than oil-based equivalents, many printmakers say that they achieve the clearest, sharpest prints with greater nuance of film weight from oil-based inks.

Different inks for different disciplines

Relief printing remains the most popular of the printmaking methods, and formulations will generally be oil (linseed or soya) or water based.

The etching process is arguably more demanding, and is certainly hard to replicate without the operator variables of inking and plate wiping. Consequently, using a suitable ink is more critical. Inks are generally oil-based or water-containing.

The lithographic process, based on the antipathy between oil and water, can only use oil-based inks. Because of the very low ink film weights achievable, a strong water-resistant lithographic ink is required.

Screen-printing generally requires one of three ink types. Plastic resin inks as used in the (albeit rapidly declining) commercial screen printmaking market are generally unpopular with printmakers because of their environmental impact and their strong, pungent solvent odour. They do, however, provide durable, versatile, opaque results resulting in a crisp and detailed print. Plastic resin inks are made from unpolymerised polyvinyl chloride (PVC) via a chemical process combining ethylene and chlorine suspended in a liquid plastic. These products do not dry through the natural process associated with either oil- or water-based inks but are cured by exposing them to high heat, which causes the plastic mixture to harden.

Screen-printing water-based inks were thought to offer a more environmentally friendly option, although there is still a core of artists that use traditional hydrocarbon solvent inks.

Screen-printing solvent inks often contain a higher solid pigment content than water-based screen inks. In general, water-based screen inks have less colour strength, and increases in colour density are usually traded with curl problems caused by greater water content reaching the paper. As with all water-based inks formulated around acrylic emulsions, they require both biocides and fungicides to retain their shelf life. What makes acrylic screen-printing inks popular is their ability to air dry. This can help when printing on demanding non-absorbent substrates and negates the need for expensive extraction.

The flexibility of acrylic formulations has made them popular with shared studios with a limited materials budget, as they can be 'made' by the printmaker by mixing a screen-print gel additive into standard acrylic paints. This allows a school or college, for example, to offer screen-printing without having to hold an extensive stock of inks.

Inks for Japanese *mokuhanga* printing

The details given previously in this chapter intentionally focus on what might broadly be classified as the traditionally European methods of printmaking, that require high-viscosity, commonly oil-based inks that are applied by roller or scraper. The specialist inks used in *mokuhanga* or Japanese printmaking methods must be treated as an entirely separate category.

Japanese block printing is a historic method of printmaking that is thought to date from the seventh century. The image is first sketched onto *washi* – a thin Japanese paper. It is then glued to the surface of the smooth woodblock, commonly made of cherry wood. The drawn lines will become the raised areas of image, while the non-image areas are carved away.

The carved wood block is not inked with a roller but with a horsehair brush called a *hakobi*. The methods vary, but traditionally a strong water-based ink is extended on the block itself with the addition of starch-based *nori* paste. Others mix the two components prior to inking the plate. Because Japanese printmaking uses a hand-held baren to apply pressure during printing rather than a printing press, the print studio is often a relatively small and simple affair. Many printmakers around the world today will not use a dedicated Japanese woodblock ink, but will make their own by mixing water-based paints, gouache or powder pigments with home-made or purchased *nori* paste. A pestle and mortar or a glass muller would not be out of place in the studio of the *washi* printer.

PROBLEMS WITH BUYING AND HANDLING INK

The most common problem is, of course, lack of knowledge by the artist regarding the qualities of the constituent parts of a particular ink and therefore the use for which that ink has been developed. For example, many artists printing lithographs and relief prints use a standard off-the-shelf commercial litho ink. The problem here is that commercial litho ink is developed first and foremost for high-speed printing. Therefore, the ink will contain surfactants, driers, anti-scumming agents and synthetic polymers, all to enhance thin coating, very fast drying and light film weight, plus additives for increased water resistance and antioxidation. None of these attributes are particularly relevant to the printmaker, and these additives can have a detrimental effect on the long-term stability and lightfastness of the ink. That means you can unwittingly create work that deteriorates noticeably over time.

Another problem is that artists commonly assume that the raw powdered pigment is standard and does not vary from supplier to supplier and from batch to batch. Awareness of this issue can help printmakers avoid disappointment. This can also become a major headache for the ink manufacturer. Suppliers of raw pigment are now rare, and if a supplier goes out of business, as has happened on numerous occasions during the first 20 years of the twenty-first century, new sources must be found. Naturally occurring earth pigments, such as yellow ochre and raw umber, are by their very nature inconsistent.

The main problem with earth pigments is the gritty nature of the pigment and the presence of impurities. If you dig up the soil from your back garden, you would not expect every spadeful to be the same colour; the same is true of naturally occurring pigment. It can be very hard to guarantee consistency of supply.

With the passage of time, the use of naturally occurring earth pigments is likely to decline further. Cranfield uses a handful of unique earth colours and one bone black; all the rest of their pigments are chemically created. The trace elements of impurities that might be found to varying degrees in inks containing earth pigments increases the chance that they will fail the chemical analysis tests for organisations such as the accreditation body Art and Creative Materials Institute (ACMI). The possible rejection of ink batches on these grounds is a risk too costly for the ink manufacturer to carry indefinitely.

WHY USE TAILOR-MADE DEDICATED PRINTMAKING INKS?

There are three primary reasons for using an ink tailor-made for artists. The first is ease of use: an ink specifically developed for the purpose is, of course, going to be much easier to use. The second and third reasons are related to conservation and lightfastness. A newspaper or magazine is commonly thrown away after a week or a month; therefore, the ink used does not need to be permanent. Newspaper inks are interesting, as in many respects they set sufficiently to be read at the breakfast table but only finally cure (that is, become completely inert and dry) long after they have gone into the compost or been sent off for recycling.

An artist's original print is not normally created for a very short lifespan; therefore, the ink needs to be permanent. A purpose-made ink that uses only single, high-quality pigment colour will be easier to test for lightfastness and is indeed less likely to fade. Most artists' inks use linseed oil or derivatives, and possibly the addition of a drier, but very little else; it is therefore possible to predict their potential lifespan. A word of caution, however: it does not pay to assume any ink is lightfast unless you have checked with the manufacturer or there is a Blue Wool Scale or similar denotation of lightfast quality on the tin.

HOW TO COMPARE VARNISH NUMBERS TO POISE AND COPPERPLATE STRENGTHS

Perhaps the most confusing element in the manufacture of ink is the measurement of the thickness and strength of the printing varnish. Even for manufacturers in the industry, it is not easy to make comparisons from country to country. Viscosity is measured in a number of ways, dependent upon which country you are in or the age of the convention used for a process. Viscosity is also temperature-dependent, and typically decreases as the temperature rises. To confuse matters further, it is also dependent on whether your ink is a Newtonian or non-Newtonian fluid. The simplest are the Newtonian ones, such as water, dilute suspensions, aqueous solutions, emulsions and oil-bound inks.

Non-Newtonians are a group of thixotropic liquids, i.e. they change viscosity when they are stirred, shaken or otherwise agitated. Some water-based screen-print inks are thixotropic, hence the confusion.

Viscosity can be measured in different unit systems. The SI (International System of Units) unit for measuring all liquids is Newtons per square metre (N/m^2). The SI unit for measuring dynamic viscosity is the Pascal second (Pa·s).

Fig 4: Chart comparing poise strength to American lithographic varnish numbers

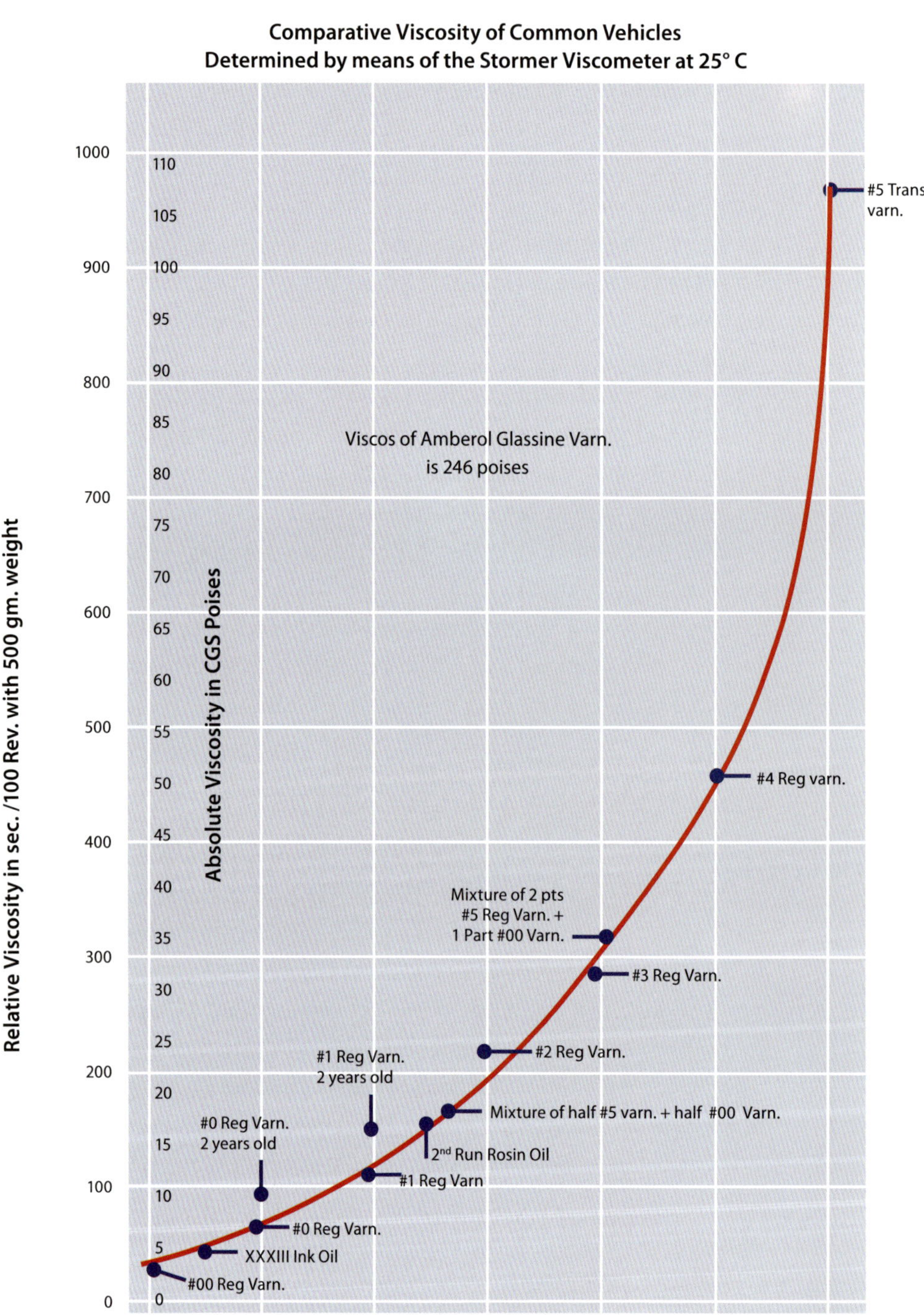

Fig 5: Poise conversion table

Consistency/poise	European litho varnish number	American oils	Copperplate varnish	European litho
Very runny	1 poise	00	Weak copperplate	Weak litho varnish
	2 poise	1		
	25 poise	2		
	30–40 poise			
	32 poise	3		Medium litho varnish
Medium oil	40–50 poise		Medium copperplate	
	50 poise	4		
	60 poise	5		
	200 poise			Strong litho
	330 poise		Strong copperplate varnish	
	500–550 poise	7		

Ink for printmakers is not measured by this standard system. An older unit, the poise or dyn-s/cm^2, remains in common use; if the force of one dyne is needed to move 1 cm^2 at 1 cm per second then the viscosity is 1 poise. The European system of measuring viscosity in printing oils ranges from 1 poise for the thinnest oils through to 700 poise for extremely thick and very viscous varnishes with a toffee-like consistency.

The American system of measuring viscosity in printing oils is completely different and uses lithographic varnish numbers ranging from litho varnish #00000 for the thinnest through to litho varnish #10 for the extremely thick and viscous varnishes, with #7 being the strongest in most cases.

To make matters even more confusing, etching oils/varnishes are measured in weak copperplate, medium copperplate and strong copperplate. For the printmaker, this profusion of different strengths and numbers for measuring viscosity in varnish allows for no means of making a comparison between one system and the next. Figs 4 and 5 attempt to clarify some of this confusion. The table in Fig 5 is offered as a rough guide, and should not be considered accurate.

VARNISH/OIL STRENGTHS USED IN MANUFACTURE

To provide a general guide to the oil strength or viscosity the ink manufacturer will use when creating an ink for one of the main printing processes, the following is offered:

- In a *lithograph* ink, the average varnish used is about 200 poise. This is because the ink must be a thin film with strong binding properties and good tack to transfer a heavy pigment loading in order to make a strong colour with low film weight.
- In *etching*, a 30–40 poise varnish is used, and a 1 poise varnish is added to assist wiping. The pigment loading for an etching ink is much less, and the varnish needs to be able to transfer from the lines to the plate. However, less tack is needed than for litho or relief printing as no rollers are required; it is also easier to push the ink into the lines.
- In *relief* printing, a combination of 200 poise and 30–40 poise is used. The ink needs a fair amount of body to deal with the higher film weights, but it also needs a lighter varnish in order to roll out a fairly heavy deposit of ink, and you will need an ink with sufficient tack.

INK LENGTH AND FLOW

Ink length is a more traditional term used to describe the viscosity and elasticity of ink; printmakers are familiar with the term, and measure the length of ink

Fig 6: Knife drop test

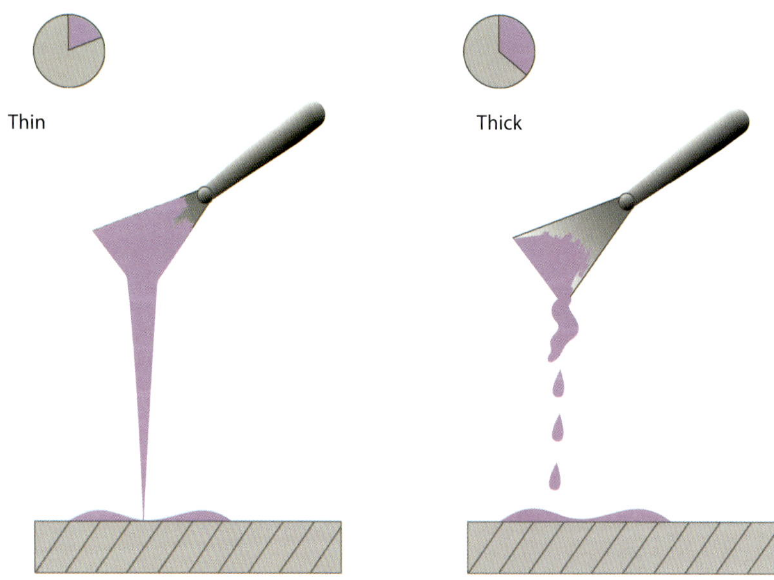

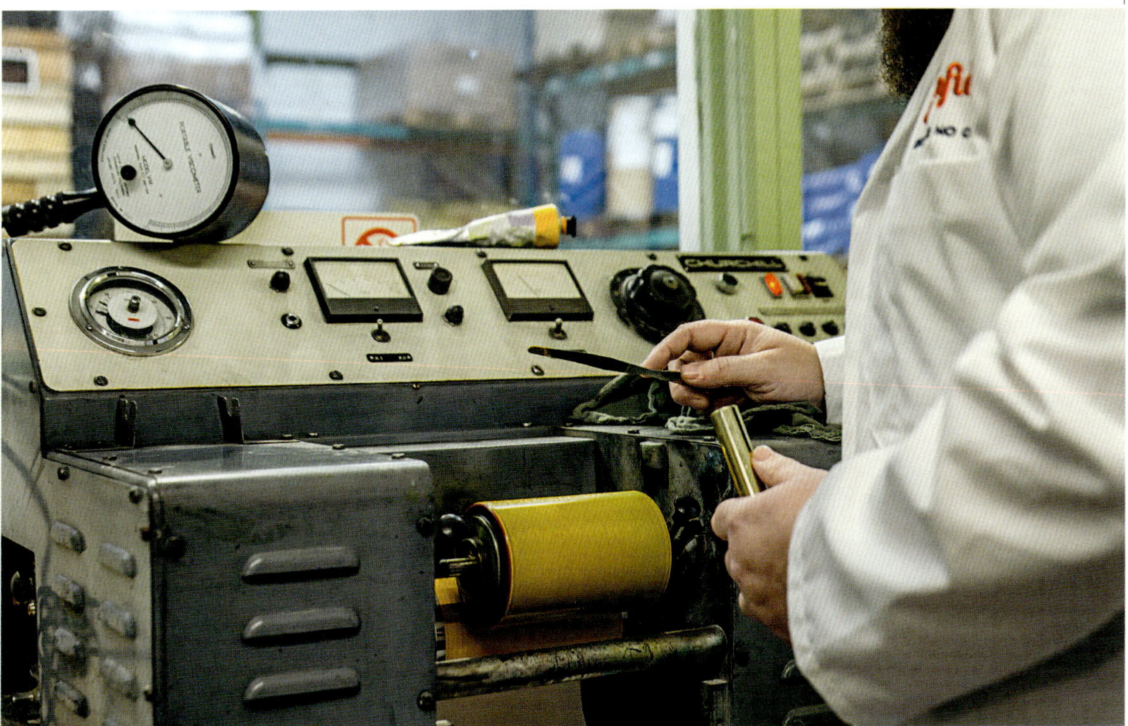

▲ Churchill tackmeter.
Photo: Jo Hounsome
Photography © Cranfield
Colours

with a palette knife or spatula. If the ink is lifted into the air and allowed to drop from the knife, its viscosity can be determined by the speed at which the ink falls away from the blade (see Fig 6).

Yet another quality, length, describes an ink's tendency to form long threads when stretched or pulled. Long inks flow well but form long filaments that tend to sling (splatter or produce strands) or mist (spray particles of ink), especially on high-speed presses. Short inks have limited flow and the consistency of butter. They tend to build up on rollers, plates or blankets.

TACK

In essence, tack refers to the stickiness of ink. Tack can be described as the ability of an ink to act as an adhesive, or, more technically, the force required for an ink to split between two rollers. Commercially, tack is measured by a tackmeter (see Fig 7). The units used by these machines are specific to each manufacturer. Therefore, comparisons can only be made between inks tested on the same machine.

Tack also determines whether the ink will pick (see p.200) the surface of the paper; ink tack that is higher than the strength of the paper surface will tear it. Tack also influences whether an ink prints in sharp lines and images or squashes out on the plate, blanket or substrate.

Fig 7: The principle for measurement using a Churchill tackmeter

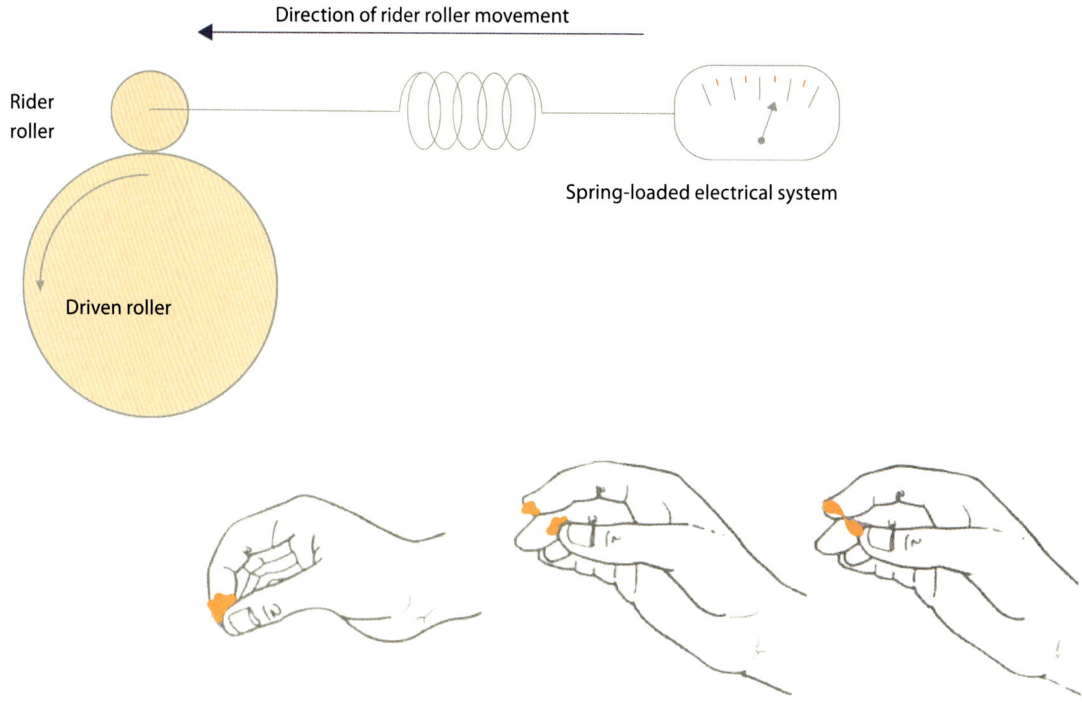

▲ Feeling the tack of ink using your fingers.

CARE OF INK

Ink is supplied in several kinds of containers, the most common being tins, closely followed by tubes and, more recently, builders' caulk guns. The container you buy is usually dictated by choice and personal preference but, whichever you choose, all ink needs to be treated with some care. There is one basic rule that applies: ink oxidises and dries in contact with air, forming hard lumps or a skin on the surface. Therefore, try and keep your ink sealed away from the air when you are not using it.

How to use a tin of ink

The following advice may seem simple, but it is surprising how often it is not followed. When taking ink from a can after having lifted the sealing ring, remove the ink required with a flat-ended palette knife in a smooth sweep across the top of the tin, keeping the level of ink in the tin even. If you push the knife down into the tin, after a couple of weeks, owing to oxidation, the ink will skin in the hole left by the knife. Then a great lump of ink has to be removed from the tin and discarded to avoid contaminating the ink with tiny pieces of dried ink skin. Once you have removed ink in the correct manner with a square-ended palette knife, it is advisable to make a greaseproof paper ring and use an antioxidant.

Preventing skinning

Antioxidants are usually very light oils of less than 1 poise, and are frequently supplied in an aerosol can. They are used to prevent skinning in a tin of ink or, in some cases, to allow a printmaker to leave out a patch of ink on the slab overnight without it drying out. They work by putting a very thin film of oil over the ink, which forms a barrier to prevent the air (oxygen) from reaching the ink and causing oxidation.

They should be used very sparingly to prevent the oil contaminating the ink and affecting its properties. To seal a can of ink to prevent skinning it is advisable first to cut a ring of greaseproof paper that fits snugly in the can, then to spray both sides of it lightly. The paper is then placed on the surface of the ink and gently rubbed down to make sure there is no air trapped under it. The lid can then be replaced, and the can stored. This method is preferable to putting a layer of water in the top of the can, as tin cans tend to rust over time, thus contaminating the ink.

Builders' caulk guns

These have become increasingly popular in communal studio environments. They allow you to squeeze out a controlled amount of ink without the tube drying up rapidly. A few tips: do not hang them up with the nozzle facing downwards, because the oil in the ink will cause the ink to seep out – hang them horizontally or with the nozzle facing upwards; always release the switch at the back after use; try not to lose the end caps and they will last longer.

Tubes of ink

'Weight for weight' tubes are the least economic method of buying ink: first, the small quantity is going to be more expensive; and second, it is harder to get all the ink out of the tube as the product ages. However, there is less wastage than using a tin if the printmaker is not using a colour regularly. The basic rules for using tubes are simple: always squeeze from the very bottom of the tube; and do not let the tube split, otherwise the ink will oxidise in the tube and create hard lumps. Do not lose the caps. Some printmakers like to hang their tubes from a hook by the crimped end, using a bulldog clip and with the cap facing down. This makes for a tidy studio, and mitigates the chance of small quantities of oil leaking from the crimped end of the tube.

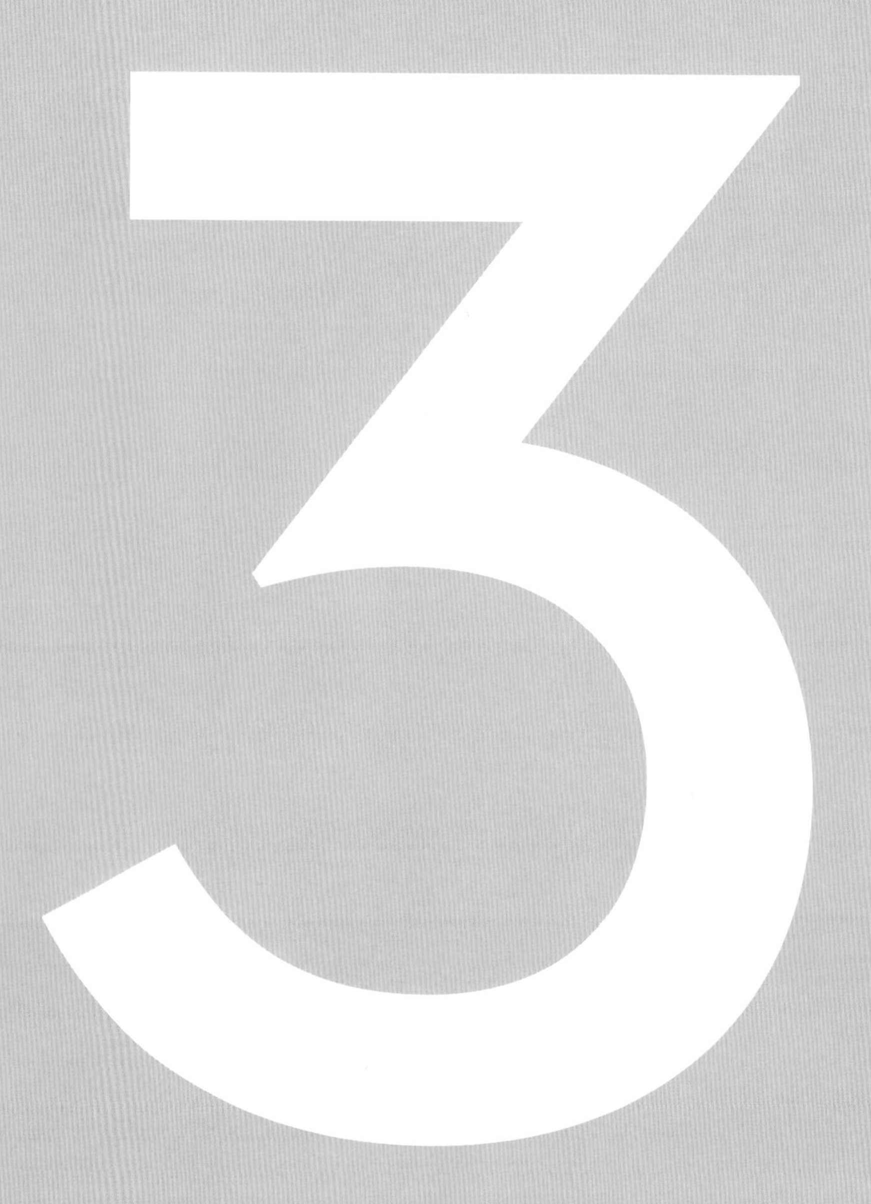

CHAPTER

3

COLOUR AND CHEMISTRY

Colour serves so many purposes for us. Is the fruit ripe or unripe? Is that a lemon or a lime? Is that my red car under the sodium yellow street light? Colour perception is at the same time objective, subjective and emotional. It is the interplay between light, surface structure and the brain. Colour vision has been described as the finest combination of physics, chemistry, biology and psychology.

Science's understanding of the extent of the computational component of vision is increasing. The human brain, armed with phenomenal colour memory capabilities, can achieve colour constancy by drawing upon its computing power. Because we know that the apple is red, the brain has been educated to compensate for the shade of the apple as it changes when viewed under a tungsten bulb, LED or candlelight to provide a mental constant.

Aspects that contribute to our colour perception

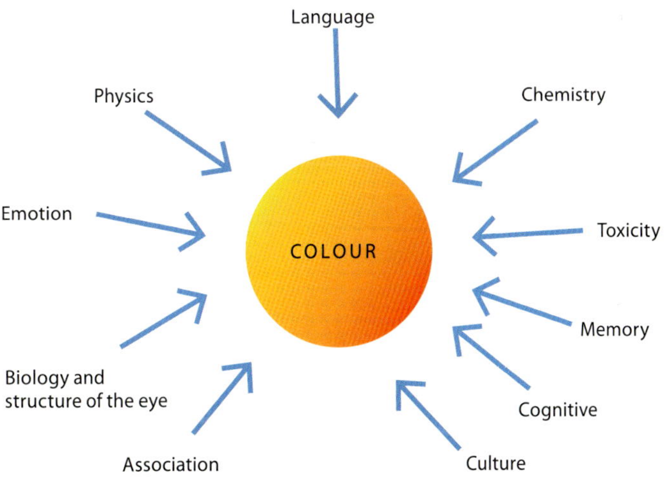

The human brain has capacity to balance all the various components of colour perception because we are subconsciously able to make contextual subconscious calculations and compensations to make colour sense of the world around us.

This can only be replicated in the digital and photographic world with highly complex algorithms. A camera does not have the benefit of knowing that we are holding an orange, and that it should therefore be rendered in the typical colour of an orange to convey what it is. The brain, however, brings personal history into the equation. It provides remembered knowledge, probabilities and statistics, even when looking at an orange.

The printmaker and the eventual viewer of a print know tens of thousands of colours, which the eye can discern with extraordinary accuracy; yet the printmaker only has access to a printing palette of perhaps 15 favourite colours that they keep in the studio. Printmaking must therefore involve some kind of colour compromise.

Colour is defined in two ways: additive and subtractive. The colour you see on the television screen, or the spectrum created by light refracted through a prism or stained glass, is known as additive light. The colour that we see on the printed page, and therefore the colour created when using an ink, is reflected from the surface of the paper it is printed upon or, in the case of ink on a mixing slab, reflected from the surface of the ink. This is known as subtractive colour.

ADDITIVE COLOUR

Light is constructed from three basic primary colours: red, green and blue. This forms the basis for all colour science. When these three are combined, they will form white light. Pure white light is composed of a number of coloured wavelengths. The primary wavelengths of light are red, green and blue (RGB), not red, yellow and blue. This phenomenon is usually demonstrated by projecting circles of light through red, green and blue filters and then overlapping them. The area where all three overlap will appear as white. The overlap of blue and red will appear as magenta, the overlap of blue and green as cyan, and the overlap of red and green as yellow.

SUBTRACTIVE COLOUR

While adding the colours of the visible spectrum together creates white light, printmakers start with white paper and subtract from the white reflected light

Additive colour mixing

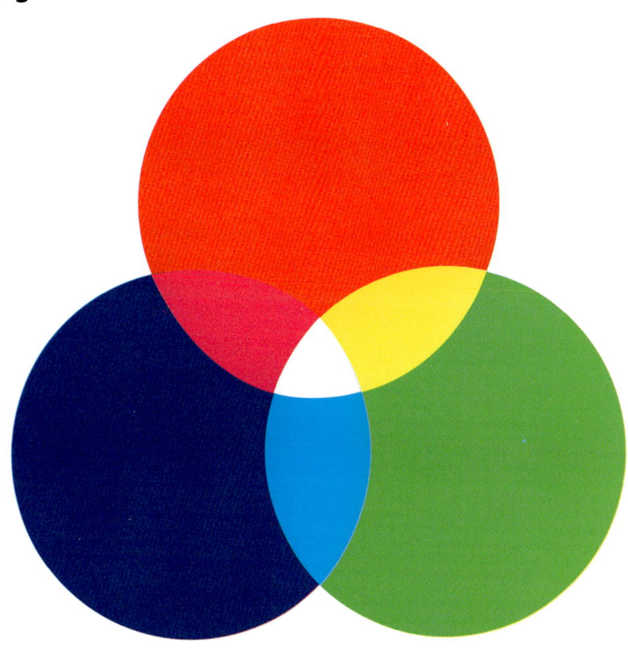

Additive colour mixing,
Red, Green, Blue (RGB).

Subtractive colour mixing

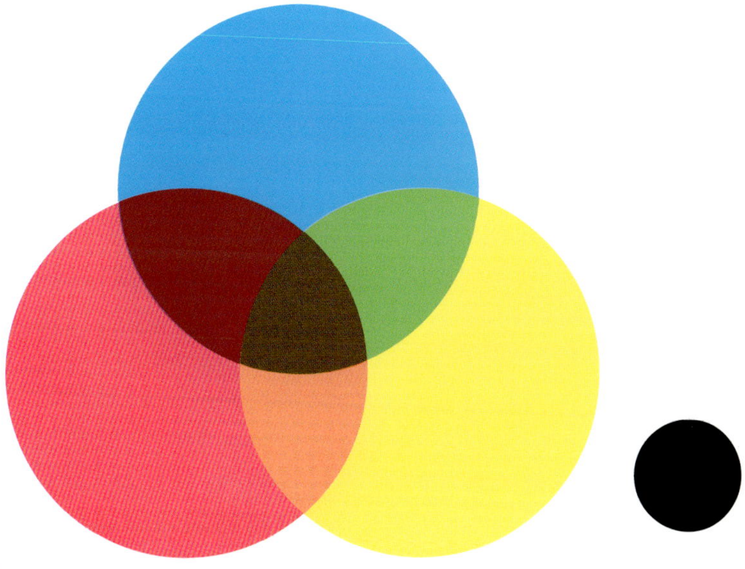

Subtractive colour mixing,
Cyan, Magenta, Yellow and
Keyline Black (CMYK).

by laying down colour. If each colour of the spectrum were overprinted, the result would be black or, more commonly, a very dark brown.

Reflecting light off a coloured surface, in our case, paper, creates subtractive colour. Subtractive colour mixing does not revolve around projected light; instead, it revolves around the absorption and reflection of light by various materials. It is the increasing layers of ink that progressively subtract from the whiteness of the paper beneath. When pure white light strikes an object, the object absorbs some of the wavelengths of light and reflects others. When you mix pigments together, they combine the number of colours they absorb, decreasing the number of wavelengths that they reflect, hence the term 'subtractive colour'. In colour science terms, the colours seen are cyan, magenta and yellow – the opposite of those used in additive colour.

Pigmented mixed colour is subtractive, and in practical terms relies on a fairly old set of colour values. The traditional view of fine artists and users of more opaque pigmented ink is that there are three primary colours – red, yellow and blue – and three secondary colours – green (yellow and blue), orange (red and yellow) and violet (blue and red). The admixture of these three is dark brown or black. To create white, they are either diluted or mixed with white pigment.

In contemporary colour science, the traditional art view is no longer the accepted norm. The reason needs to be explained, first with a bit of colour history, and then with the reasons why the views of art and science are so diverse.

HISTORY OF COLOUR THEORY

There has always been dissension between theorists and practitioners; the problem is that both are usually right in their own ways. Sir Isaac Newton is the father of modern colour theory; in 1704 he published his treatise *Optics*, the culmination of his research into colour and light.

Newton first announced his 'New Theory of Light and Colours' in a famous letter to the Royal Society in London. In it, he described several experiments, including the classic one in which a beam of sunlight refracted by a prism casts an oblong spectrum onto a wall. This spectrum ranges from red through orange, yellow, green, blue, and indigo to violet, thus providing the basis for rejecting Aristotle's theory that colour came from the object. Newton further proved his theory by setting up a glass prism in a darkened room. Sunlight was directed into the prism through a slit in a piece of card. When this beam of sunlight passed through the glass prism, a spectrum was produced. He then proved that light is the source of all colour by redirecting the spectrum

Newton White light experiment

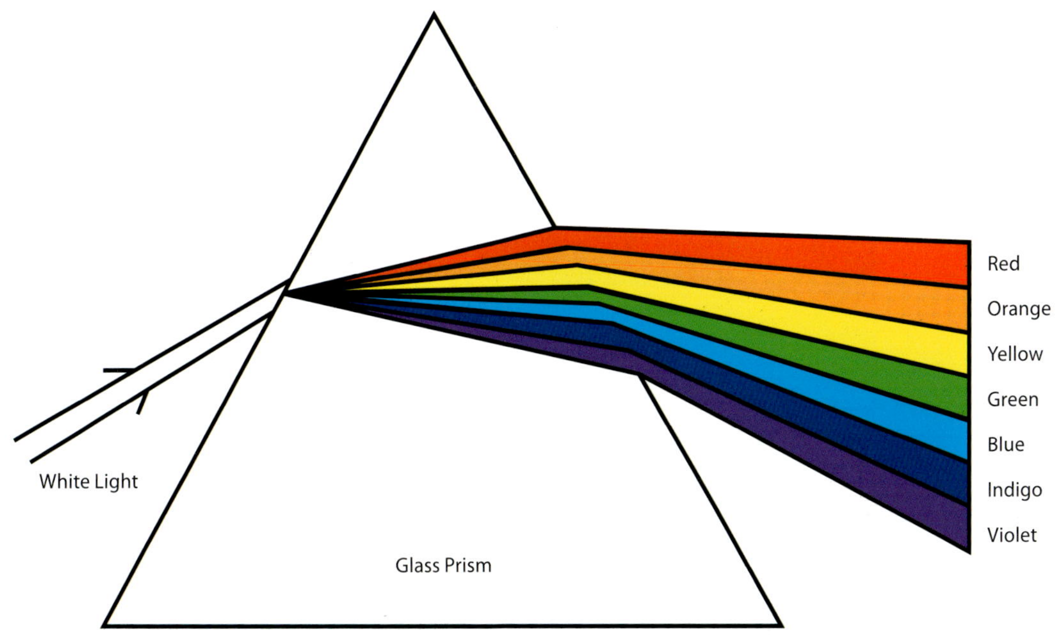

back through a second glass prism and producing white light. In doing so, he proved that white light is the sum of all colours and all colours in the spectrum are present in white light.

Newton also discovered that the colour of an object is determined by selective reflection of light. When light strikes an object, some light rays are absorbed and lost, but some are reflected to produce the colour an observer perceives. Newton expressed the spectrum of colour in a circular form by rolling up the spectrum and putting red next to violet, producing a colour wheel with seven colours. Newton was both a physicist and a theologian, and it was this latter interest which made him uncomfortable with his earliest description of the spectrum, which named six general colour groups. Feeling that six was an ungodly number, Newton designated a small section of the visible spectrum 'indigo', thereby giving seven colours – a more wholesome and holy number to Newton's mind.

Newton established the principle that all colour could be mixed from a small number of primary colours. But, while Newton proved this was so for additive colour, it was not as easy to do for subtractive colour.

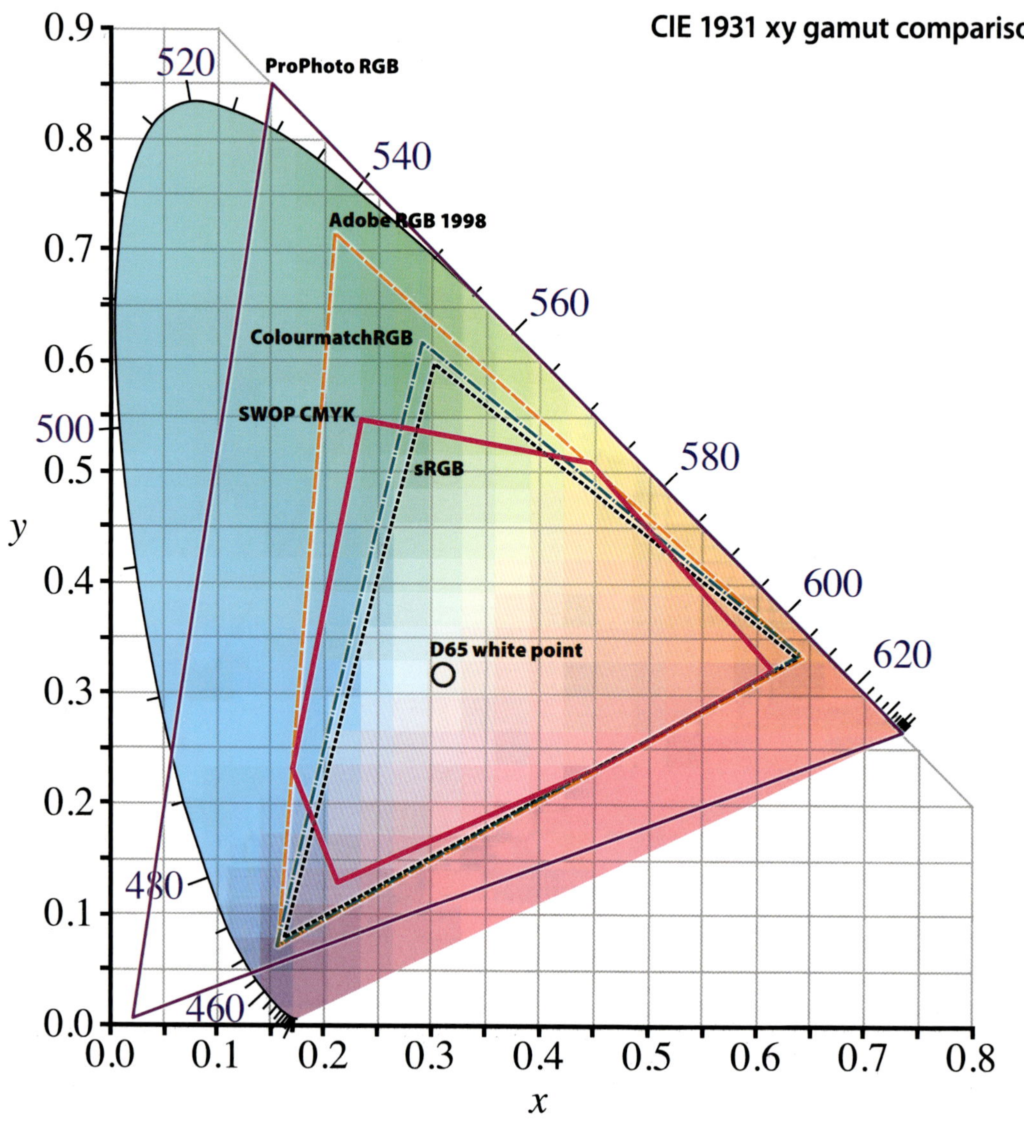

Jakob Christoph Le Blon, who in 1717 set up The Picture Office for the manufacture of coloured reproductions of paintings, has a unique place in the history of colour printing. Le Blon was the inventor of four-colour process printing. He developed a system of printing using four separate mezzotint plates, each with a different colour: red, yellow, blue and black.

Initially, in 1725, Le Blon wrote, 'Painting can represent all visible objects with three colours, yellow, red and blue; for all other colours can be compos'd of these three which I call primitive.'[42] Several years later, Le Blon found he had to add the black plate to create better colour rendition. The pattern of a 'rosette' of halftone dots of varying size on each printing plate allows the four colours to optically mix on the paper. It is the juxtaposition of these process colours through careful registration of each plate that gives the viewer the appearance of a continuous tone of shades. While the black was originally introduced to overcome the inefficiency of the process – the three colours make only a brown at best – over time there would prove sound economic reasons for its use. The black (also referred to as K, for key plate, in CMYK) is the cheapest of the four process pigments. With the advent of computer technology, the under colour removal (UCR) system was developed. This meant that where areas of the print had colours overlapping underneath black as a result of traditional colour separation at the platemaking stage, these unnecessary colours could be removed, saving considerable amounts of both ink and money.

Systems of colour theory and notation changed rapidly over the two centuries following Le Blon's work. The colour theories developed by James Clerk Maxwell demonstrated the theory of all colour additively mixed from three primaries – red, green and blue – with the use of spinning discs on which were painted samples of vermilion, ultramarine blue and emerald green. With these painted in varying combinations onto the discs, which were then spun, he demonstrated that most colour combinations could be achieved by optical mixing. Most notable for the printmaker are the theories of Michel Eugène Chevreul, who was employed by the Gobelins textile factory to improve the apparent dullness of their dyes. Chevreul experimented and found that, 'In the case where the eye sees at the same time two contiguous colours, they will appear as dissimilar as possible, both in their optical composition and in the strength of their colour.'[43]

All the colour additives discussed in this chapter fall into the broad category of absorption pigments. That is, they produce colour shades by selective absorption and reflection of visible light.

Colourimetry is 'a branch of color science concerned with numerically specifying the color of physically defined stimuli such that two stimuli that look the same (under certain criteria) have identical specifications.'[44] It could perhaps be described as applied spectrophotometry. While the physics of colour science is generally settled, the manner with which colours are described, defined, classified, grouped, plotted and presented graphically are numerous, and new methods and styles continue to be developed to this day. Many are on the interface between pure science and practical application in various disciplines.

The Munsell system, developed early in the twentieth century by Professor Albert H. Munsell, is one such method of colourimetry that specifies colours in a three-dimensional way based on three properties: hue (the basic colour), chroma (the colour punch or intensity) and value (lightness). Munsell was the first to use the idea of a three-dimensional colour space as a framework on which to hang colour, and his was one of the first systems to be based on human visual responses to colour, putting colour's subjective element on a firm experimental scientific footing.

Munsell's system outlasted its contemporary colour models and, although it has been superseded for some uses by models such as CIELAB (or L*a*b*) and CIECAM02, it is still used and taught today.

PANTONE SYSTEM

The Pantone colour measurement system was initially developed for commercial printing, but in recent years it has evolved to cover colours on computers (computational colour information transfer). The Pantone system has become a household name, as Pantone colours (both the numbered variety and the named Pantone bases such as Warm Red, Reflex Blue etc.) have become end products in their own right. The word 'guide' is often overlooked when the Pantone system is used. It is not primarily a scientific system, or a method for colour categorisation or analysis. It originated as a method by which an editor or designer could 'speak the same language', even when many miles apart. Both parties could hold in their hand the guide showing what the colour should look like given the variables introduced by paper choice and printing method.

CIE L*A*B*

In order that more scientifically objective colour information can be transported accurately without needing to transfer actual physical samples of colour, a standard mathematical system of colour transfer has been developed. This was proposed by the Commission Internationale d'Éclairge (CIE) in 1931, and is an international standard for colour measurement. In 1976 the model was refined and named CIE L*a*b*.

The purpose of the model was to address the problems associated with reproducing a colour exactly on different video monitors and printing devices by creating what is known as 'device-independent colour output'.

CIE L*A*B* Colour Space

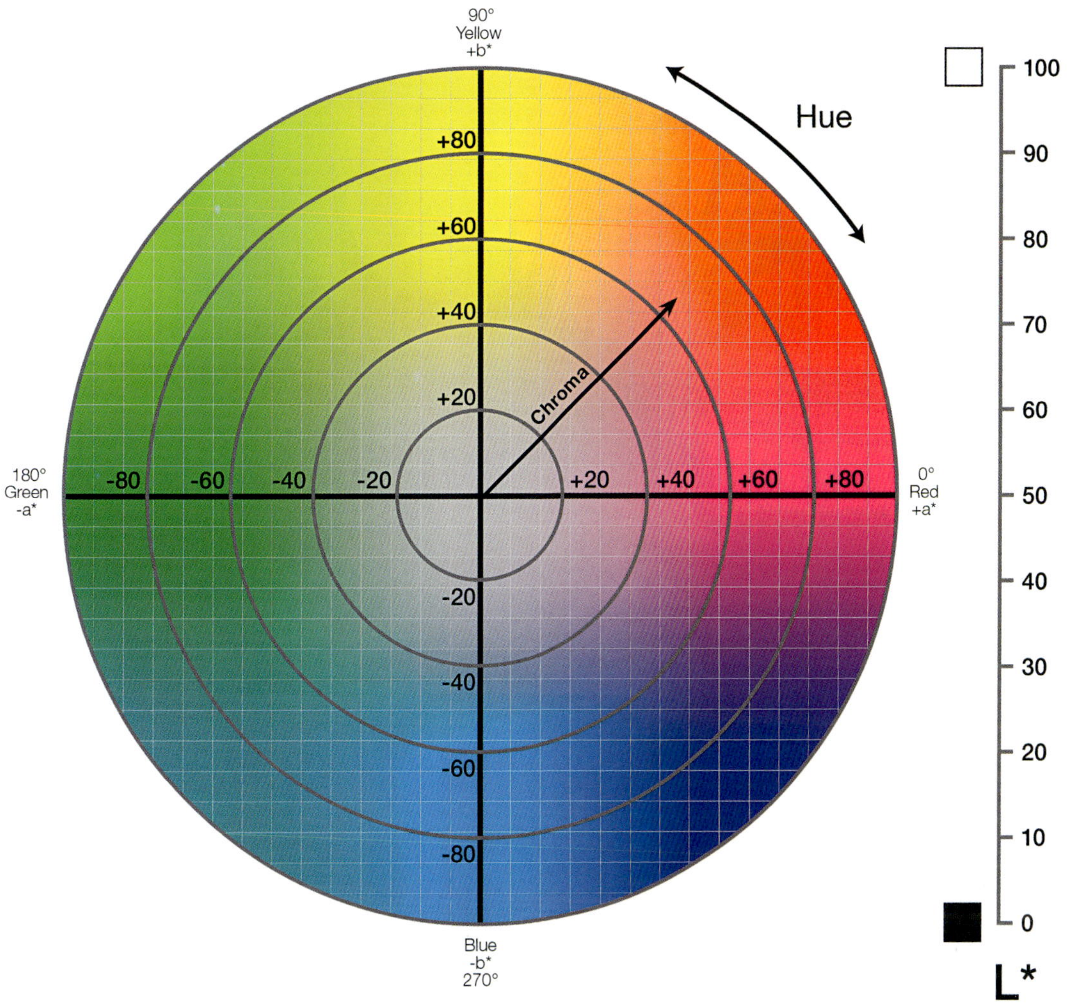

CIE Colour Space Notations

ΔL* - difference in Lightness/darkness value	"+" lighter	"-" darker	
ΔA* - difference on red/green axis	"+" redder	"-" greener	
ΔB* - difference on yellow//blue axis	"+" yellower	"-" bluer	
ΔC* - difference in chroma	"+" brighter	"-" duller	
ΔH - difference in Hue			
ΔL* - total colour difference value			
ΔE. total acceptable colour difference value			

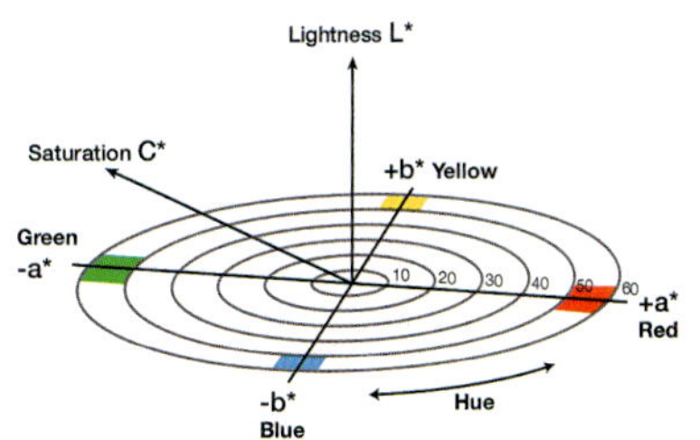

The L* value is represented on the centre axis of the a* and b* axis.

CIE L*a*b* is a means of mathematical notation for colour based on an XYZ three-dimensional graph, where L* is represented by the *z* axis and denotes lightness between white and black, a* is represented by the *x* axis and denotes colour difference from red to green, and b* is represented by the *y* axis and denotes colour difference from blue to yellow. By plotting a colour's position on the graph, it is possible to produce a mathematical formula for any colour on the visible spectrum, and therefore, theoretically, to store the information for any colour on a computer, convey that colour to a third party and reproduce it.

DELTA E

Delta E, also written as ΔE, is a numeric value ascribed to a just noticeable difference between two colours. Another way of describing this is as the largest perceptible colour difference that is acceptable between two printed samples of the same piece of artwork. Delta E is used to describe the colour shift between one printed sample and another in a reproductive process, in order to ascertain the colour sample's accuracy in relation to the digital file or original artwork.

The Delta E is essentially the sum of all the differences between the standard and the colour being analysed.

These mathematical notational systems are necessary for transcribing digital colour data from one piece of computer memory to another. These systems transcribe to the popular term of a profile. A profile is a means of transferring digital data about colour from one computer system to another without corrupting the information, and ensuring, for example, that what one computer reads as blue is the same blue when the information is read by a different computer.

In digital colour these systems are necessary to ensure consistency of colour from one print to the next. If you want to record an image and then reproduce it multiple times with as great an accuracy as possible, you need to use profiles and colour-matching systems. However, if you are creating an artwork from many digital sources – for instance photography, digital capture and scanning – and you only want to print a few copies, profiles can restrict the type of output you are printing. You still need a profile optimised for the sheet of paper you are printing on, and you also need to know how you are transferring your file from one computer to another, but a sealed profiling system will probably reduce the colour available to you rather than help increase or retain the available colour gamut.

Metamerism

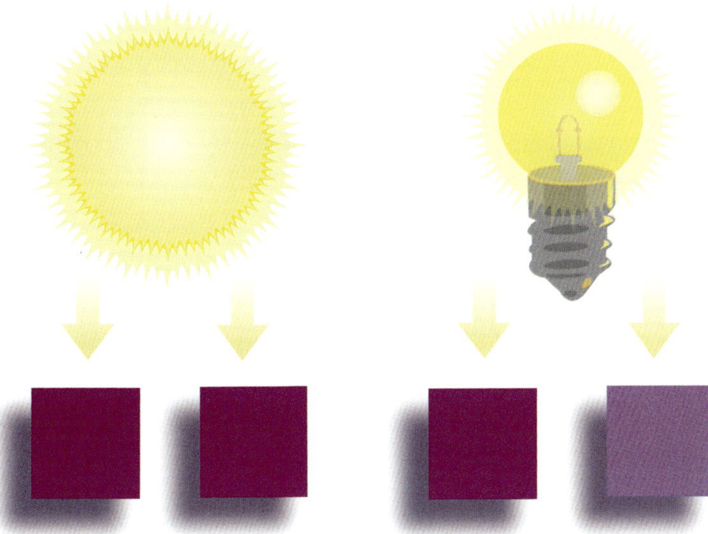

METAMERISM

Metamerism is usually defined as a change in appearance under different lighting conditions, where two colour samples appear to match under one set of conditions but not under another. Metamerism is usually discussed in terms of two illuminants (in which case it is known as illuminant metamerism), whereby the two samples may match under one illuminant but not under the second. In simple terms, illuminant metamerism means that if I match a jacket with a pair of trousers under fluorescent light in a department store, there is no guarantee that when I take the two garments outside into the daylight the colours will still match. In this case, the match is said to be conditional. Two samples that conditionally match are said to be a metameric pair.

If two samples have identical reflectance spectra (in other words, look the same under all lighting conditions) then they cannot be metameric and are therefore an unconditional match. Other types of metamerism include geometrical metamerism and observer metamerism.

This happens because there are several different ways to match colour. For example, one could make a green ink from a single green pigment or from a number of blends of blues, greens, yellows, etc. No one formula is right or wrong, but each will require a particular gamut or spectrum to reflect the colour accurately. Different light sources give differing profiles or nuances, thus increasing the chances of metamerism.

LIGHTFASTNESS

All inks fade when subjected to light, but some inks fade more than others; the problem for the printmaker concerned about the lightfast quality of his or her work is how to judge whether an ink will fade quickly or is relatively permanent. Lightfastness as a concept comes down in the end to a subjective judgement: how long should something last to be deemed permanent? Primarily, it's a matter of matching a suitable ink to the use to which it will be put. A newspaper does not need to be printed with permanent ink; most consumers will read it once and then dispose of it. An artist's original print, by a blue chip artist, does need to consider permanence if the print is to be purchased at a high price, due to its standing and rarity value, then kept for many years on display in a museum. It would not make sense if the print were to fade rapidly in front of the public's eyes.

MEASURING LIGHTFASTNESS

There are three primary measurement values for lightfastness. The traditional measurement in the UK and Europe is the Blue Wool Scale, and this has been adopted as the international standard. This has a British Standards number of BS 1006 and a set of International Organization for Standardization (ISO) numbers: ISO 105-B01 (Colour fastness to light: Daylight); and ISO 105-B02 (Colour fastness to artificial light: Xenon arc fading lamp test). The latter scale is in more common use, as it is much quicker to apply.

The xenon arc test, as it is known, is an accelerated-light test. In other words, the test sample is subjected to intense light for a short period of time, usually a month, and the sample is checked for degree of fade. Once this is determined, a mathematical interpolation takes place to equate the intense light fade over one month to a longer period of years. This test regime was originally developed for the textile industry, and the test scale is based on a series of subjective comparisons to a set of eight blue-coloured woollen samples, all with known and measured fading characteristics. The scale runs from numbers 1–8, with 1 being extremely fugitive and fading very rapidly, and 8 being as close to permanent as is possible to predict. An ink that gains a score of 6 or above in the Blue Wool Scale is usually deemed to be fairly permanent.

The American system is a series of ASTM ratings running from I–V in Roman numerals, with I being the strongest, and V the weakest.

They are as follows:

I. Excellent
II. Very good
III. Fair
IV. Poor
V. Very poor

The length of time this equates to, according to the artists' ink manufacturer Daniel Smith, is as follows:

- **Excellent** means that it will be somewhere over 100 years before a change may occur.
- **Very good** indicates that it will be 100 years before a change.
- **Fair** is somewhere between 55 and 100 years before a change occurs.
- **Poor** means that there could be a change as early as 25 years.
- **Very poor** is a category that does not apply to Daniel Smith paints, but refers to paint that can change in 5–10 years. This would apply to anything with a fluorescent pigment, for instance.

The third system is Delta E (see p.82). This system tends to be used when measuring colour change from a previously printed artwork, rather than denoting the lightfastness of the ink at the point of purchase. Delta E is increasingly used as a quantifiable value (using a spectrophotometer) in preference to the subjective interpretation of the results of Blue Wool tests.

There are three current ways of measuring lightfastness in ink. The first method is to pin the prints up in daylight, indoors, in a place where they will have unobstructed exposure to daylight over a given period, and then to measure the colour change. This is a real-time colour-fading experiment. The second is the xenon arc light test described on p.84. The third method is to use an Atlas Weather-Ometer®, which not only uses the xenon arc lamp but also controls heat and humidity. This provides the most standardised environment, but how it equates to normal, everyday variable exposure is harder to quantify.

WHAT IT MEANS FOR PRINTMAKERS AND CONSERVATORS

First, the printmaker needs to be cautious. It is worthwhile using the best ink you can lay your hands on. This is not always an available option; any number of factors from availability to cost may affect your decision. One thing that conservators agree on, however, is that more information regarding how a work of art is created makes long-term creation easier; knowing whether work has

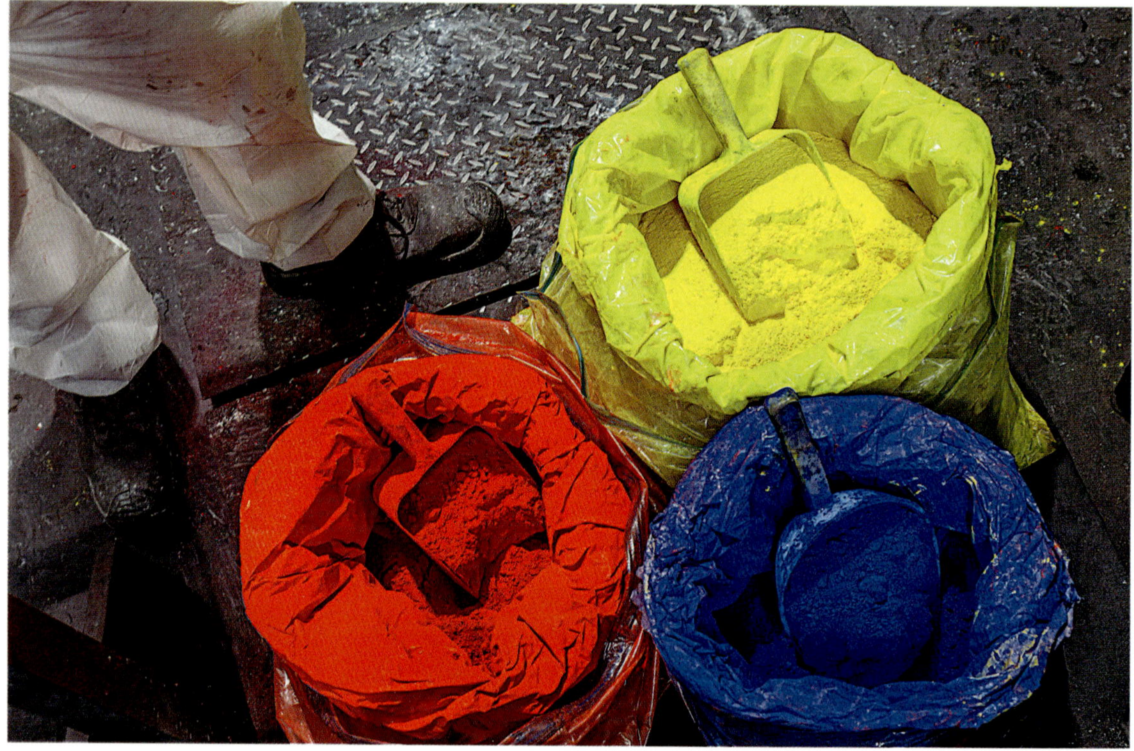

been created with a fugitive ink or not makes the decision of where and how to display it much easier. Therefore, I am advocating better information all round, rather than a change of ink. Ink manufacturers should label their cans with an indication of the lightfast properties of the ink within. (Note: a measurement of lightfastness is only ever an indication of the possible life.) For their part, artists should label their work more clearly to show how a particular piece was created and what combination of paper and ink was used.

▲ **Red, yellow and blue pigment.** Photo: Jo Hounsome Photography © Cranfield Colours

PRACTICAL COLOUR MATCHING

For the artist, a means of sophisticated colour measurement is usually irrelevant. Most artists keep good practical colour records, either by making drawdowns of colour on the paper that is to be printed, or by dabbing the colour out with a finger. Some artists will also keep wet samples of a colour, which is the most accurate method of practically recreating it. Drawdowns (see p.57) are extremely simple: take a square-ended palette knife (about an inch across at the end) and dip it into a blob of ink. Then place the square end of the knife onto a sample of the paper, hold the paper and draw the knife firmly towards you at an angle of about 70° (or nearly upright). This will draw out the patch of ink across the paper in a thin film the width of the knife. This film should equate to the strength of colour you would obtain if you printed a solid patch of litho colour. If you are printing a relief block, you will need to learn to vary the pressure, or else pack up the edges of the knife blade, to replicate the film thickness you are printing. Even if the colour obtained is not exactly the same as when it is printed, a drawdown is an excellent method of comparing one sample of ink to another before you print. When mixing colour, it is the best way of judging what is required to change a colour. A straight drawdown, for instance, is often the best method of assessing the colour of an etching ink.

Some people combine a drawdown with dabbing out to get a true evaluation of a colour's strength, and dabbing out colour with a finger is another effective way of testing colour strength and tone. Place a small blob of colour on a sample of the paper you are going to use, then with your forefinger tap away gently at the ink, slowly spreading it out into a thinner and thinner film that becomes paler at the edges, until you have run out of ink. With experience, you will find this the most accurate method of assessing how an ink will blend from light to dark tone, and it is also the best method of simulating relief-ink films.

Traditionally, many commercial printers compared subtle undertones by reducing ink with opaque white for testing purposes. If you add 30–50 per cent opaque white to the inks you want to test, it is then possible to evaluate comparative ink strengths and to gain a better insight into the nuances of colour. This method is particularly useful when trying to work out the undertone colours that have been added to create a colour's tertiary effects.

CHROMOPHORES

The crossover between theory of colour and its function in ink manufacture occurs in the chemical construction of the pigment or dye. At a molecular level, there are certain chemical groups that determine the absorption of particular wavelengths of light; these groups are called chromophores and are responsible for the colour of materials. In organic materials, colour is associated with particular molecular structures that absorb and emit light of specific frequencies – chromophores are groups of atoms within a molecule.

The molecular structure of a pigment can be closely controlled, by means of the chromophores, to obtain a desired and reproducible colour. Current theories about chemical bonding are based on either the valence-bond or the molecular-orbital approaches and can provide a more sophisticated account of colour and constitution relationships than chromophores within colour chemistry.

TRANSIENT CHROMOPHORES

Certain conditions, including whether a print is allowed to dry in ambient studio light or in darkness, can momentarily change the colour of a printed film of ink. The most common of these phenomena are the transient yellow chromophores formed by and within linseed oil when it dries without light. Thankfully, the yellow caste is reversible, and an unexpected and unwanted yellow undertone that forms in transparent colours within days of printing can usually be dissipated by exposure to daylight (not direct sunlight).

MIXING COLOUR AS A PRINTMAKER

In contemporary practice, printmakers need to be aware of the three separate means of understanding colour: additive or RGB; subtractive, normally associated with CMYK; and a subset of subtractive using red, yellow and blue, which is the traditional artists' approach to mixing paint or ink.

It is now also important to understand the difference between colour theory as applied to additive colour used in photography and image capture, which also controls your computer screen. Subtractive colour mixing using the CMYK process is used for commercial printing. With the advent of digital technology, the inkjet printer and random algorithms, this four-colour set has expanded to up to a 12-colour set: cyan, magenta, yellow, red, green, blue, light cyan, light magenta, light grey, mid grey, black and a varnish overprint.

Printmakers invariably mix colour, and the immediate mixing of colour creates a problem for colour theory. Subtractive colour theory, as explained above, relies on placing a spot of colour on a sheet of white paper and measuring the reflected light bounced off that paper through the colour. Once you add colour particles of different sizes from different colours – especially white or a transparent medium – to the colour you are mixing, the light is going to reflect differently through the ink. If one then adds white to the ink, that adds further complications, and that is without starting to layer colours on top of each other, which is when you start to get real problems with reflectance.

One theoretical attempt to deal with this problem is known as the Kubelka-Munk theory, which was an attempt by Paul Kubelka and Franz Munk in 1931 to model the appearance of paint films. Nearly 100 years later, although it is in widespread use, the theory has limitations because it is not valid for strongly absorbing materials.

$$R_\infty = 1 + \frac{a_0}{r_0} - \sqrt{\frac{a_0^2}{r_0^2} + 2\frac{a_0}{r_0}}.$$

THE KUBELKA-MUNK THEORY

What does this mean for printmakers in practical terms? For digital and reproduction purposes using inkjet and commercial printing technology, you need to understand both additive and subtractive colour. You need the widest available colour gamut when you scan or photograph an image. For practical purposes this is usually Adobe RGB (1998), which is transferred from device to device until the point of printing. At this point in the process, you may adopt a different colour transfer or profile.

If you are mixing physical colour, then it makes sense to return to traditional artists' colour-mixing and painting colour theories, the best being that of Johannes Itten, who published his *Art of Colour* in 1961. Itten follows the three primaries of red, yellow and blue with secondary colours of green, orange and violet. When mixing colour, it is worth remembering that the combination of all three primaries creates brown. So, to keep your colour clean, you need to avoid mixing parts of all three primaries; for example, to mix a bright yellow/orange, you need to use a red-shade yellow and a yellow-shade red. If one used a green-shade yellow and a blue-shade red, you would end up with a yellowish brown.

The Itten colour circle

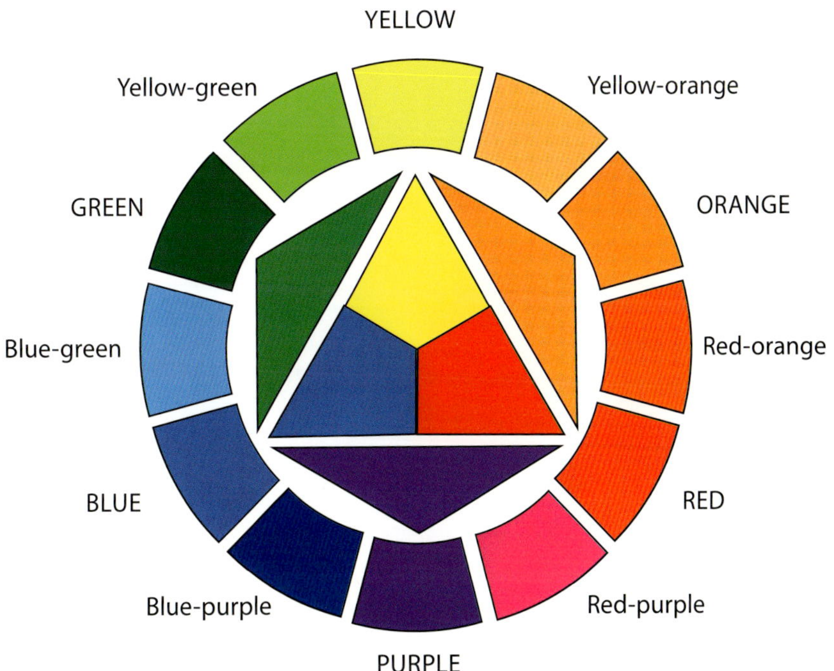

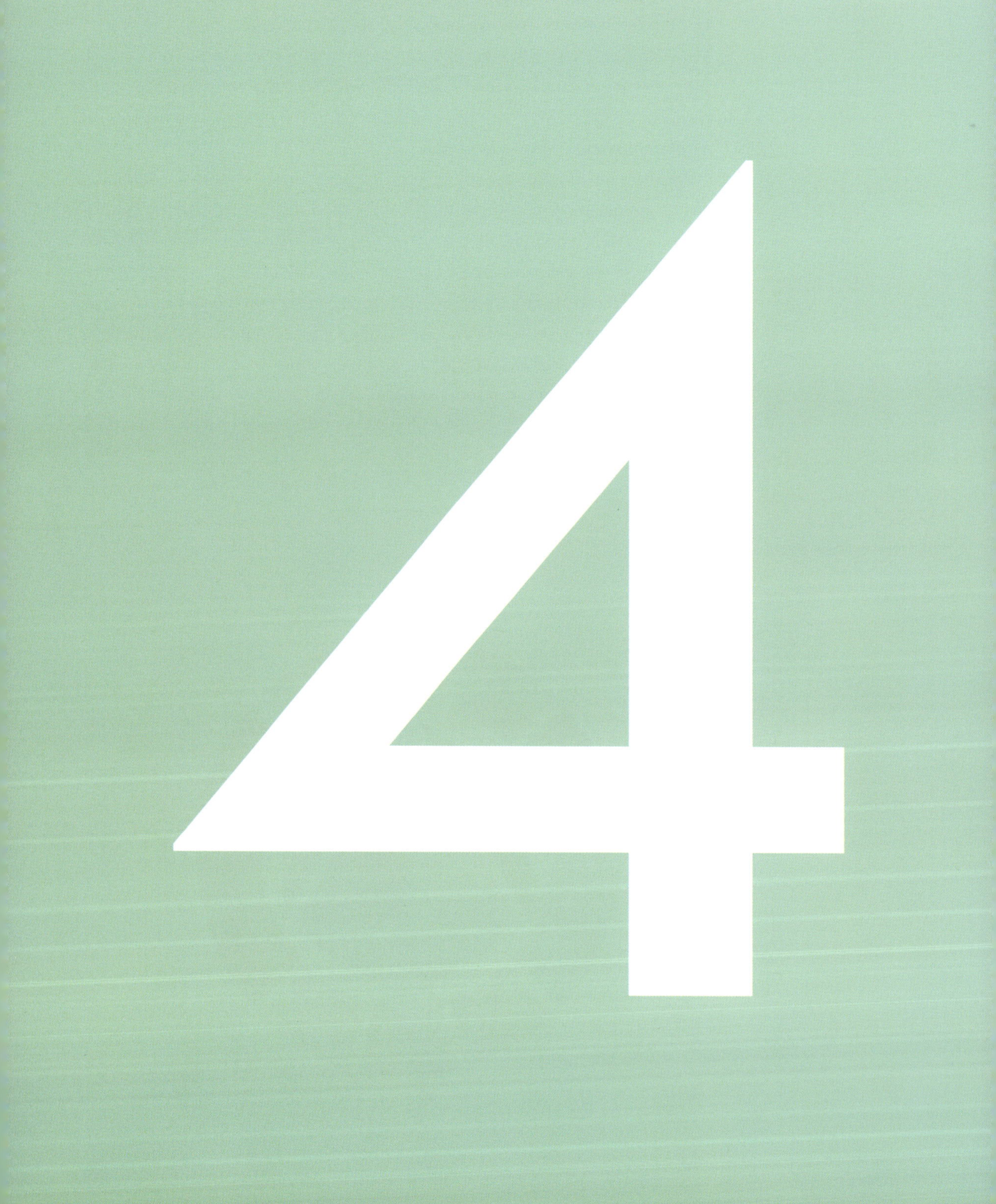

CHAPTER

4

INK FOR ETCHING

In Chapter 2, we covered a number of recipes for etching ink over the period since it was first used. The purest, simplest construction of an etching ink – linseed oil plus carbon black in some form – has remained constant throughout the last 500 years. This is not really surprising, as the etching process itself has changed little since Rembrandt's day. Etching purists try to keep it that way, but that is to deny that some change will naturally occur over time. For example, even if you were to attempt to manufacture your own ink in the style of Rembrandt, most pigment colour used today, as already mentioned, is artificially manufactured and the oils are subtly different from a true burnt oil; the result will never be quite the same as the original.

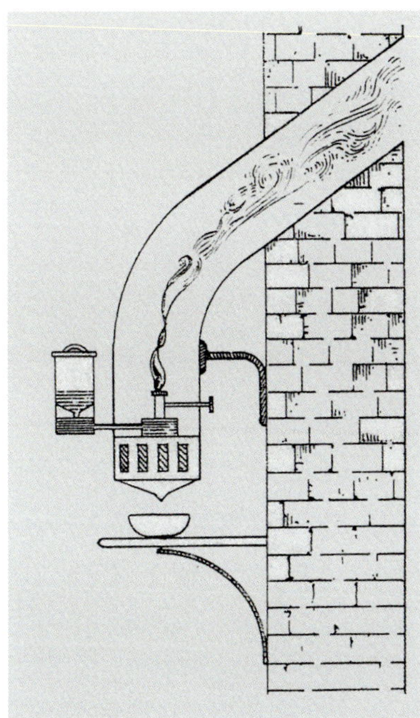
▼ **Lampblack apparatus.**
Source: Dr Joseph Bersch,
*The Manufacture of
Mineral and Lake Pigments*

Rembrandt and the earliest chronicler of etching knowledge, Abraham Bosse, used Frankfurt black as their black pigment. This pigment was available up until the 1960s and can still be found today, although there is some debate as to whether it resembles the original product. Also known as vine black, it was made either by heating vine twigs in a closed crucible to create charcoal, and extracting the residue with water, or else by burning dried wine lees (the sediment left at the bottom of the vat after wine is made). This was burnt until carbonised and then ground.

Birgit Reissland, in an article entitled 'A Practical Guide to the Production of Black Pigments & the Preparation of Black Watercolours, 1350–1700', cites Pomet who, in 1694, described:

'Black from Germany. It comes from Frankfurt, Mainz, & Strasbourg, as black stone & powder, which is burnt wine lees & thrown in water & after being dried we pass it through special mills. This waste product of winemaking gained later fame as Frankfurt black, widely employed as a pigment for intaglio printing ink.'[45]

Reissland also cites Krünitz from 1801 on how Frankfurt black was made.

'The wine yeasts that remained in the vessel after the distillation of brandy are poured onto a coarse stretched cloth so that all remaining liquid can run off. The residues are then pressed into balls and left to dry in the air or in the sun. These dry balls are inserted into pots; the pots are covered with well-fitting lids, carefully glued with clay, put into a potter's oven, and burnt with the other goods. After taking it out, the vine-yeast has burnt to a completely black charcoal, the so-called "Frankfurt black".'[46]

Other recipes added burnt ivory, peach stones and the bones of sheep's feet. These ingredients were all burnt and carbonised, then ground with the vine black.

The reason for the preference for vine black over lampblack in copperplate ink is to be found in the structure of the black, as articulated by Bloy.[47] Lampblack is light and floccular (particles tend to clump together). Frankfurt black was heavy and granular. This means the pigment was more likely to reside in a deeply bitten line on the etching plate, thus transferring more pigment to the print.

The choice of a granular particle in black ink highlights the primary difference between etching and lithographic ink. In lithography the printed film layer is very thin; therefore, the particle size has to be very small to obtain the maximum colour effect from the particle. In an etching, the deposition of ink creates a very heavy film deposit, so the colour is naturally strong. Combined with this is the need to be able to fill the line on the etching plate with ink, then to wipe the surface of the plate clean. A larger, heavier particle sticks in the line but is easy to wipe from the plate surface without leaving the stain that very small particles would leave.

The reason that many people make their own etching ink from pigment and oil can be found in the need for larger particle size in etching ink. It is not necessary to grind the pigment and oil together for long periods under the high shear that would be required for lithographic ink. (To qualify this statement: this is a reference to etching ink, not ink for photogravure or very fine aquatint. A handmade ink would almost certainly scratch the delicate surfaces of the fine-detail plates required for photogravure.)

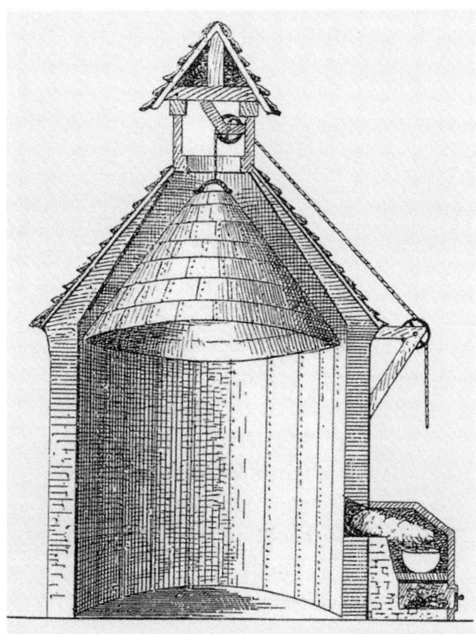

▲ Lampblack chamber.
Source: Dr Joseph Bersch,
*The Manufacture of
Mineral and Lake Pigments*

There is no doubt that when it comes to printing etching plates, even though there are certain given parameters, printing is a matter of subjective preference. Perhaps here it is easier to quantify what those preferences and parameters might include and why.

In recent years there has been much debate and confusion about so-called 'safe' etching. This is somewhat of a misnomer when it comes to ink, and it needs to be clarified. In terms of health and safety and the environment, a standard etching ink is not viewed as hazardous. A straightforward etching black, for example, will be made from linseed oil, carbon and a small quantity of calcium carbonate (whiting). Linseed oil is a naturally occurring plant oil extracted from the flax plant, carbon is the most commonly occurring chemical and is inert, and calcium carbonate is derived from common chalk, another common inert chemical. None of these ingredients would merit a hazard warning on the packaging.

The misconception lies in the method of cleaning up the ink after printing. Most etchers clean up with white spirit or turpentine substitute; this chemical is mildly hazardous and toxic. *Sax's Dangerous Properties of Industrial Materials* rates white spirit as 1 (a low hazard rating: Sax ratings run from 1 to 3, and it is useful to add that whisky is rated as a 3 on the same scale) and its safety profile states, 'Slightly toxic by inhalation. An experimental teratogen. Human systemic effects by inhalation: conjunctive eye irritation, cough and gastro-intestinal changes. When heated to decomposition it emits acrid smoke and irritating fumes.' This sounds dire, and care should be taken when handling white spirit. Do not confuse white spirit with pure turpentine, which has a hazard rating of 3.

White spirit's harmful properties can be mitigated if it is used in a controlled manner. Good ventilation of any room where white spirit is used is crucial, as is wearing appropriate protective gloves when cleaning plates after use. The International Programme on Chemical Safety (IPCS) states in its guidelines on white spirit that the constituent parts are readily absorbed into the bloodstream following inhalation of the vapour.[48]

An exposure level of 150–240mg/m^3 after eight hours continuous use in a well-ventilated room can rise to 6,200mg/m^3 in a closed or poorly ventilated room. The estimated level of solvent in the atmosphere is 150–240mg/m^3 after painting in a well-ventilated room for seven to eight hours. With sparing use of white spirit for plate cleaning in a well-ventilated environment, exposure is many times less than the limits set for painting a room with a solvent-containing paint. Therefore, exposure can be kept to a safe limit. Rags used for cleaning need to be kept in a closed metal bin before disposal, and containers of white spirit should be closed after use. These two precautions will significantly reduce the amount of white spirit vapour in the atmosphere. It is difficult to assess the difference in environmental terms between traditional ink and white spirit, and safe etching methods. However, unlike acrylic polymers, the ink and white spirit will biodegrade in the soil over time. The future lies in the new generation of linseed oil-based inks that are cleaned up with cold water and liquid soap.

WHAT MAKES A GOOD BLACK ETCHING INK?

This is entirely a matter of subjective preference, borne out by the fact that each major manufacturer makes a range of black inks, but there are some useful guidelines. Black inks vary in three ways: strength of colour, colour tone and consistency, i.e., viscosity and tack. These relate to ease of wiping, plate tone, tonal range, etc.

Strength of colour is a subjective judgement and is primarily dictated by the demands of the print itself. If a soft, calm appearance is required, then a weak-coloured ink is more likely to be used on a toned paper than the strongest, most contrasting black. There are occasions when this decision is dictated by the requirements of printing. If a large area of very even aquatint is to be printed, a smoother, more even-looking print can usually be obtained with a weaker-coloured ink mixed with weaker oil of a lower poise, which makes the ink easier to wipe evenly across the surface but harder to wipe clean without leaving a plate tone. Likewise, if a number of colours and plates are to be printed together, then a weaker black will not conflict in tonal strength with the coloured inks.

Colour tone is again a somewhat subjective judgement, but any printmaker must be aware that black inks are not entirely neutral when printed as a lighter tone. This applies in particular to aquatint: as the black gets progressively lighter through the aquatint tones, so the ink will reveal its colour tone. The majority of blacks will either appear less neutral and bluer (cooler) or less neutral and browner (warmer). Very few blacks will show true colour neutrality as they get lighter. This, in the main, is an advantage to the printmaker, as they can select an ink with a colour tone to suit the image. If a neutral black tone is required, then mixing two or more blacks will invariably be necessary.

Selecting an etching ink from a dedicated supplier of printmaking supplies can be extremely complex; for example, most suppliers offer not only a range

▶ **Laura Clarke Oaten**
Baba Yaga, **2024.**
Etching, 56 x 76 cm.
Photo: Laura Clarke Oaten
© Laura Clarke Oaten

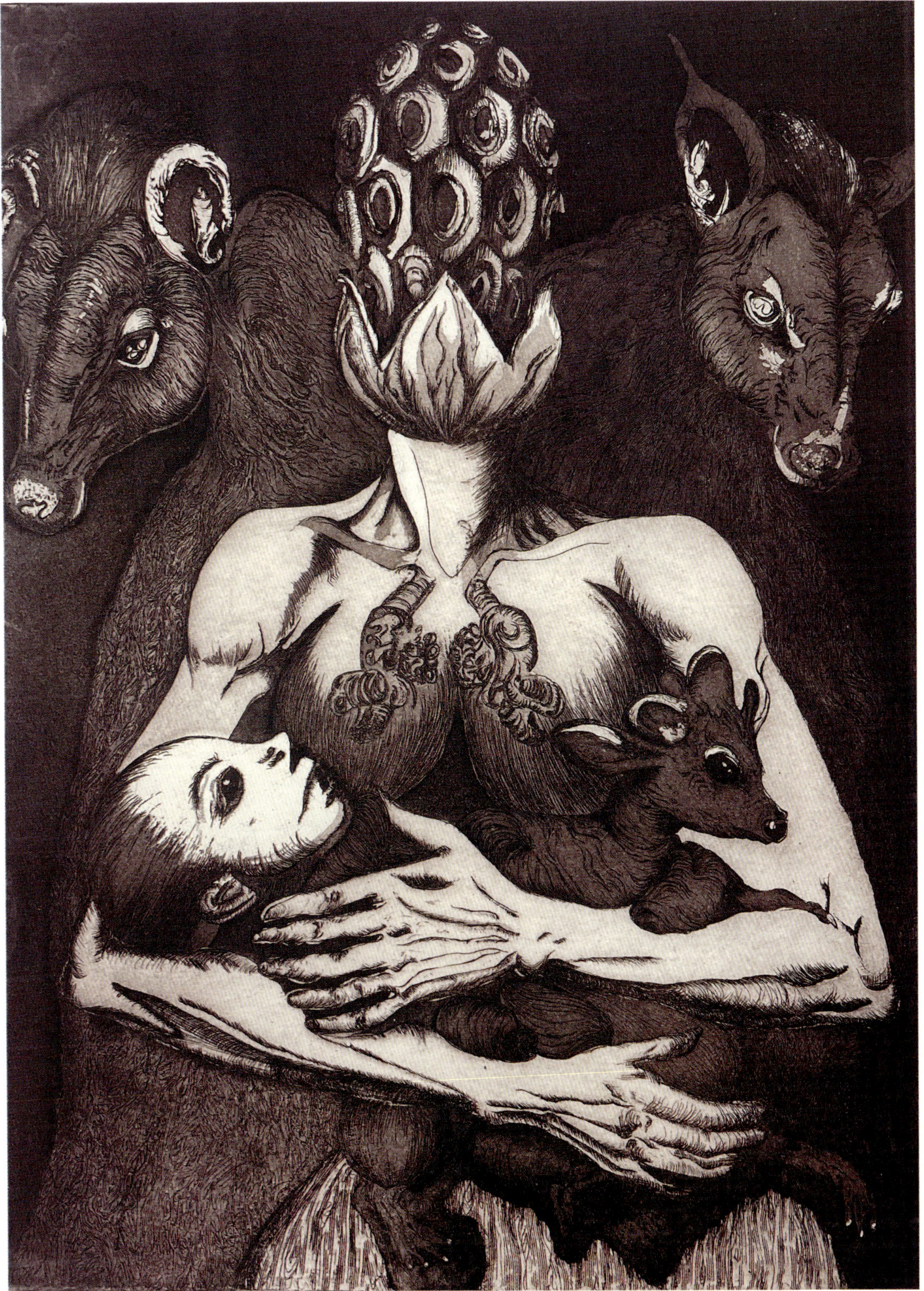

of different black inks from a single manufacturer, but often offer several ranges from different manufacturers. Things are further complicated by the commentary on an ink's use, which often differs from one supplier to another.

Therefore, it is useful to compare the commentary published by a range of suppliers on the properties of a particular range of inks from a single manufacturer. This set of comments could be applied to almost any manufacturer's range of inks, and almost any set of colours. I chose Charbonnel as an example, as it was easy to find and compare comments on a set of eight black inks. The point is that the comments produced – presumably by or for the retailer – differ greatly, and are subjective in relation to the use and performance of the inks.

The following comments from a number of supplier websites have been anonimised.

1. Black 55985

- A very deep, slightly blue-black used to strengthen other blacks. A mixture of ivory and carbon black and Prussian blue. Highly viscous and on its own, can be challenging to wipe. Completely lightfast, even when lightened. Opaque. Pigments: PBk9-PBk7-PB27.
- Has high viscosity and is difficult to wipe. This ink is an intense black and designed for aquatint plates where a mottle free, jet black is essential. It is a very deep, slightly blue-black and can be used to strengthen other blacks.
- Very deep slightly blue-black well suited to dry point, aquatint and mezzotint. Highly viscous, difficult to wipe.
- Composition of Ivory Black, Carbon Black, Prussian Blue. Highly viscous, difficult to wipe. Very deep slightly blue-black. Used to strengthen the other blacks. Lightfastness: Completely lightfast, even when lightened. Opacity: Opaque Pigments: PBk9-PBk7-PB27.

Stephen Hoskins' comments: In terms of performance, it is not difficult to wipe when warmed on the plate. It then wipes very cleanly, without leaving much plate tone, but retains a crisp line if the paper has been well damped overnight. It was my general preferred ink from the Charbonnel range when I taught. However, I ran my class with a hotplate on all of the time and paper was damped the previous day, wrapped in plastic overnight, and then blotted before printing.

2. Black 71303

- A warm black with a hint of red, made from a mixture of ivory and carbon black and Prussian blue. Viscous, greasy, takes time to wipe. Completely lightfast, even when lightened. Opaque. Pigments: PBk9-PBk7-PB27.

- Composition of Ivory Black, Carbon Black, Prussian Blue. Viscous, wiping takes time.
- Composition of Ivory Black, Carbon Black, Prussian Blue. Viscous, wiping takes time. A thick ink.

Stephen Hoskins' comments: In terms of performance, this was always the ink I used when a plate was under-bitten, or I needed to leave a lot of plate tone on an image.

3. Black Luxe C

- A soft black composed of a mixture of ivory and carbon blacks and Prussian Blue, slightly blue tinted with a low viscosity. Completely lightfast, even when lightened. Opaque. Pigments: PBk9-PBk7-PB27.
- Low viscosity supple black. Used as 55985 but easier to handle, it is a black with hints of blue.
- Composition of Ivory Black, Carbon Black, Prussian Blue. Low viscosity. Supple and gentle black. Slightly blue. Lightfastness: Completely lightfast, even when lightened. Opacity: Opaque. Pigments: PBk9-PBk7-PB27.

Stephen Hoskins' comments: In terms of performance, here I agree with the above descriptions: a soft black with a hint of bluish colour. I would always use 55985 from preference. I found this ink a little cold in colour.

4. Black 55981

- A universal soft black, composed of ivory and carbon black. Very viscous but supple and easier to wipe than Black 55985. Completely lightfast, even when lightened. Opaque. Pigments: PBk9-PBk7.
- Composition: Ivory Black, Carbon Black. Viscosity: Very viscous. Easier to wipe than 55985. Characteristics: Universal, supple black. Lightfastness: Completely lightfast, even when lightened.
- Universal supple black. Viscous but easier to wipe than 55985.
- Composition of Ivory Black, Carbon Black. Very viscous. Easier to wipe than 55985. Universal supple black. Lightfastness: Completely lightfast, even when lightened. Opacity: Opaque. Pigments: PBk9-PBk7.

Stephen Hoskins' comments: In terms of performance, easier to wipe than 55985, but the colour is less strong in the lines.

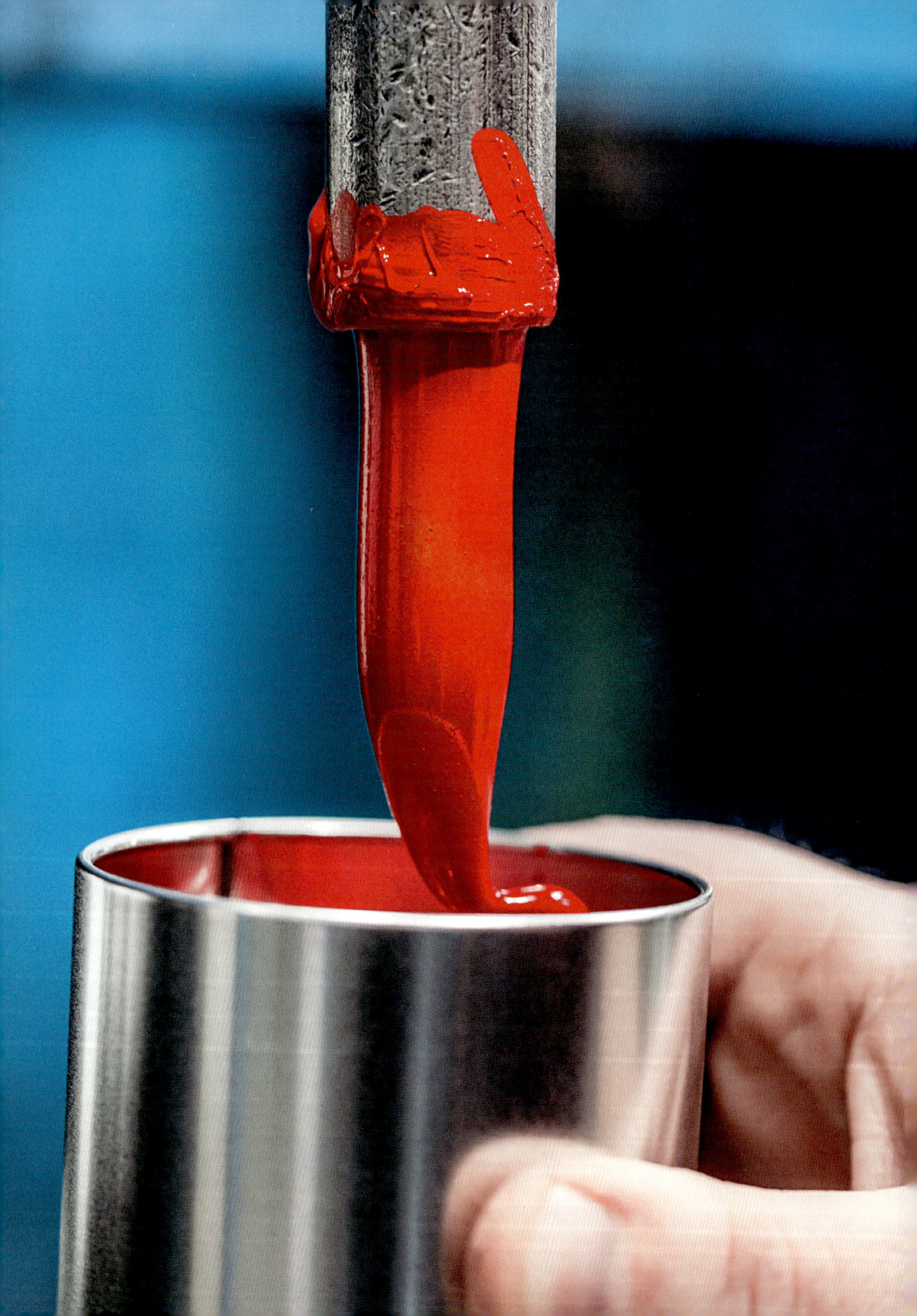

5. Carbon Black

- A warm black with a low viscosity, extremely easy to wipe. Particularly useful for test run prints. Completely lightfast, even when lightened. Opaque.
- Low viscosity, very easy to wipe. Used in particular for test print runs.
- Composition of Carbon Black, Low viscosity, easy to wipe. Can be used in particular for test print runs. Lightfastness: Completely lightfast, even when lightened.

6. Soft Black (Doux)

- Composition: Ivory Black. Viscosity: Low viscosity, easy to wipe. Characteristics: Very supple and relatively opaque. Can be used for lowering the tones of a plate which is too heavily engraved. Lightfastness: Completely lightfast, even when lightened. Opacity: Opaque. Pigments: PBk9.
- Low viscosity, easy to wipe. Very supple and relatively opaque. May be used for lowering the tones of a plate which is heavily engraved.
- Composition of Ivory Black. Low viscosity, easy to wipe. Very supple and relatively opaque. Can be used for lowering the tones of a plate which is too heavily etched. Lightfastness: Completely lightfast, even when lightened. Opacity: Opaque. Pigments: PBk9.

7. F66 Black

- Low viscosity, easy to wipe. Medium intensity, handles well, for all types of etching.
- Composition of Ivory Black, Carbon Black, low viscosity, easy to wipe. Medium intensity. Lightfastness: Completely lightfast, even when lightened. Opacity: Opaque. Pigments: PBk9.

Stephen Hoskins' comments: In terms of performance, my go-to ink for a rich black aquatint or photogravure plate.

8. RSR Black

- Viscous, powerful and supple black. Useful for deeply engraved or bitten line.
- Composition of Carbon Black. Viscous. Powerful, supple black. Lightfastness: Completely lightfast, even when lightened. Opacity: Opaque. Pigments: PBk9-PBk6.

The most important thing to remember is that every printmaker prints differently, and you will most likely only need three different blacks at most to be able to print a full range of plates. There are so many variables to printing an etching plate that it is very difficult for anybody to advise you on the best ink to choose unless they are printing with you, in your studio conditions. Which ink to use will depend on whether you have been taught to heat the plate or print cold, what type of press you have and what combination of blankets you use. In addition, your printing will depend on how you damp your paper: do you put the paper in a bath of water for 20 minutes and then blot it and print, or do you damp the paper with a sponge, stack it up wrapped in plastic, and leave it overnight to print the next day? Then there is the choice of paper to print on, how deeply your plate is bitten, whether it has a coarse or fine aquatint, or is a dry point or engraving, the sort of scrim you use and whether your plate is copper, steel, zinc, Perspex or flexographic. The final variable is down to you and how you personally ink and wipe your etching plate.

WATER-BASED AND WATER-SOLUBLE ETCHING INK

There is much confusion between water-based ink and water-soluble or water-washable ink. A water-based ink uses water as one of its main component parts, alongside a vehicle such as gum arabic. An example is the ink used for *mokuhanga* or Japanese water-based woodcut printing. A true water-based ink would not work for etching or intaglio.

Water-soluble, water-miscible and soap-and-water-washable inks are not entirely the same, but each, either in the presence of a soap surfactant, will mix the water and oil to make an emulsion that can then be easily cleaned up with water and a cloth. A good range of manufacturers make water-soluble or washable inks today: Cranfield makes Caligo Safe Wash and Charbonnel makes Aqua Wash – both traditional linseed-based inks – and Speedball makes Akua Intaglio Inks, which are soy-based; all three are washable with water.

Printmakers and ink makers hold various, sometimes strongly held views about the comparative advantages and disadvantages of soya and linseed oils. Linseed, despite being the more traditional oil used in printmaking inks, has lost none of its appeal or reputation with the increasing concern about the environment. Generally, modern modified crops, including rapeseed, flower at clearly defined times, making harvesting agriculturally efficient – a great economic advantage for farmers. One of linseed's 'failings' is, however, one of its charms; the linseed plant, with its characteristic blue flower, matures over a longer period. The farmer will therefore have to choose a moment to harvest

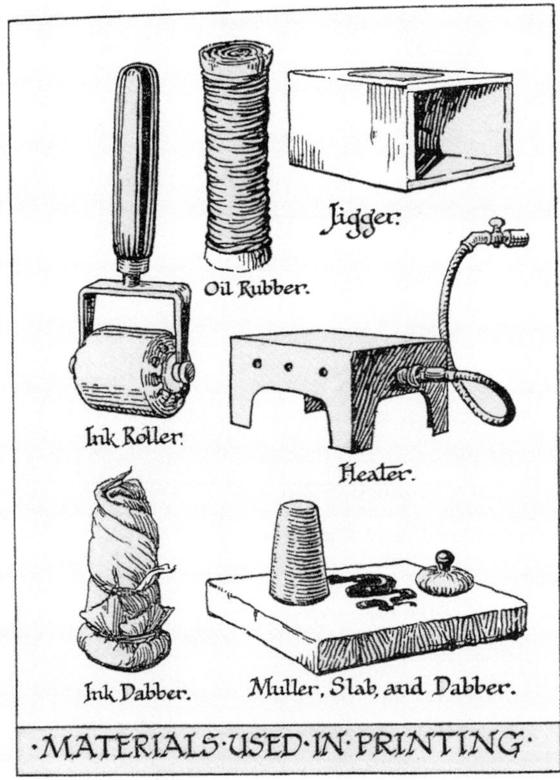

▲ **Materials used in printing.** Source: Eric Hesketh Hubbard, *On Making and Collecting Etchings*, 1920

the crop before all the plants have bloomed, and after a proportion of the seed has fallen back to fertilise the ground.

Certainly, oil-based inks benefit from paper damping. The method preferred by Stephen Hoskins is to damp the paper the previous day and keep it wrapped in plastic overnight. The water will cause the fibre in the paper to swell, softening it and making it more likely to pull the ink from the line on the etching plate. We are not trying to make the paper wet, only to swell the fibre, using as little water as possible. In the worst-case scenario, if you just dunk your paper in a bath of water and leave it for 10 minutes, you will have a hard layer of dry fibre in the middle of the paper and a layer of water on the surface. If you print this in the press, the roller will chase a thin line of water across the plate between plate and paper, rejecting the ink as you go. In addition, there is the potential for the excess water to begin to emulsify with the surfactant in a water-washable ink and begin to create a spread of ink away from the etched line, forming a softer and fuzzier-looking print.

VISCOSITY AND TACK

Viscosity and tack are the least subjective factors. However, personal preference does greatly influence the choice of ink, which is made in relation to the type of plate being printed and the effect one wishes to obtain. A deeply bitten line plate would normally require a stiff ink to fill the line and remain in place, with very little excess oil in the ink so that the surface of the plate can be wiped clean, leaving no plate tone. In this context, a larger pigment particle is desirable, as a very small particle can adhere to the surface of the plate, leaving an uneven stain; this is separate to plate tone, which is usually consistent in its colour.

If a plate with a deeply bitten line is to be printed with plate tone, a weaker oil can be added to the stiff ink to make sure that it will not wipe as easily, thus leaving tone on the plate. A very lightly bitten aquatint plate may require low viscosity and loose tack, so that the ink can be evenly spread across the surface of the aquatint and not easily wiped off the surface of the plate. Conversely, an aquatint may need an even tone across its surface, but the rest of the plate may need to be wiped clean. It is in this instance that a proprietary compound such as Graphic Chemical Easy Wipe may be added to the ink.

OXIDATION

Oxidation is a chemical reaction between the metal plate and the pigment in the ink. It happens to some extent with all colours, some much more noticeably than others. White and yellow are the two colours that demonstrate the greatest effects of oxidation. If you are concerned with clarity of colour, steel is least affected by oxidation, followed by copper, with zinc most affected. Most artists who wish to use clear, bright colour will have copperplate steel-faced before printing.

As a general rule, the less you wipe a plate, the less you provide new pigment with a fresh metal plate surface to oxidise with, and the less colour change you create. In real terms, wiping less is not a very practical option. With whites, oxidation can be reduced by using titanium white with a copperplate, and zinc white with a zinc plate. For a clean, crisp yellow that does not turn green, steel-facing of a copperplate is the only answer. Once a colour plate has been steel-faced, the colour quality is so improved that using an unfaced copperplate for colour printing is disappointing.

ADJUSTING INK VISCOSITY FOR PRINTING

If a colour is too stiff for printing, adding copperplate (linseed) oil is straightforward. Primarily, medium to weak copperplate oil will adjust the viscosity in order to make an ink easier to apply to a plate, or easier to wipe. The alternative is to add small amounts of a proprietary compound such as Easy Wipe. Some etchers add petroleum jelly to their ink in order to make the plate easier to wipe. This can have a detrimental effect on the ink, and the solvent nature of this product can stain the paper in the long term.

If the ink is too thin and liquid, then the options can be more limited. The first option is always to add in more pigment. This is relatively easy if the ink is a black. Adding coloured pigment will substantially alter the quality of colour of the premixed ink. Care must be taken with mixing and mulling the ink in order to render the ink particles of a similar size.

The second option is to add calcium carbonate (whiting) or French chalk

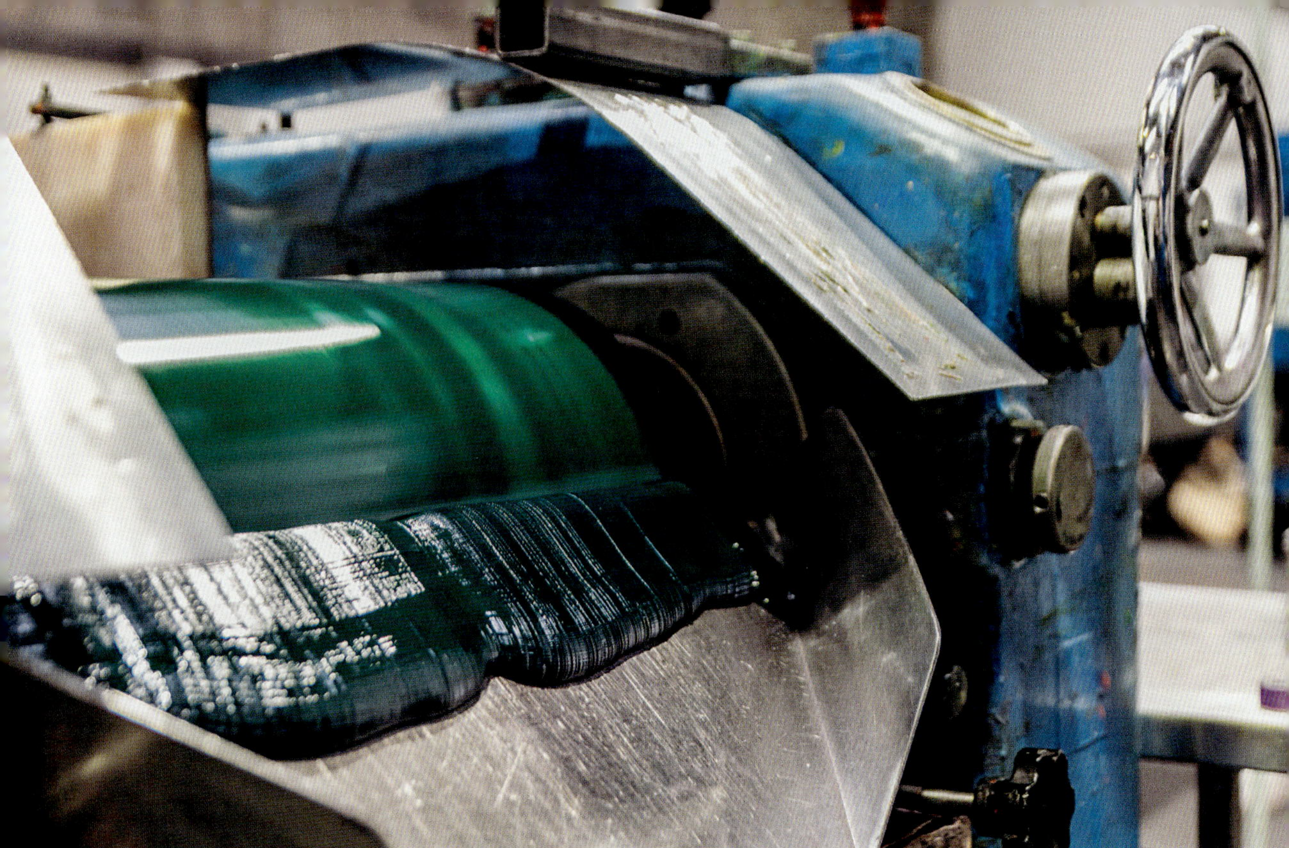

(talc), which will stiffen the ink and make it shorter. Take care, as it will severely alter the printing properties of your ink and tend to make it more transparent.

If the quality of colour is to remain the same, the more drastic option is to absorb some of the oil from the ink. This is achieved by placing a patch or pool of the ink on a clean, fresh sheet of blotting paper. The ink is then left for one or two days. You may need to spray an extremely light dusting of antioxidant oil over the ink to stop it drying out too quickly and skinning, but use this sparingly or you will undo all the work of removing oil from the ink. The ink is then carefully scraped off the blotting paper and used; again, take care to not disturb the fibres of the blotting paper when removing the ink.

INK FOR PRINTING *À LA POUPÉE*

Printing *à la poupée* is a method by which multiple colours are applied to an etching plate at the same time using a rolled and folded piece of scrim for each colour, known as a 'dolly' – a direct translation of the French word '*poupée*'. The scrim, after it has been rolled and folded, looks like an old-fashioned child's rag doll. Popular in the nineteenth century, advances in commercial colour printing ended its use as a mainstream technique, but it has remained a printmaking discipline. The requirements of the inks are similar to those of other etching

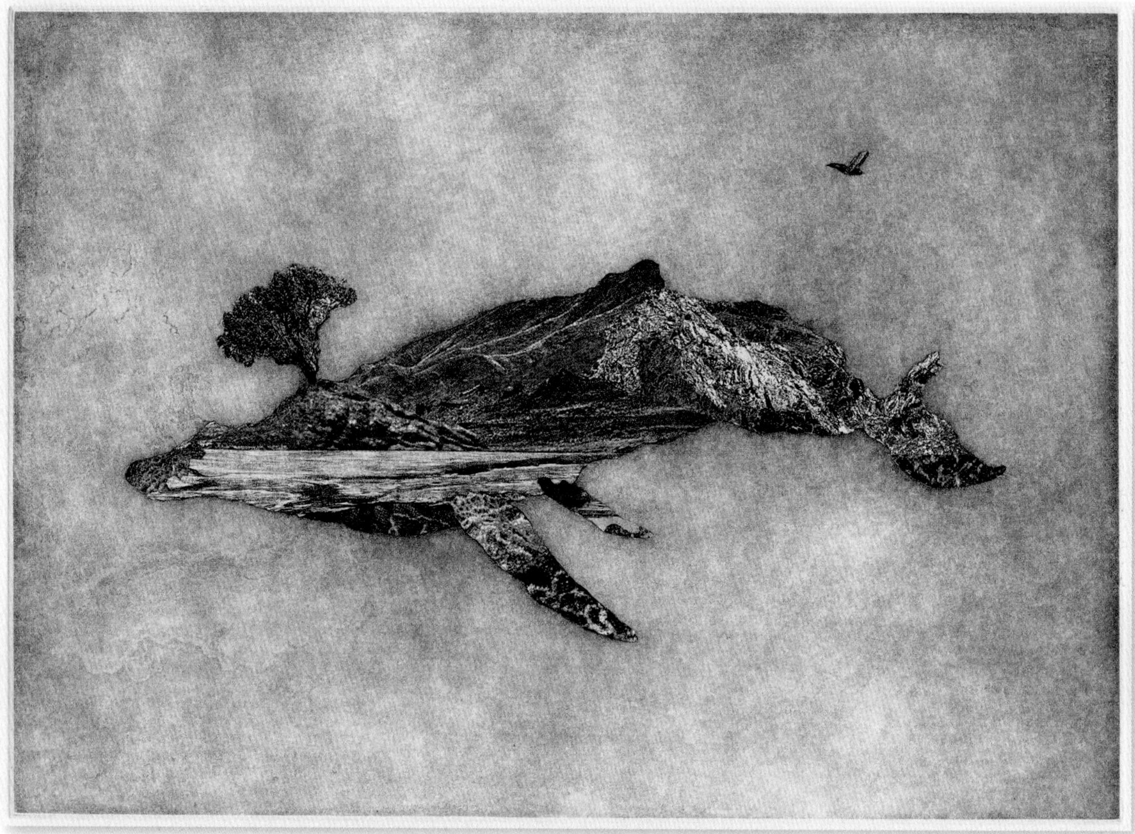

forms, but with a particular need for the chosen inks to have similar viscosity and tack to maintain uniformity as the colours are applied to the plate. Two methods are still in use for printing a multi-coloured etching plate.

The first historic method is usually used for printing from a single plate. First, the plate is inked with a transparent pale colour such as a pale beige. This colour is usually fairly weak and fluid in etching ink terms. Then the colour is worked into each section of the plate with a dolly. The plate is then carefully wiped, creating a tendency for the colours to blend from one area to another.

The second, more contemporary method is usually used when printing multiple plates one after the other in register to create the image. Often the coloured areas are separated from each other on the individual plates, and the image is built across several plates. The ink is then applied to the relevant section of a plate and the plate is wiped clean. The next colour is then applied and carefully wiped in a direction away from the first colour with a clean piece of scrim. This process is repeated for each colour across the plates. When all the colours have been inked and wiped, the plates are then printed in register. The ink used for this method is usually stiffer and easier to wipe clean.

MAKING YOUR OWN INK

The advantages of making your own ink are twofold: first, you can make the ink to suit your own personal requirements, adjusting fineness of grind, tack and viscosity; second, you can mix the colour to your own requirements, starting with single pigments of known quantity. To make your own ink, begin with dry pigment, still obtainable from suppliers such as Cornelissen & Son in the UK and Daniel Smith in the US. Build a heap in the middle of a large piece of plate glass or an old litho stone. Make a small hollow in the top of the mound and add about 10 per cent by volume of heavy copperplate oil. Slowly work the pigment into the oil with a broad-bladed palette knife; as you are mixing, the excess on the knife, and the pile, can be controlled by using a second palette knife to scrape the ink back into the pile. When the pigment is almost completely worked into the oil, the mixture should begin, in Anthony Gross's words, 'first to take on a flaky consistency and then to appear maggoty'[49] – meaning the mixture will have broken into something akin to a crumb base in pastry terms.

At this stage, the pile should be forcibly worked with the wide palette knife. Draw the knife through the ink, then turn it over with the wrist. Gather up the pile, turn the knife and draw it through the ink once more. When all the pigment is well worked into the mixture, it is ready for mulling with either a glass, marble or, in some cases, limestone muller. This is best undertaken by dividing the mound of ink into sections and mulling the ink in small parts. Spread a patch of the ink across the glass with the broad palette knife. Then rub the muller backwards and forwards across the patch of ink with an even movement while leaning onto the muller, applying as much pressure as possible. The ink will gradually become looser in consistency and appear shinier. Repeat this for the remainder of the ink in the pile.

While mulling, the ink should feel less gritty and the muller should move smoothly through the pile. Medium copperplate oil can be added in small amounts, to ease the mulling process and to bring the ink to the desired consistency. Do this with caution: it is very easy to add oil too quickly and find you need to add more pigment due to overzealous use of oil, beginning a cycle. Be warned: mulling your own ink is not a quick or easy process; to benefit from making your own ink, you need to give the whole process time and care. It is not for the faint-hearted or weak-wristed; it takes time and patience, but for good, strong black ink that is easy to wipe and print, the rewards are usually worth it.

CASE STUDIES

Thumbprint Editions

CORNIELIA PARKER

Thirty Pieces of Silver (Exposed), 2015
A series of 21 polymer gravure etchings on Fabriano Tiepolo Bianco 290 gsm paper.
Paper and image size: 66.3 x 54.3 cm (some landscape / some portrait format).
Editions of 20, plus five artists proofs and two printers proofs.
Published by Alan Cristea Gallery, London, 2015.
Printed and proofed at Thumbprint Editions Ltd, London.
Case study of two polymer gravure prints, *Silver Tray* and *Broken Tureen*, from the series *Thirty Pieces of Silver (Exposed)* by Cornelia Parker, printed by Pete Kosowicz at Thumbprint Editions, who tells us more below.

'*Thirty Pieces of Silver (Exposed)* is a series of 21 polymer gravures that Cornelia created in 2015. The prints were made by exposing Toyobo Printight plates in a Theimer Copymat exposure unit through large-format photographic glass negative plates. The plates, which were found by Cornelia at a junk market, were made to catalogue an auction of silver items, and we exposed the plates in their original glassine sleeves.

   The resulting image is a soft shadow of the glass plates themselves and, as it was exposed by a single source lamp, there is more tone towards the edges of the plates where the light was less strong. Polymer gravure plates tend to have a surface that is difficult to print completely clean, and this was exacerbated at the edges of the plates where they were less exposed. My preferred ink for photopolymer gravures is Charbonnel RSR, a very particular ink developed for printing engravings. It has a very dry, chalky texture, and a very finely ground and concentrated pigment, which

is easier to clean off the tacky surface of the polymer while keeping the intensity of the blacks. The images are torn down full bleed but have a clear area around the objects. It was hard to keep these areas clean, so we blended the RSR into some Charbonnel Doux, similar in feel to the RSR but much softer and therefore easier to blend, which wipes off the surface much easier to give the nice, clean surround.'

Cornelia Parker was born in Cheshire in 1956. She studied at the Gloucestershire College of Art & Design and at Wolverhampton Polytechnic before receiving her MA in Fine Art from the University of Reading in 1982. Her first major solo exhibition, *Thirty Pieces of Silver*, took place at Birmingham's Ikon Gallery in 1988. In 1997 she was shortlisted for the Turner Prize, and in 2010 she was elected to the Royal Academy of Arts and became an OBE. Parker was later appointed a Commander of the Order of the British Empire for services to the Arts in 2022. She was the UK's official Election Artist for the 2017 General Election, and in 2023 was commissioned by the UK Government Art Collection to create works in response to the Coronation of King Charles III. Parker's most recent major solo exhibition was a retrospective at Tate Britain, London in 2022.

Thumbprint Editions Ltd is a printmaking studio in Camberwell, South London. It was founded in 2003 by Pete Kosowicz, and produces intaglio and relief prints for many important British and international artists, including Anish Kapoor, Antony Gormley, Cornelia Parker, Damien Hirst and Harland Miller.

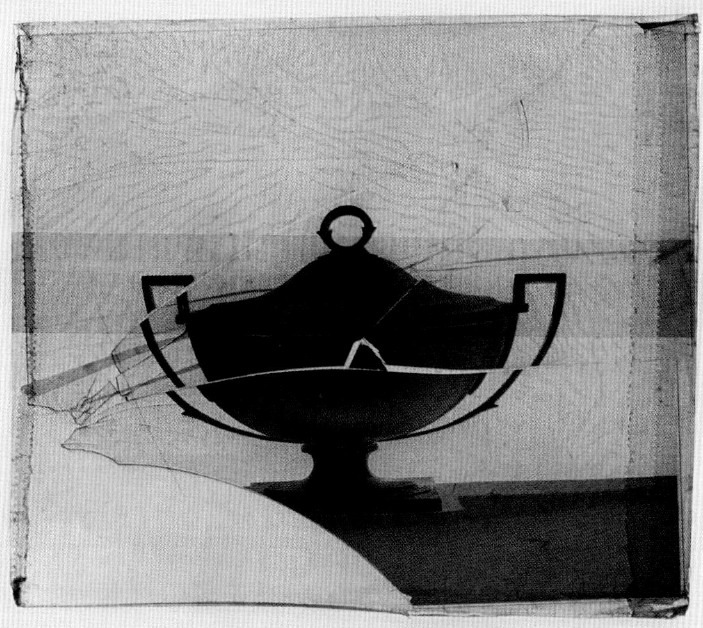

▲ *Broken Tureen* from *Thirty Pieces of Silver (Exposed)*, 2015. Polymer gravure etching, 66.3 x 54.3 cm. Courtesy Cornelia Parker and Cristea Roberts Gallery, London © Cornelia Parker. Photo: FXP Photography, London

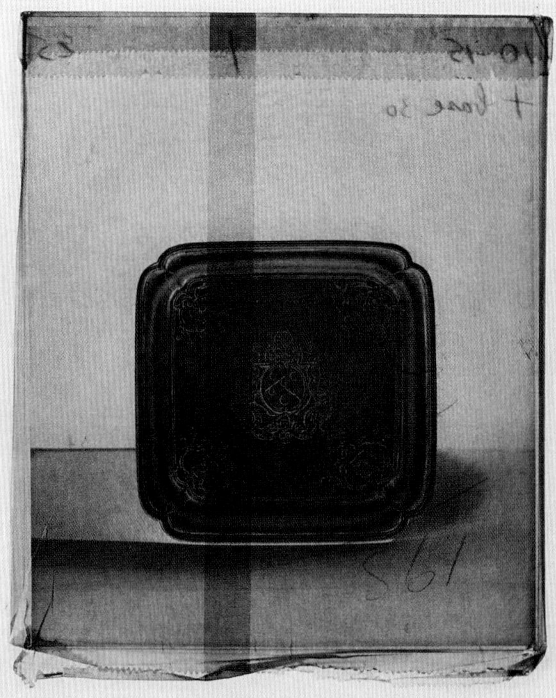

▲ *Silver Tray* from *Thirty Pieces of Silver (Exposed),* 2015. **Polymer gravure etching, 66.3 x 54.3 cm.** Courtesy Cornelia Parker and Cristea Roberts Gallery, London
© Cornelia Parker. Photo: FXP Photography, London

PETER MOSELEY

'The two photogravure prints are monochromatic prints showing landscape views taken in the Thingvellir National Park in Iceland in September 2023.

The original colour images were taken on a Nikon D3X and subsequently edited in Photoshop – a challenging process for securing satisfying monochromatic tonal differentiation, as the digital image files contained many subtly different colour hues but exhibited very similar levels of luminosity. The choice of etching inks helped realise these differences in the prints.

The prints are from photopolymer gravure plates (Toyobo Printight KM73) produced using calibrated and colourised digital positive film transparencies (Agfa CopyJet), themselves printed from an Epson SureColor P800. The dual exposure method was employed: each plate was initially exposed to a fine stochastic screen from Keith Taylor (keithtaylor.shop/products/aquatint-screen) for 58 units and then for 52 units under the transparency films. The vacuum UV exposure unit holds eight 20w black-light fluorescent tubes. Wash-out of the plates was for three minutes at 20°C.

The prints are on Hahnemühle 300 gsm natural etching paper using Gamblin Portland Cool Grey ink gently coloured with a touch of Intaglio Printmaker's Burnt Umber. Portland ink has a very high printed reflectance density and a high level of contrast.

I felt both were needed to express something of the bleak landscape which, for me, retained its dark foreboding and deep shadows despite the autumn sunlight. I experimented with added Burnt Umber to mediate the strong black, and later with added viscosity printing to give a tint to the highlights.' Further experimentations with these and other Iceland images lie ahead – Chine collé with thin natural Gampi paper on a white receiving paper to start with.

I have no single favoured ink or favoured brand. Ink choice depends entirely on the unique image in question, the qualities of the plate I've made, the type of paper and

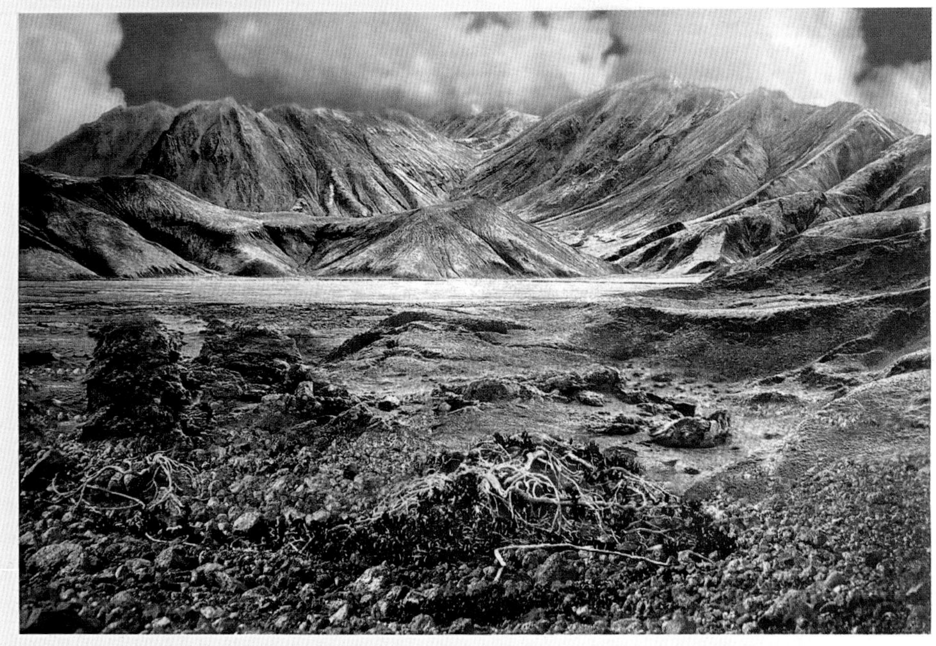

▲ **Peter Moseley** *Iceland 1*, **2023. Photogravure, 40 x 27 cm.** Photo: Peter Moseley © Peter Moseley

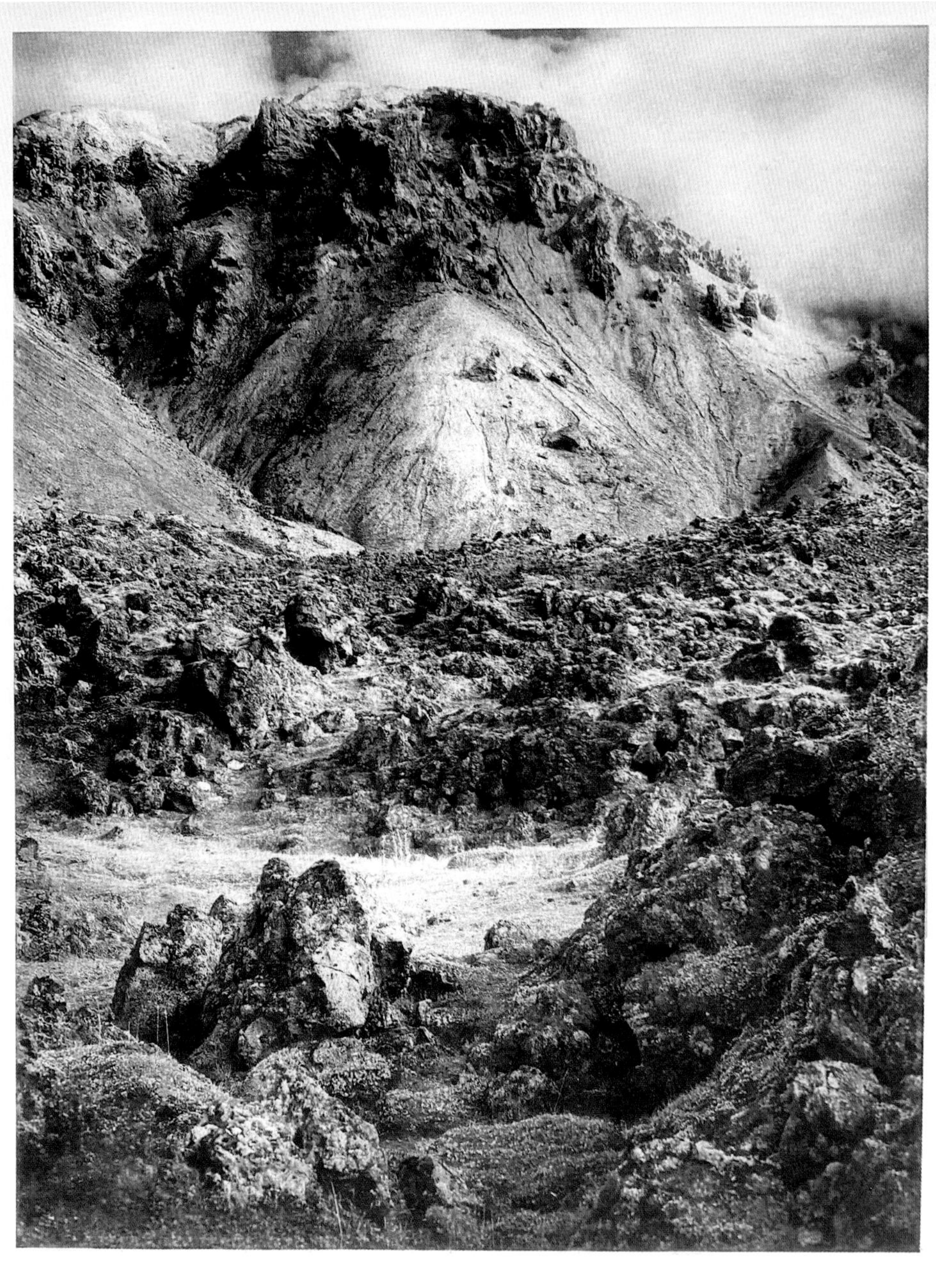

▲ **Peter Moseley *Iceland 2*, 2023. Photogravure, 40 x 27 cm.** Photo: Peter Moseley © Peter Moseley

what passes for my artistic imagination. However, I can offer some general observations:

- For prints where I wish, or the quality of plate production requires, to enhance the density of the shadow areas or increase the contrast in the print, two of my favoured etching inks are Gamblin Portland Black and Graphic Chemicals Vine Black. The Portland Black series gives me the highest shadow density and is relatively easy to work with using a plate warmer. Charbonnel 55981 is my standard go-to black for most test and many final printings.
- Where I wish or, because of platemaking issues, need to reduce print contrast or open up shadow areas, on most occasions I use Intaglio Printmakers Shop Mix Soft Black, with Cranfield Soft Black as a good alternative. Both give a "convincing" black, although, when placed side by side with 55981, the difference is obvious.
- I generally print black monochrome; where I wish to warm or otherwise modify the print colour, I use Intaglio Printmaker's range.
- Unless I'm doing viscosity printing, I rarely need to use Easy Wipe, plate oil or magnesium carbonate additives to alter the qualities of the inks. I find the standardised and very moderate depth of etching and complete absence of burr with photopolymer plates renders their use unnecessary.
- For duotone printing, I rely on Intaglio Printmakers' extensive own-brand range of colours (rumoured to be made by Cranfield). For four-colour work, I use Cranfield's process colours; I find their Cyan not to be so overpowering as some manufacturers and their Yellow to give both better yellows and greens in the print. I like the way these inks "sit" on the plate, are easily worked and don't take off quite so much of the previous colour when printing wet. When leaving each colour print to dry before overprinting, I use Hawthorn Stay Open process inks. This might seem a contradiction in terms – letting each printing dry before overprinting and using a stay open ink that's very slow in drying, but I find it works.'

Dr Peter Moseley practices photographic printing processes of the nineteenth and early twentieth centuries, including copper plate and photopolymer gravure, specialising in photogravure portraiture and landscapes. Following retirement from a career in educational management, his interest in photography was extended by a MA in Printmaking. He completed a PhD project at the Centre for Print Research at the University of the West of England, investigating aspects of the textuality and tonality of early printing processes and the contributions these make to audience 'readings' of the prints. He has had work selected for exhibition at the National Portrait Gallery, the Royal West of England Academy and the Royal Society of Painter-Printmakers, and has exhibited three solo shows of portraiture. He has taught workshops at several UK universities and colleges, and has taught abroad in Russia, China, the US and Iceland. He cites his exploration of photogravure and the haptic of its prints within the context of portrayals of the skin, the body and the person and, similarly, in the 'skin' and texture of the landscape.

Ian Chamberlain

Summit, 2024

The print *Summit* is inspired by the National Air Traffic Control System radar station, located at Clee Hill in Shropshire, UK. It forms a part of a broader collection of works that documents architectural forms associated with communication and investigation, emphasising the shared aspects of inquiry and curiosity in both the arts and sciences.

Original drawings have been translated into the etching process, which uses its inherent qualities to edit and build up layers of information – a balance between the slow build-up of the graphic image and subtle tonal variations of the intaglio process.

Ian was originally trained using Charbonnel ink at the University of the West of England (UWE). It became his ink of choice due to its consistency, ability to capture and retain subtle mid tones, and its ease of wiping. A creature of habit, he has always stuck with what he knows.

He only prints in one colour – Charbonnel 55985. This offers graphic strength, yet retains the mid tones and tends not to over wipe. It is very good when printing large areas of aquatint. Depending on the plate he is printing, he may add more copperplate oil to obtain an even tone, aquatinted sections or a touch more chalk to hold up in deeply bitten areas of line work.

Cellular 2nd State, 2024

Ian has been developing a current body of work that deals with communication, focusing on the repetitive design and sculptural qualities of mobile phone masts. The *Cellular 2nd State* etching is a dichotomy: a celebration of the fast pace of technology and the slow pace of making with the etching process, juxtaposed

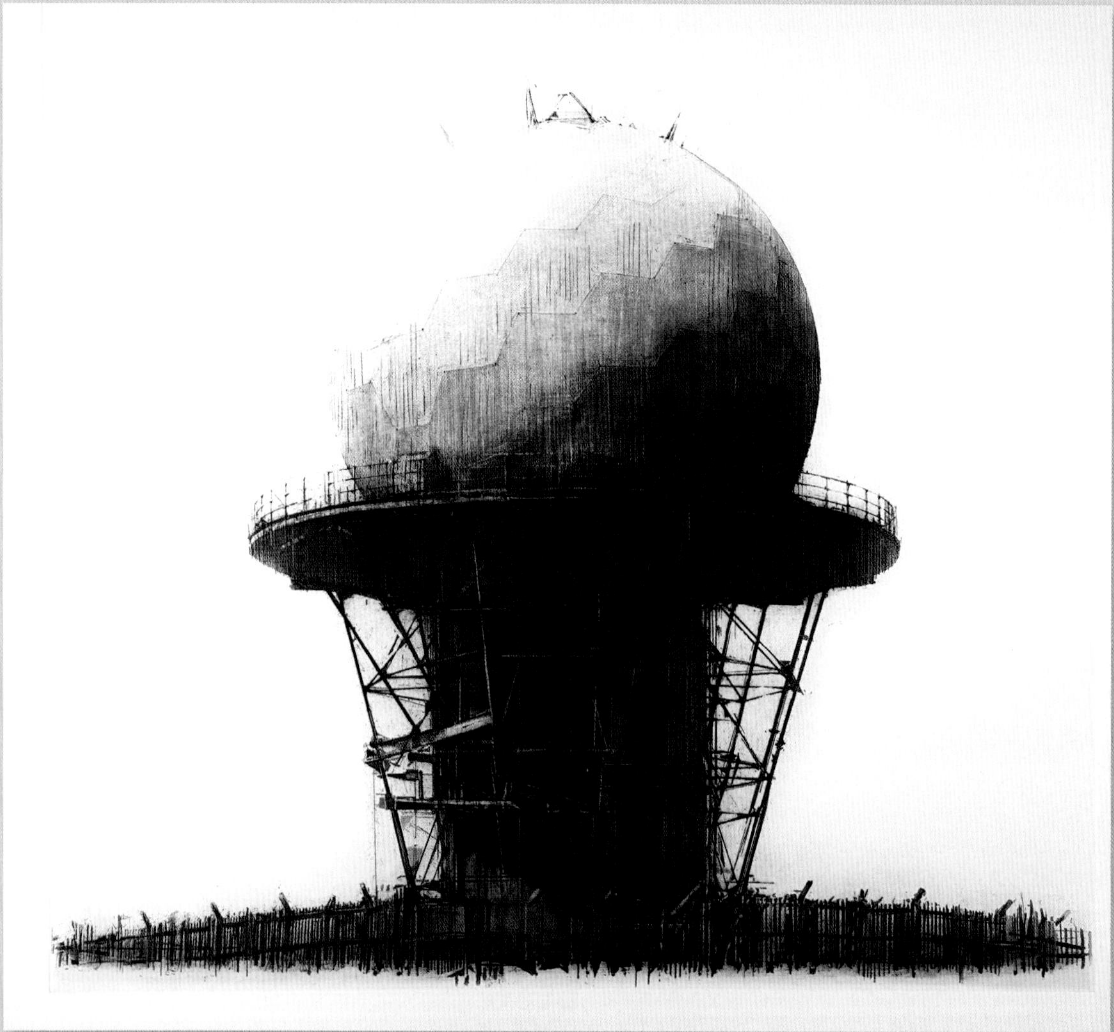

▲ **Ian Chamberlain** *Summit*, **2024. Etching, 56 x 76 cm.** Photo: Ian Chamberlain © Ian Chamberlain

with the quick and slow aspects of communication.

Necessary yet controversial structures, the masts are transformed into powerful symbols representing the omnipresence of modern communication networks, conveying a sense of time, change and continuity in our ever-evolving digital world. This is evidenced in the print, the copper plate continually reworked and edited, each layer adding new elements of information: a journey of recording the object.

They become subjects of artistic inquiry, questioning a deeper reflection on the role of technology and its overlooked infrastructure in our contemporary lives.

Ian currently only prints in one colour and using one plate (apart from *Dish Colour 1* – a collaboration with CFPR. See p.9.)

He spends a long time building up the copper plate, and enjoys the sculptural physicality of the process of layering and building up information through cyclical reapplications of grounds, drawing, etching, burnishing and drypoint. The copper surface is constantly revisited and altered, so that it is continually evolving. He spends large amounts of time burnishing and scraping away, especially in the aquatinted tonal areas. The Charbonnel ink really helps to pull out and bring attention to the highlighted areas. He finds the hardest thing is to know when to stop. Further states are used to explore the

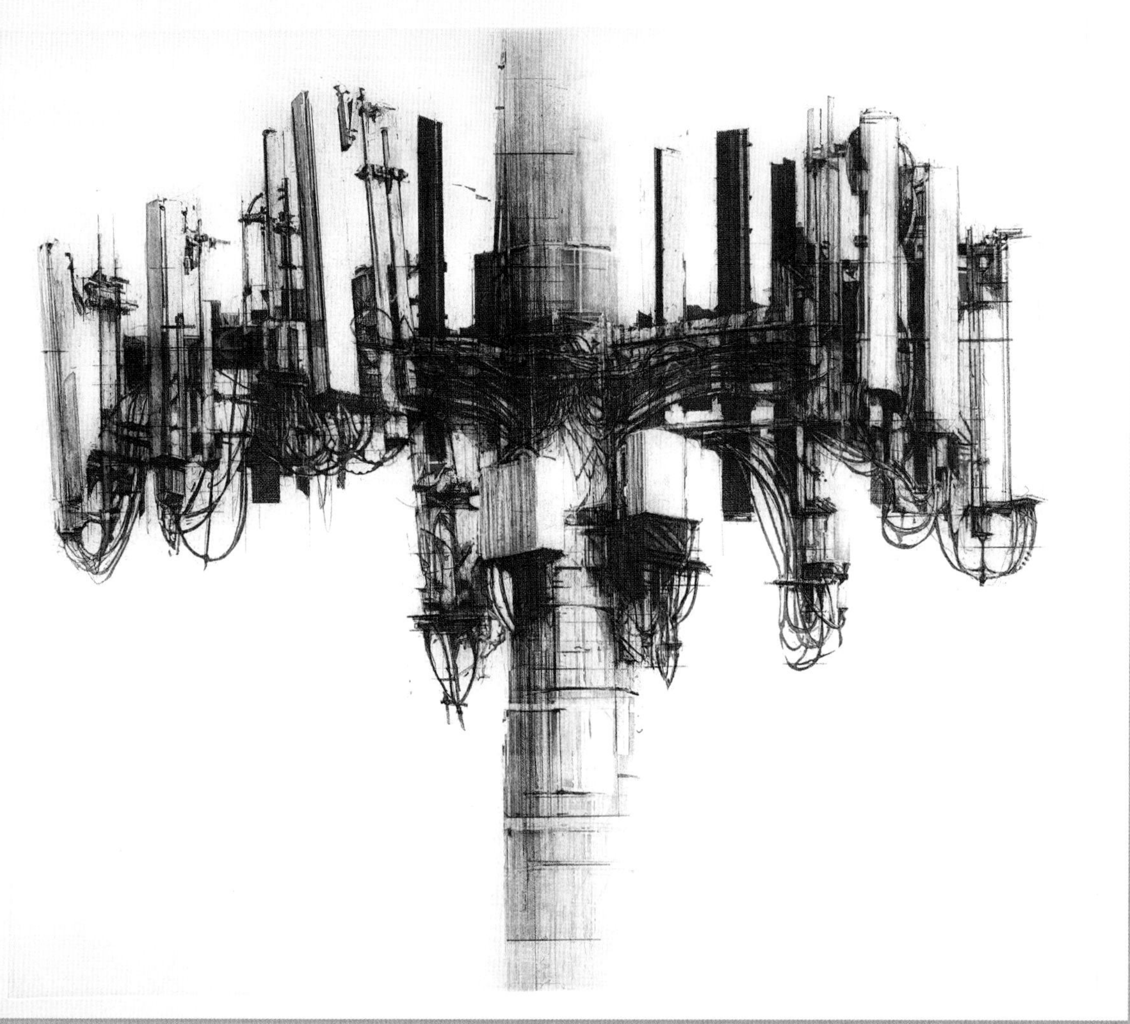

▲ **Ian Chamberlain** *Cellular 2nd State*, **2024. Etching, 56 x 76 cm.** Photo: Ian Chamberlain © Ian Chamberlain

possibilities of under wiping to gain tonal variations and a painterly effect; this in turn could inform new areas to include tone and aquatinted areas.

Ian Chamberlain is a Bristol-based artist whose work is influenced by manmade structures. He has a long-standing fascination with technology and architectural forms, including agricultural, industrial, scientific and military structures.

His work aims to reinterpret these manmade structures as monuments placed within the landscape. Ian is interested in the use of a traditional print process like etching to record subject matter that is generally at the cutting edge of technology.

The etching process has not significantly altered in over 500 years, which adds to Ian's interest in juxtaposing new technologies with traditional processes.

Ian has exhibited nationally and internationally, in London, Hong Kong, New York, Barcelona and Berlin. His prints and drawings are held in the collections of the Victoria and Albert Museum, London; Tate Modern, London; Bristol Museum; Royal West of England Academy, Bristol; Pallant House Gallery, Chichester; The University of Chichester collection; The Ashmolean, Oxford; and Chippenham Museum.

He is also a senior lecturer at UWE, Bristol, where he teaches on the MA in Multi-Disciplinary Printmaking.

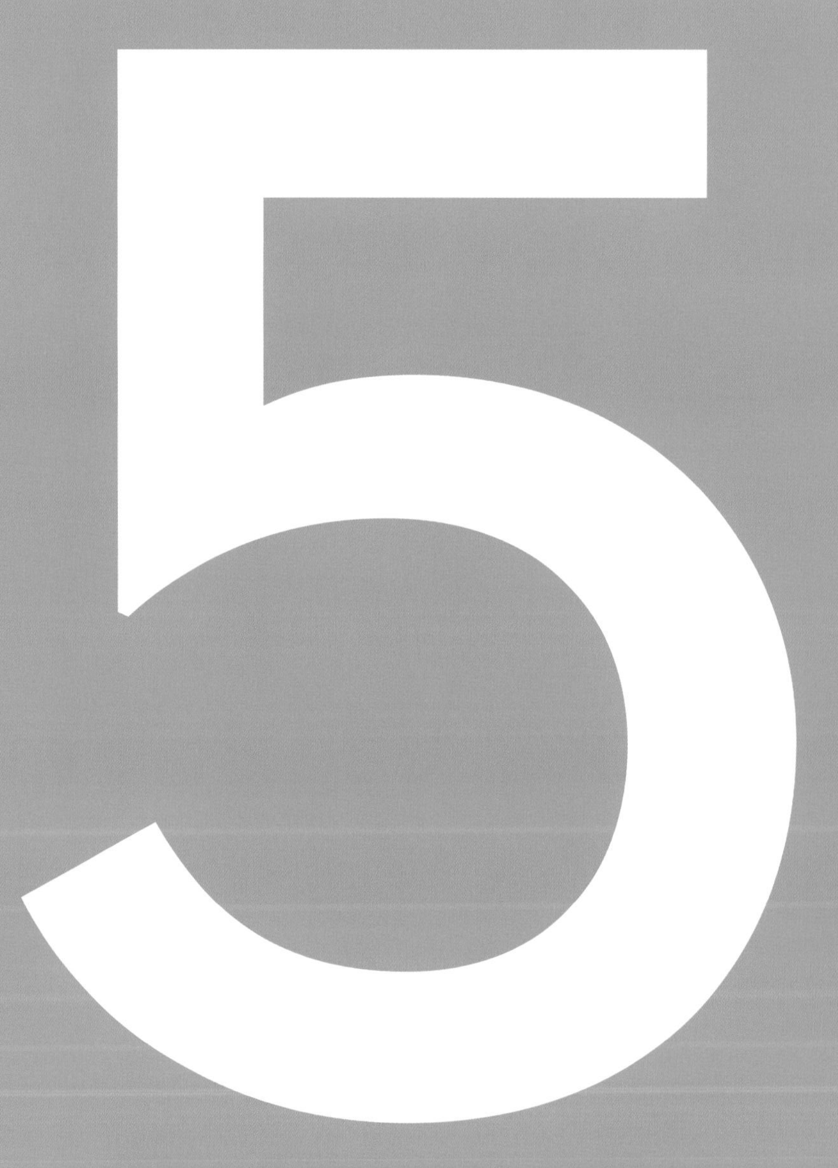

CHAPTER

5

INK FOR LITHOGRAPHY

To appreciate the attributes required by a lithographic printmaking ink, we first need to understand the process itself, which rests upon the principle that oil and water do not mix. The image to be printed is formed as a greasy mark on a flat lithographic limestone. The stone itself is naturally hydrophilic (water-loving) so when water (often termed the 'fount solution') is applied to the stone by sponge, it will cover the stone but will be repelled by the hydrophobic image area. The requirement of the lithographic ink to be rolled across the surface of the stone is that it should adhere to the greasy image area but be repelled by the damp, non-image area of the stone.

Given that the process is based on the chemical antipathy of oil and water rather than the contours of the plate (as with relief and etching), the margin for error for a lithographic ink is small. It needs to be sufficiently hydrophobic that it will not emulsify, while not being so very greasy that it will be difficult to roll out and transfer.

The ink needs to print a strong, clear colour but at a very thin film weight. This is achieved by the ink chemist, who must formulate an ink with a high proportion of pigmented colour in relation to the vehicle or varnish. Because the process is planographic, meaning that the plate is flat and the ink sits only in a very thin film upon a grease mark, the density of the ink deposit is in direct relation to the density of grease supporting the ink. Due to the nature of the grease deposit of the image area that supports the film of ink as it is rolled out, there is very little leeway for increasing the density and weight of the ink deposit. If the ink is weak and the printmaker attempts to apply a thicker film weight to achieve the colour, the ink is likely to spread, creating scum and giving rise to ink squash within the image.

The entire lithographic process is arguably the least forgiving in terms of ink selection by those using oil-based inks. Whereas relief printing can use almost any combination of colourant and vehicle, the list of things that a lithographic ink must *not* be is long!

The lithographic ink must be oil based; it should be highly pigmented; it should have the correct rheology to allow the ink to be rolled out on the stone without small droplets of ink misting or flying from the roller onto the non-image areas of the stone. At the same time, it should be able to compromise to a small degree in terms of invisible emulsification. Inks that are very oily and accept no invisible droplets of fount solution are generally too cohesive and can give a mottled appearance when printed, which creates an 'orange peel' effect, especially in solid areas of the print.

These same constraints on the ink equally apply to printmakers who use aluminium or zinc lithographic plates and the commercially available photoplate technologies.

EARLY LITHOGRAPHIC INK RECIPES

Colin Bloy lists an original ink recipe from Senefelder, dated 1818, alongside a recipe from Mairet in France also dated 1818, and a further French recipe from Charleville, dated 1821. It is interesting to compare Senefelder's recipe (detailed below), and then to compare the common elements of the other two inks:

> 'Take good old linseed oil, and place in an iron vessel up to one-third of its capacity. Heat over a good fire until it ignites. Remove from the fire and stir with an iron rod from time to time. When it is burning with a great flame, and bubbles and froths, cover the kettle and keep it covered until it no longer takes fire when the cover is removed. Test for threading. A good varnish does not need the addition of dryers.
>
> Several strengths of varnish are required, thin, medium and thick. The thin is about the consistency of honey and has been reduced one-third by combustion: the medium is reduced by one-half and threads well. The thick must be cooled quickly as it can solidify. The thin takes 1 hour and the thick about an hour and a quarter.
>
> Another method is to heat the varnish without burning. This gives a clearer varnish but takes longer to produce.
>
> Add roasted lampblack and grind well with a muller. Be careful not to over pigment.'[50]

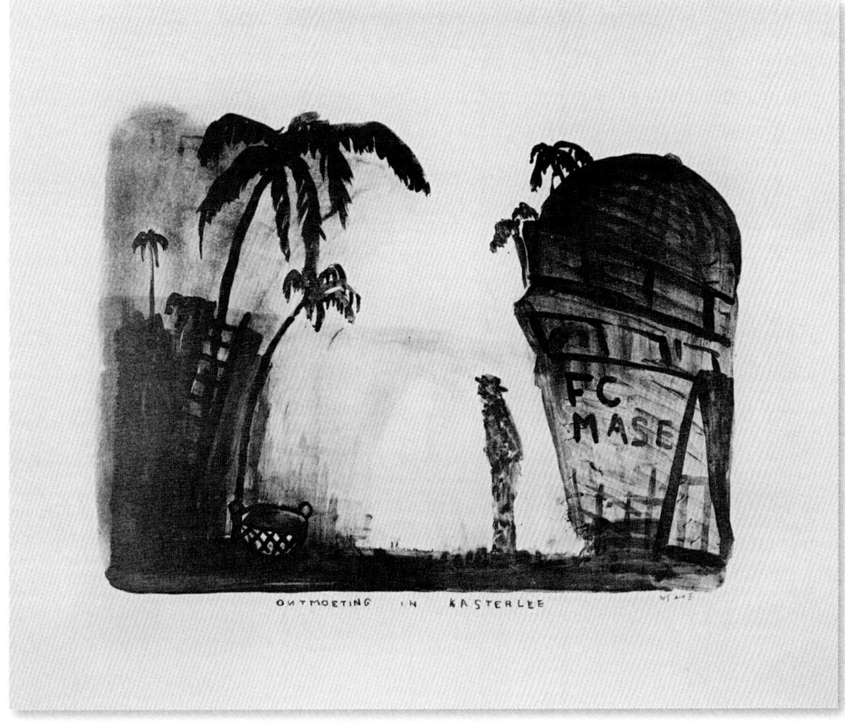

▶ **Walter Swennen** *Ontmoeting in Kasterlee* **(Encounter in Kasterlee), 2021. Lithograph, 70 x 57 cm.** Photo: Frans Masereel Centrum © Frans Masereel Centrum

The other two recipes are very similar, both requiring a mixture of several strengths of varnish. However, the Mairet recipe requires the addition of one part fatty soap and two parts white wax, while the Charleville recipe advocates the addition of sugar candy while burning to make the ink glossy.

It is interesting to note that the recipe for a good tailor-made artists' lithographic ink has changed very little over the last 200 years, apart from the fact that there are probably fewer additives in the ink than there were originally.

TAILOR-MADE ARTISTS LITHOGRAPHIC INK

A good-quality tailor-made ink for lithographic artists is usually a single-pigment ink. Having this single colour tends to assist the clarity of colour within the ink, enabling the ink to take a high degree of transparency without becoming muddy in appearance. Other advantages are that single-pigment inks containing the most suitable pigment are often more lightfast, so the ink should be less prone to fading. Mixing two lightfast pigments is not a problem, but weakening inks is, and pastel colours are always prone to fading at a faster rate. This is particularly important in a litho ink, as the thinner the film and the more transparent the overlays become, the more likely the ink is to be susceptible to fading. This is because there are simply fewer particles of pigment in a transparent thin film, so the particles are more exposed to UV light and any change of colour in these particles is going to be more noticeable than in a thicker film ink packed with strong, rich colour, such as a screen-printing ink. A single-pigment ink is also less likely to be prone to metamerism (see p.83) than ink made from a number of pigments. It also means that when mixed with other ink, the colour should remain bright and not cause unexpected tertiary colour.

If you buy a good-quality ink, in most cases (apart from mixing with other colours) it should perform satisfactorily without the need for adjustment; around 10 per cent of inks have poor performance relative to expectation, and a small amount of adjustment is necessary, but adjust your ink with caution. The ink manufacturer has spent time and thought making an ink to the specification you are about to change. There is usually a very good reason for the behaviour and engineered characteristics of a particular ink. Below is an example of a typical lithographic ink recipe developed for artists' use:

Lithographic Ink – Hansa Yellow
36% Hansa yellow pigment
62% linseed stand oil (150–200 poise)
1% wax
1% antioxidant

Note that the formulation principles include a relatively high pigment loading, which, as we have stated, is finely ground, and with few or no driers – this will vary from pigment to pigment. The example above, of Hansa yellow, is a pigment that will not affect the drying property of the ink too much and, given the thin film weight, the 1 per cent or less of antioxidant is there to make sure you can roll out the thin film without it drying on the slab or plate too quickly, before the colour is printed. This formulation is for a relatively long ink: in other words, when you put a knife into the ink and pull it upwards, the bead of ink will not break easily. This property ensures good adhesion of the thin film of ink and pigment particles to the paper, and the ink will also show less tendency to emulsify with the water. It will transfer well to the roller and be easy to work.

WHAT IS IN COMMERCIAL LITHO INK?

Commercial lithographic ink is formulated for a very different use, primarily high-speed printing. This involves much faster drying properties, as each sheet is stacked within seconds of printing. The inks have different skin-forming properties, antioxidants, reagent resistance as required, and the ability to withstand alcohol font solutions, as well as added driers and other chemicals to control film weight and dispersion. These inks, though cheap to buy, are invariably not sufficiently lightfast for art purposes and may be made from a number of different pigments. Most tend to form a skin on their surface caused by the added driers.

USING COMMERCIAL INK

A commercial ink might be the only choice if you need to use a low-cost ink that is readily available locally, or for students in an open-access workshop where ink management may be a problem and therefore cost is an important consideration. The user must bear in mind that most commercial litho inks will contain surfactants, driers, anti-scumming agents and synthetic polymers, all to facilitate a very thin, high-speed printing film weight. These are not necessarily the properties conducive to printmaking, and can in fact cause more problems for the printer. The surfactants can cause the ink to bleed when used in thicker films that naturally occur by hand rolling a plate and the greater quantity of water by using a sponge rather than automatic damping.

For the professional printmaker who needs to understand the ingredients of his or her ink, a commercial ink can be a problematic choice over the long term, especially if a gallery or museum asks if the print can be exhibited without risk of fading. Colour quality is also an issue; there is no substitute for good-quality materials. We have described elsewhere how quickly a commercial litho ink may fade. The average expected lifespan of a colour magazine or brochure is often no more than a few months, rather than the multiples of years expected by the fine-art printmaker. The low tack and the presence of antioxidants can also make images feather as filament along the lumens (hollow cavity) of the paper fibre. This can result in disappointing prints without definition.

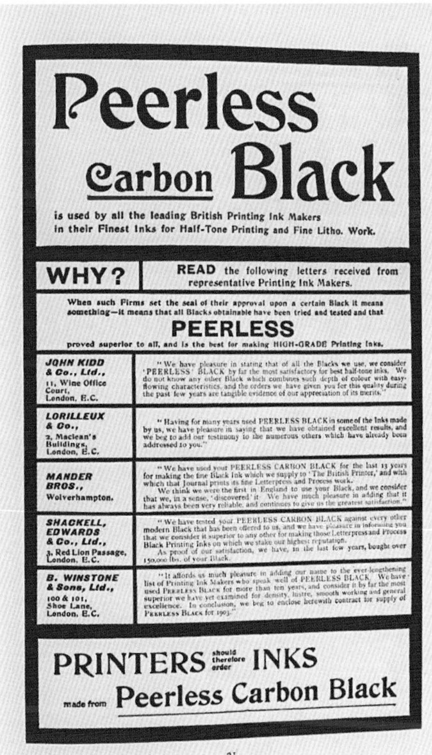

▼ Peerless Carbon Black advertisement from the *Penrose Annual*, 1905. Photo: Jo Hounsome Photography

A typical commercial blue lithographic ink may consist of:

50% Varnish (oleoresinous/alkyd)
25% Soya oil
18% 50% phthalocyanine blue water paste (C.I. Pigment Blue 15)
5% Extender (white pigment TiO_2 (titanium dioxide))
2% Additives

Additives may be any or all of the following: silica, talc, clay, dispersants, PTFE waxes, driers and stabilisers.

The price advantage of using a commercial ink can also be offset by the potentially higher level of wastage. Commercial lithographic printing inks are generally supplied in vacuum-packed 1 kg or 2.5 kg tins. Once the lid is removed (often distorting in the process) and the seal is broken, the ink will begin to dry and, unless used relatively quickly, it will deteriorate. While more expensive per gram, a tube of lithographic printmaking ink is significantly less likely to dry inside the packaging.

USING VARNISHES

The printing of litho ink can be controlled by the use of varnishes (here referring to a stand oil). It is common to use a range of varnishes between 40 and 60 poise, to reduce the tack and create an ink that is easier to roll and transfer. To quote the *Tamarind Book of Lithography*, 'a hand-printing ink should permit easy inking of solids and permit halftones to stay open.'

If you alter the properties of an ink to prevent one problem, you are almost certainly building up another, so be careful and add sparingly. It is also worth bearing in mind that lithographic varnish, beyond the usual problems of transferring a pigment and acting as the glue that binds it together, also possesses the inherent property of rejecting water through its natural greasiness. Therefore, any adjustments made to the ink must bear this characteristic in mind.

A very thin varnish of 1 poise (#00 in American varnish numbers) may be added in tiny quantities to avoid 'picking' of the paper. This is where fibres of the paper pull away from the surface due to the

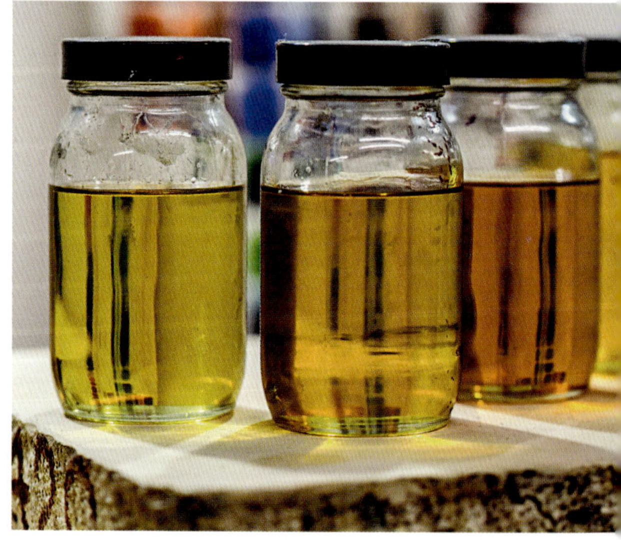

▼ **Varnishes of varying strengths.** Photo: Jo Hounsome Photography © Cranfield Colour

strength of the ink. It is traditional to use very small amounts of petroleum jelly for this purpose but, if possible, use thin varnish – it avoids adding the solvent present in the petroleum jelly to the ink. A thin varnish may also be used to add greasiness to the ink, causing it to pick up detail on the plate more readily. However, too much will cause the ink to become too greasy, causing all manner of problems. Consider trying a different brand of ink if this is a problem.

If your ink is not stiff enough, it is better to add a strong litho varnish of 250 poise (American #7 or #8) or a strong copperplate oil. This, in addition, will make the ink appear less greasy and increase tack.

MAGNESIUM CARBONATE AND OTHER ADDITIVES

It has long been common practice in lithography to add magnesium carbonate to ink that is too tacky or liquid. The reasons given are to create shorter ink that is stiffer and less tacky, and to take away some of the greasiness, therefore rendering the ink less likely to spread on the plate and to scum it up. Magnesium carbonate will stiffen your ink; some authorities recommend the addition of large amounts to the ink, but care should be taken with the addition of magnesium carbonate. Too great a quantity can alter the drying properties of the ink and, if an excess amount is added, then the ratio of ink to pigment can be affected, causing the pigment to rub off or the print to scuff. Magnesium carbonate in quantity will affect the colour strength of your ink, making it more transparent. It is always worth remembering that a different brand of the same colour may solve your problems.

FLOCCULATION WHEN ADDING DRY POWDER

In lithography, adding dry powder to ink increases the potential for the powder to become saturated by the water, which will then allow the ink to emulsify with the water and so increase scumming on the non-image areas.

It is a particular problem for the fine particles in lithographic ink if flocculation occurs in the manufacture of ink. When the printmaker comes to use such an ink, problems can arise if water then reaches the dry particles of ink that have not been coated by oil. The water can mix with the oil in the ink, forming an emulsion and causing the printing plate to scum up. With this in mind, the printmaker should always be cautious when adding any powder to a lithographic ink. Poor mixing may well make things worse through flocculation, rather than curing the problem as intended.

FURTHER MODIFYING LITHOGRAPHIC INKS

As with etching and relief, the most common modification is to strengthen with the addition of an extender, sometimes called a 'tinting medium'. This is essentially a colourless ink, but as it contains a solid, albeit translucent, pigment it has the structure of ink and is therefore very easy to fold into the coloured ink using a plat-blade ink knife. Extending the ink allows the printmaker to obtain a range of shades of varying intensities from the one colour. Many litho colours are so highly pigmented that they behave almost as concentrates, and would be too strong for many printed images without the addition of an extender.

If the artist wishes to reduce both the colour strength and the viscosity of the ink simultaneously, the addition of an appropriate linseed oil will achieve the desired effect. Essentially, the oil dilutes or thins the ink by changing the ratio of the existing components of oil and pigment. It is important that the ink is not overly diluted, as an ink with a high proportion of oil will produce prints without definition and may stain the reverse of the paper with oil as it strikes through the paper.

While not intended primarily for lithography, wiping compounds and tack reducers can be used sparingly to change transfer properties. However, the solvent content can cause emulsification problems on the stone, as these mediums introduce a Vaseline®-like solvent into the ink which will impact print quality, ink drying time and the rub resistance of the finished print.

Printmakers' wax drier paste is a combination of wax with suitable metallic salt driers that is squeezed from a tube rather than poured from a bottle. It is therefore easier to mix with ink. The wax content increases the rub resistance of the dried ink film while the drier speeds up the whole process.

The addition of talc of any kind will introduce more solids into the ink, which will increase the ink viscosity while not proportionally increasing the tack. With all ink modifications, the printmaker needs to test at each stage and not lose sight of why the modification was required in the first place. Each of the aforementioned modifiers, when used to excess, will adversely affect the ease of use, the quality of print or the drying profile and behaviour of the ink once printed.

Add any driers sparingly. Driers are carried in spirit (e.g., manganese in naphtha), but remain a catalyst only; adding more drier will result in excess solvent, creating a greater emulsion and, perversely, slowing the drying process. The balance, as with all litho ink, is a delicate one.

The often-overlooked modification that, when used, negates the requirement for the use of material modifiers is the addition of heat energy.

Either a heated surface to warm the etching plate, or the vigorous use of a palette knife to warm the ink can be used. Oil-based ink, being by nature thixotropic, will fall in viscosity with comparatively little effort.

PRESS BLACK, ROLL-UP OR NON-DRYING BLACK

In recent years, hand lithographers have had problems finding a good press black. In *The Tamarind Book of Lithography*, Antreasian and Adams describe the requirements of a press black. Only the stiffest lithographic ink is used for the roll-up process. Its minimum fatty content and stiff consistency help to prevent fill-in of the partially desensitised stone. Traditionally, many large studios have used an ink manufactured by Charbonnel called Noir a Monter. However, due to changes in pigment suppliers, manufacturing base and ownership, this and similar products are no longer the same as the traditional press black described by Antreasian and Adams in the 1960s. Other roll-up blacks are available, and it is up to the individual to find one that best suits their personal circumstances. However, in the hand-printed lithograph community there is an ongoing desire to find the perfect roll-up black.

COLLOTYPE

We hope that collotype printers are not offended by the appearance of collotype as a subset of lithography, but the similarities are broad and the physical constraints and pressures on the ink similarly daunting.

This is now a very obscure process practised professionally by very few printers. In Europe, Fratelli Alinari, in Florence, was among the last collotype studios to print on a regular basis, as was Lichtdruck Werkstatt in Leipzig. Benrido, in Kyoto, Japan, is probably the last commercial collotype printer of any scale left in the world. Collotype is very similar to lithography in that it is a planographic process that relies on water to repel ink. However, collotype is printed from a layer of light-sensitive gelatine, usually on a glass plate that has been exposed through a continuous-tone film negative. The plate hardens in direct relation to the amount of light it receives.

After development in warm water, the gelatine is hygroscopic; therefore, the plate is receptive to water in relation to how hard the gelatine is in the parts that have received light. During the washing-out process, the gelatine reticulates to form a random, very finely detailed structure in the manner of a fine aquatint. At this stage, the plate is then treated in a similar manner to a litho plate: it is dampened with a mixture of glycerine and water, and rolled up with

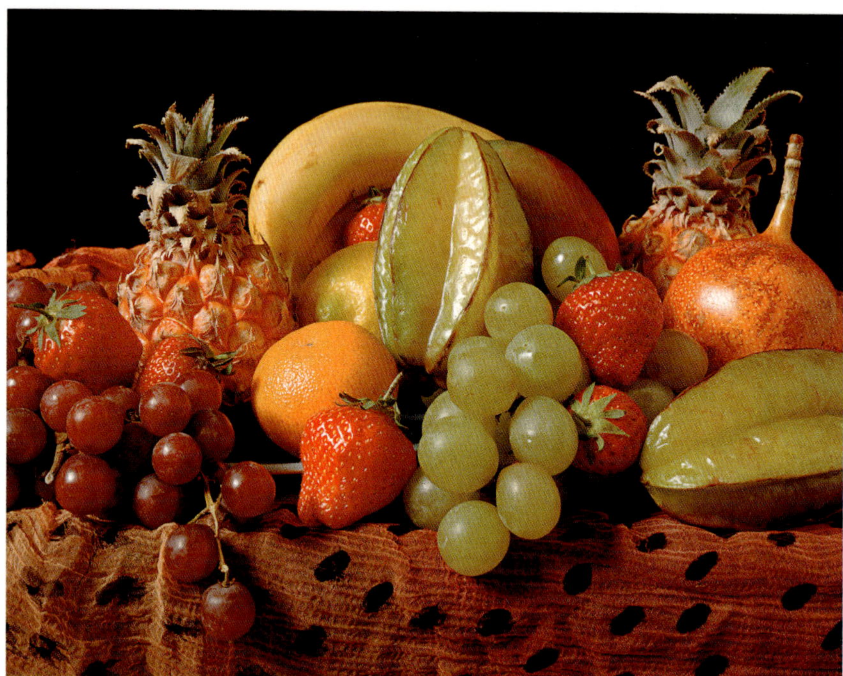

◄ **Paul Thirkell** *Fruit 2 (after Chardin)*, **2001. Collotype.** Photo: Paul Thirkell © CFPR, UWE, Bristol

ink. The parts that have absorbed the water reject the ink in direct relation to how much light they have received. The process is far more sensitive than lithography, and a result close to continuous-tone print, which has a full range of grey tones, can be achieved.

Inks for collotype are somewhat different to those developed for litho. They are usually heavily pigmented, with a ration of pigment loading close to 50 per cent. They are also tackier and stiffer than lithographic inks. Good collotype ink needs to be cut from the tin and will only become more elastic when worked with a palette knife. This is because it is harder to get a collotype ink to stick to the printing plate. With lithography, the greasy part of the plate is receptive and attractive to the ink and the water rejects it. In collotype the water is rejecting the ink across almost the whole plate and the gelatine is less attractive than grease. Therefore, the ink has to be stickier to adhere to the gelatine, and of a strong colour due to the very thin film weights printed.

The Centre for Print Research, in close collaboration with Cranfield Colours in Wales, recreated collotype ink for its own use and, potentially, for the last commercial printers left in Europe. The inks are also superb for four-colour CMYK etching and photogravure due to their stiff nature, although they are more expensive than a standard etching ink because of their high pigment loading and the costs of the small batches required. Sadly, however, this project has now ended and collotype ink is no longer made.

CASE STUDIES

Tamarind Institute

Tamarind Institute was founded in 1960 as Tamarind Lithography Workshop in Los Angeles, CA, USA. Since 1970, Tamarind Institute has been a division of the University of New Mexico in Albuquerque, New Mexico, USA. They operate a professional collaborative lithography workshop, gallery programmes, and rigorous educational training for artisan lithography printers.

VALPURI REMLING, MASTER PRINTER & WORKSHOP MANAGER, TAMARIND INSTITUTE

Valpuri was born in Rovaniemi, Finnish Lapland. After receiving her MFA in printmaking from the Finnish Academy of Fine Arts, she studied at Tamarind Institute and received her Tamarind Master Printer certificate in 2009.

Following her training at Tamarind, she returned to Helsinki and Helsinki Litho, becoming co-owner of the workshop, while also teaching lithography at the University of the Arts, Helsinki, in the Academy of Fine Arts printmaking programme. Remling was appointed the Master Printer and Workshop Manager of Tamarind Institute in 2015. Her role includes collaborations with visiting artists, managing multiple publishing projects, advising other workshops and manufacturing entities on best practices in lithography, and leading research in advances in lithographic techniques.

Valpuri chose two recent lithographs to share and discuss below. Both were created in collaboration with the artists in residence at Tamarind Institute.

'Proofing happens together with the artist during the residency. We create the matrices, choose and mix the inks and print various versions of colourways and paper options for the artist to react to. We will make as many versions as it is necessary for the artist to feel like their vision is achieved. This approval to print-proof is then signed by the artist.

The edition is printed to match the approval. Printers follow notes on the order of layers and rollers to use, along with other details, and the colours are mixed following a recipe and matching a colour sample.

We use lithographic inks that are made for fine-art hand printing. These inks are high in pigment content, slow drying and lightfast. For these two prints I have used a selection of inks from Hanco Ink and Graphic Chemical & Ink Co. Properties of inks keep changing throughout the years, but we trust these manufacturers to maintain the standards we are dedicated to.

We need the ink to transfer from the slab to the roller, from the roller to the matrix and from the matrix to the paper in a specific way. To achieve this, we modify the viscosity, length or tack of the ink according to the characteristics of the ink, the paper, the roller, the matrix, mark making and press used.

In addition to the highly pigmented colour inks used in the chosen prints, opaque white and transparent tint base play significant roles. Opaque white is used to lighten the hue without making the colour more transparent, whereas transparent tint base is used to add to the natural transparency of the coloured ink. These properties balance the colour mixing of overlapping marks from each matrix. Transparency also lets the paper hue show through and play part in the image.'

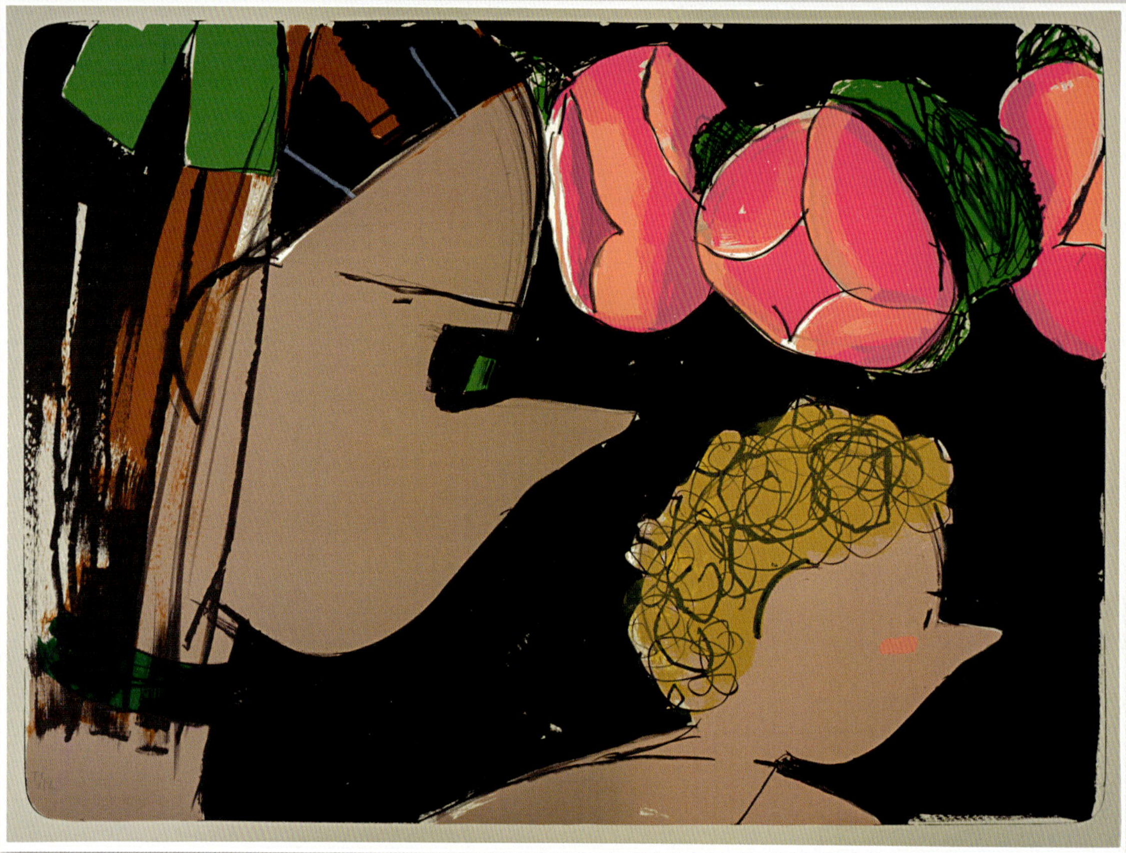

▲ Ellen Berkenblit *Night Peonies*, 2022 (22-303). **Lithograph, 68.5 x 94 cm.** Photo: Valpuri Remling, Kenton Bueche, Francis Reynolds © Tamarind Institute, University of New Mexico

ELLEN BERKENBLIT

Night Peonies, 2022 (22-303)

11-colour lithograph.
Paper size: 68.5 x 94 cm.
Paper type: Grey Rives BFK.
Collaborating printer(s): Valpuri Remling and Lindsey Sigmon.
Edition printed by: Valpuri Remling.
Edition of 20.

'Ellen Berkenblit is a painter who has decades of experience in working with various printers. She has created work with us at Tamarind on multiple occasions, which means that we have established a very comfortable way of working together. Ellen's mark making is confident and direct. She loves making the key image on a stone, using greasy tusches and crayons. We like to print her key stone on the offset press to maintain the original orientation of the image, and at the same time we're able to comfortably print the entire surface of the stone, edge to edge. Additional colour runs are mostly printed on the direct press from positive working photo plates. The artist draws on polyester film that is then exposed on to a photo plate.'

Run 1:
Colour(s):
- Dark brown: 1 part Hanco Stiff Tint Base, 1 part Hanco Opaque White, toners: Hanco Trophies Brown, Hanco Dark Red, Hanco Leaf Brown, Hanco Xmas Green.
- Light brown: 1 part Hanco Stiff Tint Base, 1 part Hanco Opaque White, toners: Hanco Leaf Brown, Hanco Fire Red, Hanco Trophies Brown, Hanco Xmas Green.

Method: Hand inked, blend roll, positive working photoplate, on a direct press.

Run 2:
  Colour(s): Hanco Leaf Brown.
  Method: Hand inked, positive working photoplate, on a direct press.

Run 3:
  Colour(s):
  - Blue-green: 2 parts Hanco Phthalo Blue Green Shade, 1 part Hanco Process Yellow, 1 part Hanco Stiff Tint Base, toner: Hanco Opaque White.
  - Warm green: 2 parts Hanco Stiff Tint Base, 1 part Hanco Opaque White, toners: Hanco Phthalo Blue Red Shade, Hanco Process Yellow, Hanco Xmas Green, Hanco Fire Red.
  Method: Hand inked, separate rollers, positive working photoplate, on a direct press.

Run 4:
  Colour(s):
  - Pink: 1 part Hanco Stiff Tint Base,1 part Hanco Opaque White, toners: Graphic Chemical Madder Lake Red, Hanco Purple.
  - Purple: 2 parts Hanco Opaque White, 1 part Hanco Stiff Tint Base, toners: Graphic Chemical 1930 Purple, Hanco Purple.
  Method: Hand inked, separate rollers, positive working photoplate, on a direct press.

Run 5:
  Colour(s):
  - Black: 1 part Hanco Trophies Brown, 1 part Hanco Dark Red, 1 part Hanco Xmas Green, 1 part Hanco Ultra Blue.
  Method: Hand inked, limestone, on an offset press.

Run 6:
  Colour(s):
  - Ochre: 3 parts Hanco Stiff Tint Base, 1 part Hanco Opaque White, 1 part Hanco Leaf Brown, toners: Hanco Process Yellow, Hanco Xmas Green.
  Method: Hand inked, positive working photo plate, On a direct press.

Run 7:
  Colour(s):
  - Hanco Opaque White.
  - Pink: 1 part Hanco Stiff Tint Base,1 part Hanco Opaque White, toners: Hanco Fire Red, Hanco Process Yellow.
  Method: Hand inked, separate rollers, positive working photoplate, on an offset press.

JARVIS BOYLAND

California Interior #3, 2023 (23-318)

12-colour lithograph.
Paper size: 99 x 66.3 cm.
Paper type: Soft White Somerset Velvet.
Collaborating printer(s): Valpuri Remling and Julia Marco Campmany.
Edition printed by: Valpuri Remling.
Edition of 20.

'Jarvis Boyland is an artist who works in both painting and drawing mediums. His residency with Tamarind was his first time collaborating on a lithograph or a print. Jarvis came to the residency with an idea about a piece and we set on our way to make his vision come to life. As he was a first-time resident, we made sure he had a chance to try various mark making techniques on all the matrices we traditionally use (limestone, ball-grained aluminium plate and positive working photoplate). He adapted to the medium rather easily. Mark making became enjoyable and seeing the colours overlap one after another gave him guidance to work on additional layers. The stone was his favourite matrix to work on, as is the case with many artists, and he kept on making changes to the stone layer until the very end. We also ended up using one ball-grained plate and multiple photoplates.'

Run 1:
  Colour(s): Light yellow: 9 parts Hanco Stiff Tint Base, 2 parts Hanco Opaque White, 1 part Hanco Process Yellow.
  Method: Hand inked, positive working photoplate, on a direct press.

Run 2:
  Colour(s): Yellow: 8 parts Hanco Stiff Tint Base, 1 part Hanco Opaque White, 1 part Hanco process Yellow.
  Method: Hand inked, positive working photoplate, on a direct press.

Run 3:
  Colour(s): Blue: Hanco Stiff Tint Base, toners: Graphic Chemical Reflex Blue, Hanco Opaque White, Hanco Xmas Green, Hanco Flame Red.
  Method: Hand inked, ball-grained aluminium plate, on a direct press.

Run 4:
  Colour(s): Cerulean: Hanco Stiff Tint Base, toners: Hanco Process Cyan, Hanco Opaque White, Hanco Flame Red.
  Method: Hand inked, positive working photoplate, on a direct press.

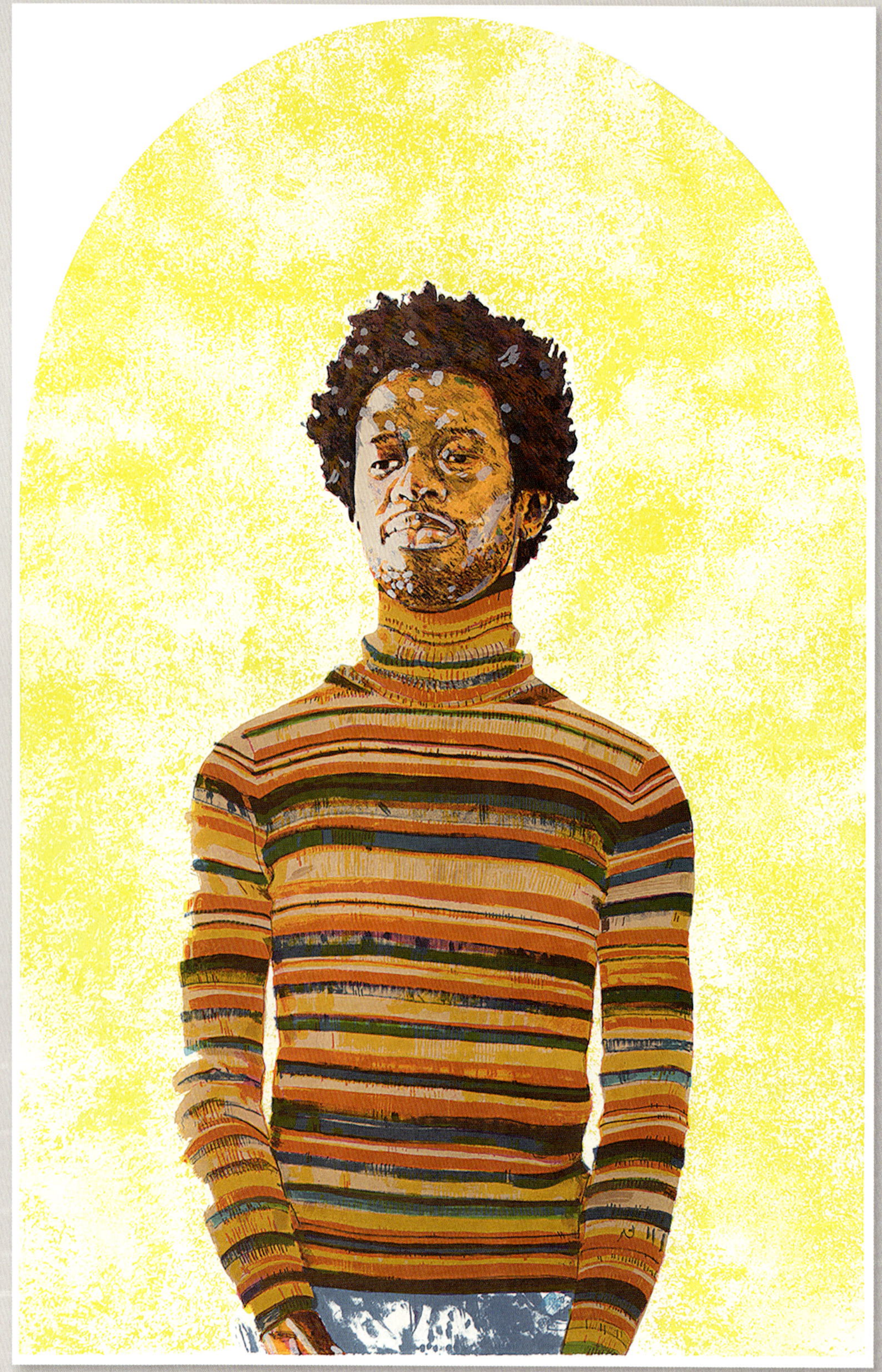

▲ **Jarvis Boyland** *California Interior # 3,* **2023 (23-318). Lithograph, 99 x 66.3 cm.** Photo: Valpuri Remling, Kenton Bueche, Francis Reynolds © Tamarind Institute, University of New Mexico

Run 5:
   Colour(s): Magenta: 7 parts Hanco Stiff Tint Base, 2 parts Graphic Chemical 1929 Process Red, 1 part Hanco Opaque white.
   Method: Hand inked, limestone, on a direct press.

Run 6:
   Colour(s): Bright yellow: 1 part Hanco Stiff Tint Base, 1 part Hanco Process Yellow.
   Method: Hand inked, positive working photoplate, on a direct press.

Run 7:
   Colour(s): Sand: 10 parts Hanco Stiff Tint Base, 1 part Hanco Opaque White, toners: Graphic Chemical Raw Sienna, Hanco Bismarck Brown, Graphic Chemical 1930 Purple, Hanco Xmas Green.
   Method: Hand inked, positive working photoplate, on a direct press.

Run 8:
   Colour(s): Clay: 10 parts Hanco Stiff Tint Base, 1 part Hanco Opaque White, toners: Hanco Bismarck Brown, Graphic Chemical Raw Sienna, Graphic Chemical 1930 Purple, Hanco Xmas Green.
   Method: Hand inked, positive working photoplate, on a direct press.

Run 9:
   Colour(s): Sienna: Hanco Stiff Tint Base, toner: Graphic Chemical Raw Sienna.
   Method: Hand inked, positive working photoplate, on a direct press.

Run 10:
   Colour(s): Brown: 8 parts Hanco Stiff Tint Base, 1 part Hanco Opaque White, toners: Hanco Bismarck Brown, Hanco Reflex Blue, Graphic Chemical 1930 Purple, Hanco Xmas Green.
   Method: Hand inked, positive working photoplate, on a direct press.

Run 11:
   Colour(s):
   • Light blue: Hanco Stiff Tint Base, toners: Hanco Opaque White, Hanco Cerulean Blue, Graphic Chemical 1930 Purple.
   • Purple: Hanco Stiff Tint Base, toners: Graphic Chemical 1930 Purple, Hanco Flame Red, Hanco Ultra Blue, Graphic Chemical Raw Sienna.
   Method: Hand inked, blend roll, positive working photoplate, on a direct press.

The Lemonade Press

STEPHANIE TURNBULL

Stephanie Turnbull has an MA in Multi-Disciplinary Printmaking from UWE (2016) and prior to this completed the professional Printer Training Programme at the Tamarind Institute, New Mexico, in 2010. Stephanie has been collaborating with artists since completing her Tamarind training, and spent five years in London collaborating with artists at the Curwen Studio. She is now based at The Lemonade Press in Bristol where she continues to collaborate with artists alongside her technical research into the sustainability of lithography. Technical research is the driving force behind her own practice. She is passionate about printmaking, especially lithography, and has co-written a book on lithography with fellow printer Catherine Ade, which was published in 2023 by The Crowood Press. Stephanie also has a number of her own works in both national and international collections. Below, Stephanie reveals the inks she uses.

'Over the years, I have used a whole range of ink brands from Graphic Chemical, Hanco, commercial offset inks, Intaglio Printmaker, Cranfield and Hawthorn. I don't necessarily have a favourite brand, but each brand does come with its own colour range and they vary, so choices are based on the colours needed for a particular project. However, there are certain colours that I gravitate to within my own practice, such as Hanco Flame Red and Graphic Chemical's Senefelder Grey.'

Heads of State, 2016

Artist: Andreas Rüthi.
Image size: 50 x 76 cm.
Collaborating printer: Stephanie Turnbull.
Edition of 25.

Heads of State is a three-colour lithograph consisting of two photoplates and one ball-grained aluminium plate, printed onto a Somerset Satin White 300 gsm paper.

Run 1: A paper texture printed as a digital film.

Run 2: 10 portraits created and printed as a digital film.

Run 3: Flats on a ball-grained aluminium plate drawn using a shop black, which is a mixture of equal parts asphaltum, Charbonnel's Noir à Monter ink and turpentine.

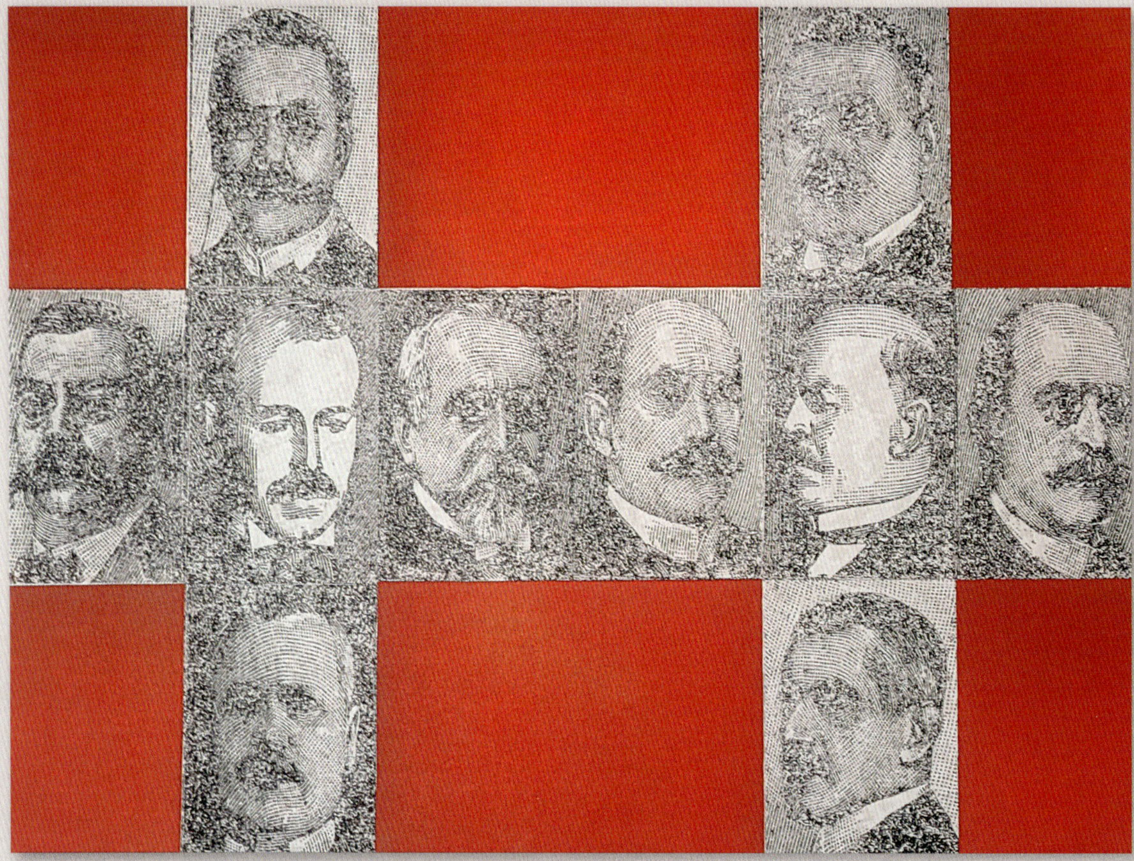

▲ Andreas Rüthi *Heads of State,* 2016. Lithograph,
50 x 76 cm. Photo: Stephanie Turnbull © Stephanie
Turnbull, The Lemonade Press

Heads of State uses a combination of inks from Intaglio
Printmaker and Graphic Chemical. The red (flats) is
Intaglio Printmakers Poppy Red Litho/ Relief ink and
the black (heads) is from the same company. The grey
paper texture is mixed from a base (transparent white)
and opaque white from Intaglio Printmaker and the
Graphic Chemical Senefelder Grey. These colours were
selected based on the artist's requirements. The red
and black were straightforward, as the artist requested
a black and a bright red. In regard to the paper texture,
four-colour variations were proofed before the artist
selected the light grey that was used for the edition.

Tattoo, 2016

Artist: Andreas Rüthi.
Paper size: 56 x 76 cm.
Collaborating printer: Stephanie Turnbull.
Edition of 25.

Tattoo is a one-colour lithograph printed from a
photoplate onto a Somerset Satin White 300 gsm paper.
The image was taken from the embossed cover of a
French cookbook.

A silicone cast was taken from the book cover to
prevent it from getting damaged and, once set, inked
up and printed with Graphic Chemical water-based
ink onto a sheet of acetate. The acetate was cleaned of
any unwanted marks and exposed to a photoplate. The
image went through an initial proofing session where
the idea was to recreate the book cover, printing the
image onto a flat and matching the colour to the red of
the book cover. Another plate was made from a rubbing
of the book cloth texture and, after this initial proofing
session, the image was scanned in, edited, rotated
and rescaled. A second proofing session was carried

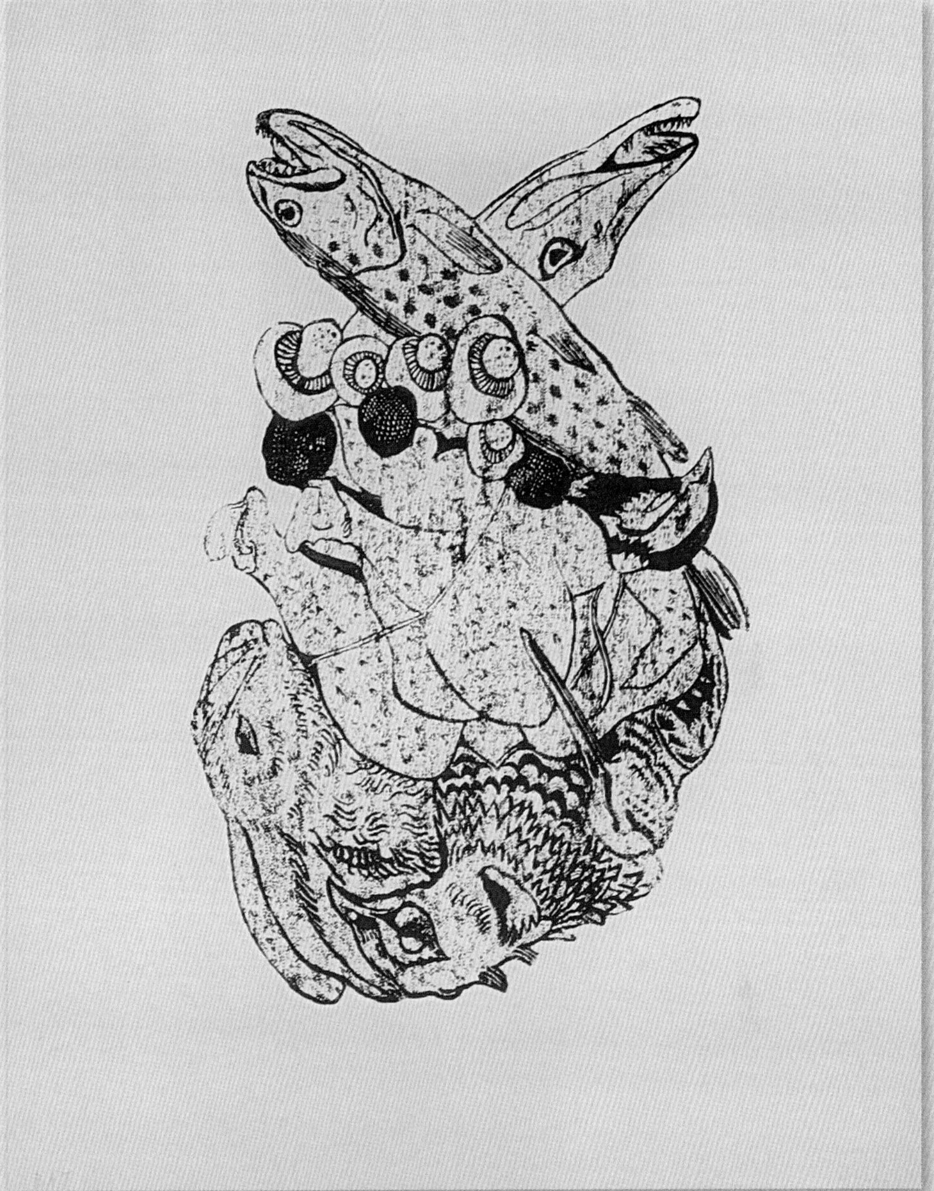

▲ **Andreas Rüthi** *Tattoo*, **2016. Lithograph, 56 x 76 cm.** Photo: Stephanie Turnbull
© Stephanie Turnbull, The Lemonade Press

out with a deep blue ink, and resulted in the edition of *Tattoo* being run.

Tattoo uses a range of Intaglio Printmaker inks. The edition was printed with an ink recipe of Phthalo Blue Red Shade and black. The other combinations were: Phthalo Blue Red Shade and Poppy Red, and Phthalo Blue Red Shade, Poppy Red and Phthalo Blue Green Shade. The first proofing session consisted of four different shades of red using differing proportions of the following colours: Crimson Red, Burnt Sienna and Opaque White. A Graphic Chemical black water-based ink was used to pull an impression from the silicone cast taken from the book cover. This ink was chosen because oil-based ink will not adhere to a silicone plate.

CHAPTER

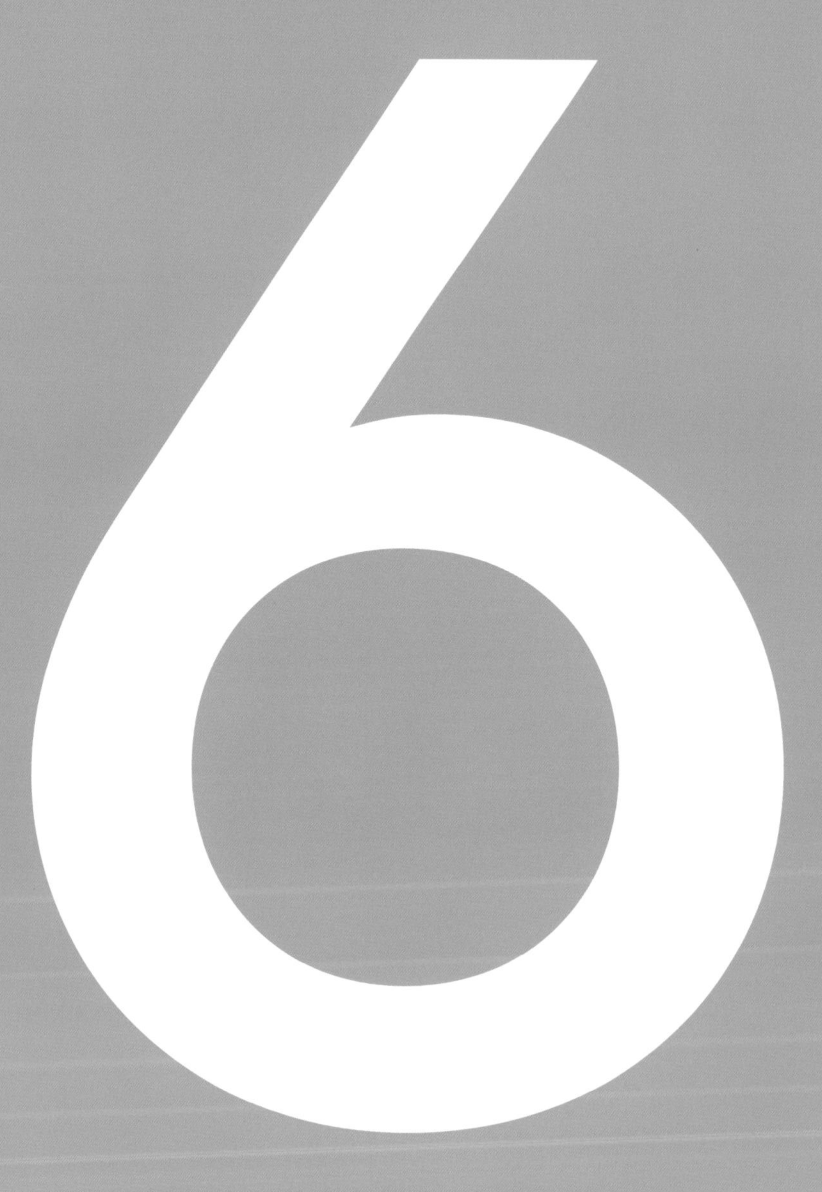

INK FOR RELIEF PRINTING

More than any other discipline, it is relief printmaking that has seen the most growth over the last 20 years. Still popular with professional printmakers, relief printing also provides a low-cost medium for entry-level printmakers. A passable print can be made using the pressure applied by the back of a spoon rather than a press. The printing plate can still be made from lino or wood, but modern composite materials can equally be used. Indeed, any raised surface can be used as a plate, prompting street art techniques such as *raubdruck-erin*, where urban fixtures such as manhole covers are used to print T-shirts and tote bags.

Smaller, lightweight presses are now available and innumerable online communities have emerged showing how a simple press can be home-made from chipboard and a car jack. At the same time, online marketplaces such as Etsy have allowed hobby artists and professionals to monetise their work. Relief prints simply as works of art or as greetings cards can easily be produced and sold online.

Relief printing covers a range of printing processes, from letterpress, the traditional woodcut processes (European woodcut, Chinese woodcut, Japanese *mokuhanga*, wood engraving, xylograph engraving), lino cutting and, more recently, the use of SoftCut and other replacements for wood and lino.

LINO CUTTING

Lino cutting is the relief process most people identify with, and it is still the most popular. Lino has, in many cases, been superseded by plastic materials such as SoftCut, Speedy-Carve and Japanese vinyl. All of these are easier to cut than lino (unless the lino has been warmed first). However, environmentally, real brown linoleum is made from natural materials such as linseed oil, pine rosin, ground cork dust and jute. Generically, ink for lino is the same as for woodcut and wood engraving, however like all of the relief processes, this will depend on the thickness of film layer chosen by the individual artist and their own personal preferences.

However, as lino is invariably the starting point for beginners to this printmaking discipline, we wish to point out that most beginners apply far too thick a layer of ink for printing. One should use the best quality ink roller they can afford and roll out a thin layer of ink. The roller should make a gentle hissing sound as it rolls over the ink, and not a splashing, slapping sound. The ink film should gently lose its shine after the roller has passed, and resemble a very fine orange peel. Place the paper on top of the print after printing and rub the back of it to help the print transfer. The best thing to burnish (rub) the back of the print with is a polished wooden spoon or a tablespoon, using firm pressure on the back of the paper.

WOODCUT

A woodcut uses the plank of a piece of wood and cuts along the grain. In Europe, the favoured wood is ply, generally birch or cherry faced. Cherry, pear and other fruitwoods are also favoured. Historically, artists such as Dürer used pearwood.

WOOD ENGRAVING

A wood engraving uses the end-grain of the wood and, invariably, wood engravings are cut from boxwood. Wood engraving had its heyday in the nineteenth century, when it was used as the pictorial element in letterpress printing. In nineteenth-century London there were very large wood-engraving studios, employing up to 60 people, such as Dalziel Brothers, who engraved blocks for illustrated books and magazines, including *Punch*. The size of a boxwood end-grain block is very small, at most a few inches in each direction. To create a large image, several blocks have to be pinned and glued together. An engravable plastic is now obtainable that is often used as a substitute for boxwood, especially for larger prints.

▶ **Taking off a white ink after milling.** Photo: Jo Hounsome Photography © Cranfield Colours

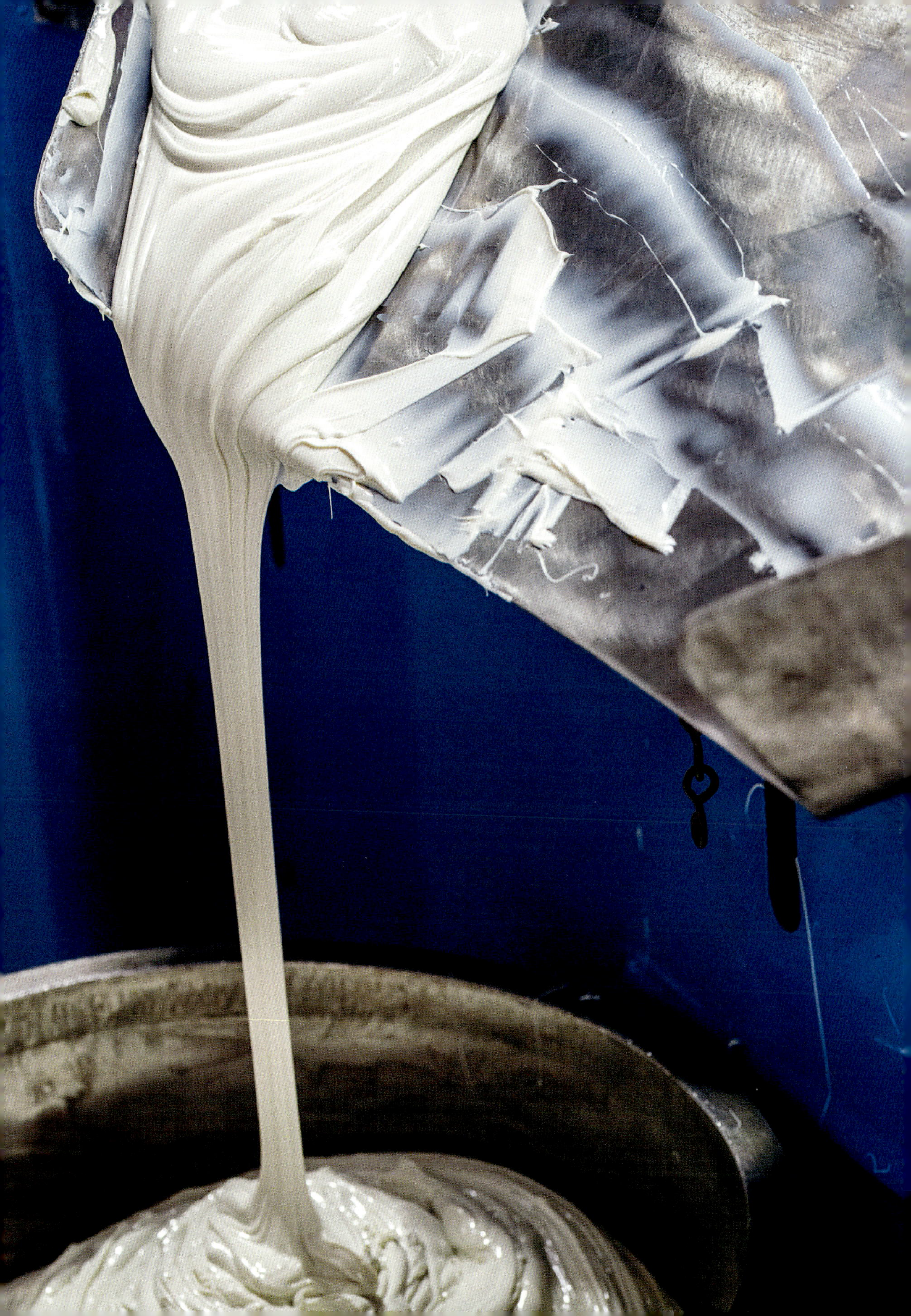

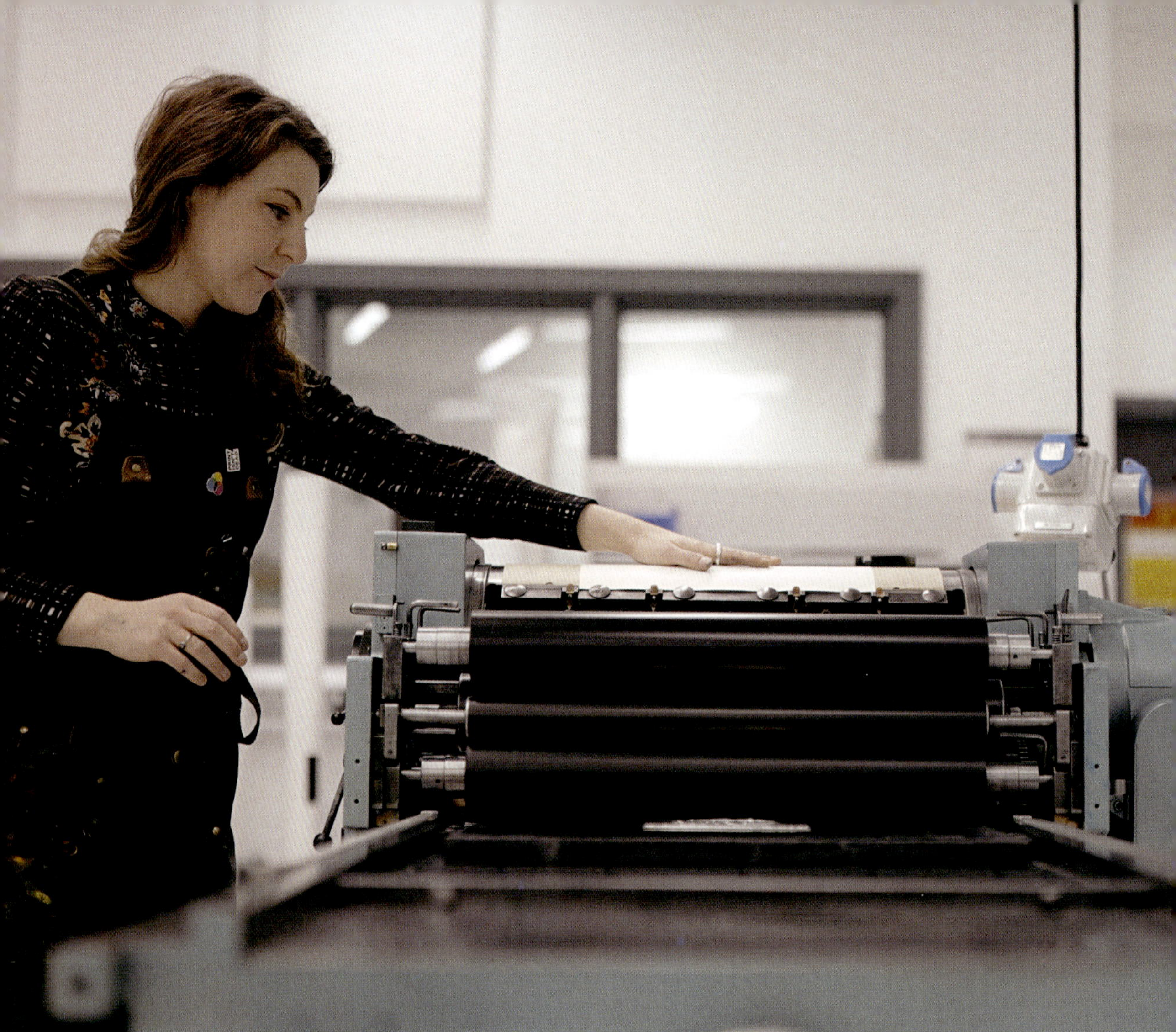

LETTERPRESS

Letterpress is a relief-printing process that generally uses movable metal type. It was first invented in Europe by Johannes Gutenburg in the 1430s, and was the primary method of commercial print production until the 1970s.

The resurgence of letterpress in recent years has grown beyond anything that could have been imagined 20 years ago. However, most of the manufacturers who made commercial ink for the letterpress industry have since disappeared. They have been replaced by the manufacturers of specialist ink for printmakers. Most letterpress printers seem to prefer rubber-based inks such as Van Son (see p.139).

The rapid growth or renaissance of relief printmaking has not been without challenges. Entry-level printmakers are often dealing with poor-quality inks

▲ Laura Clarke-Oaten operating the FAG press at CFPR Bristol © CFPR

and unsuitable papers. Relief inks require open paper surfaces with good absorbency and long fibre lengths. Printmaking on a budget will necessitate cutting corners, but cheap cartridge papers will often contain recycled content. Paper fibres are generally shorter, and the paper will be loaded with non-absorbent China clay to increase brightness and opacity. These unfavourable paper characteristics, combined with weak inks, will give rise to problems both during and after printing.

Nonetheless, relief printmaking is in its ascendency and, when using the correct materials in the specified way, can prove a safe and rewarding technique. In the last few years, attitudes to health and safety and the environment have come to the fore in new ways. Primarily, the latest consideration is the importance of environmental impact. The acrylic water-based inks that replaced the traditional solvent inks were far healthier for the user and complied with the health and safety legislation of the time. Now we know that acrylic ink (which is essentially a plastic) can, if not treated properly, introduce micro-particles that are extremely harmful to the environment into the wastewater systems (see Chapter 7).

There is much that can be done in mitigation; methods include storing waste acrylic ink in a vessel, and encouraging the solid content to precipitate through the addition of flocculants. This leaves a chemical sludge that can be disposed of appropriately, and clear water that can be reused. However, there is also much confusion and lack of research as to the best solutions. The first question is one of environmental life cycle, from manufacture to disposal, and whether it is better to continue to use acrylic water-based inks or to speculate as to whether the old solvent-based inks had a smaller environmental footprint. Currently, there is not enough research and environmental analysis to take a truly informed decision. Therefore, in consideration of health and safety legislation and the health of the user, it is probably best to keep using the current water-based inks, but mitigate the problems and reduce the environmental impact as much as possible.

Up until the renaissance of relief printing in the 2000s and the advent of kitchen table methods, many artists tended to reach for the nearest commercially available ink. However, with oil-based relief-printing inks there are some factors that need to be considered. For increasing numbers starting out as printmakers without formal training, using a dedicated printmaking ink makes life far simpler. Innumerable YouTube videos demonstrate the essentials to novice printmakers and have underscored the need for and advantages of the correct tools and inks.

OIL-BASED RELIEF INKS

In general, for relief printing, the colour construction will be broadly similar to lithographic inks, with strong, finely ground, highly pigmented formulas. A purpose-designed relief ink will generally be manufactured with certain criteria in mind, such as adding a small amount of wax to avoid scuffing when a thick deposit of ink is printed, and perhaps including additional driers to cope with the much greater film weights. The oil, as with litho ink, is a strong, stiff oil able to hold the pigment weight and create good transfer properties. However, with letterpress ink it is slightly different. Letterpress has a physical gully on every letter, so the colour tends to be a lot weaker for a greater film weight.

The predominant oil still used in traditional oil-based relief inks is linseed. Some alternative formulations successfully use other oils including soya. It is up to each individual printmaker to appraise themselves of both the technical and environmental advantages of each.

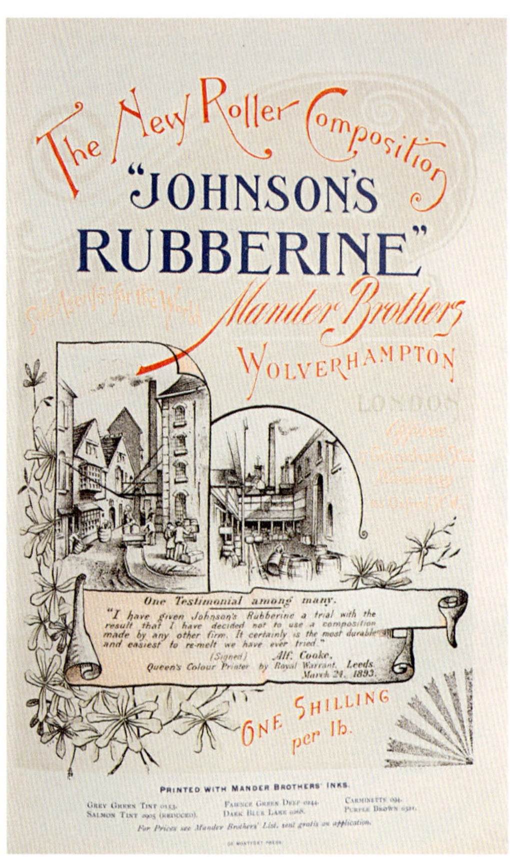

▲ Johnsons Rubberine advertisement from the *Penrose Annual*, 1905. Photo: Jo Hounsome Photography

MODIFYING OIL-BASED RELIEF INKS

Oil-based relief inks can be modified in a number of ways. As with etching and lithographic inks, this is most commonly done by adding an extender, sometimes called a 'tinting medium'. This is essentially a colourless ink, but as it contains a solid pigment particle it has the structure of ink, and is therefore very easy to fold into the coloured ink using a plat-blade ink knife. Extending the ink allows the printmaker to obtain a range of shades of varying intensities from the one colour. Many colours are so highly pigmented that they behave almost as concentrates, and would be too strong for many printed images without the addition of an extender.

If the artist wishes to reduce both the colour strength and the viscosity of the ink simultaneously, the addition of an appropriate linseed oil will achieve the desired effect. Essentially, the oil thins the ink by changing the ratio of the existing components of oil and pigment. It is important not to overly dilute the ink, as too high a proportion of oil will produce prints without definition, and may stain the reverse of the paper, resulting in excessive ink squash.

Wiping compound and tack reducers can be used to improve ink transfer and rolling of the relief plate. Such products were originally intended for etching, and should be used with care. They will reduce the tack while maintaining the body of the ink. This is an 'oily' rather than an 'inky' product, and is used to make inks thinner, reduce viscosity, and increase flow and transparency. Care must be taken when using wiping compounds, as they introduce a Vaseline®-like solvent into the ink, which will impact print quality, drying time and the rub resistance of the finished print.

Not all manufacturers include driers in oil-based inks. As these inks dry by the slow but steady process of polymerisation and oxidation, the artist will want to read the manufacturer's instructions, and add driers if required. Driers for oil-based inks include manganese and cobalt driers, depending on regional regulations. After printing, leave prints in a warm, dry environment with plenty of free-flowing air. Printmakers' wax drier paste is a more recent and valuable development that combines wax with suitable metallic salt. It is squeezed from a tube rather than poured from a bottle and is, therefore, easier to mix with ink. The wax content increases the rub resistance of the dried ink film, while the drier speeds up the whole process.

The addition of talc of any kind will introduce more solids into the ink, which will increase the viscosity without proportionally increasing the tack. With all ink modifications, the printmaker needs to test at each stage and forget why the modification was required in the first place. Each of the aforementioned modifiers, when used to excess, will adversely affect the ease of use, the quality of print or the drying profile and behaviour of the ink once printed.

The addition of heat energy as a modifier is often overlooked, but it can negate the need for material modifiers in many cases. Energy is introduced to the ink, either by a heated surface that warms the etching plate or the vigorous use of a palette knife to warm the ink. Oil-based ink, being by nature thixotropic, will fall in viscosity with comparatively little effort.

The modifiers available for water-based ink have different functions. Most water-based systems are of lower viscosity and tack, but some manufacturers nonetheless produce thickening agents, drying retarders and extenders for use with the various brands available.

RUBBER-BASED RELIEF INKS

Rubber-based inks were used extensively by relief printmakers due to their non-skinning properties, but with the decline in the number of small reprographic machines and the number of printers and stationers, the options regarding inks for 'small offset' are similarly decreasing. The term rubber-based is actually somewhat of a misnomer; the rubber refers to the vehicle (a cyclised rubber varnish), which has to be dissolved in solvent to make it into a useful ink. It is the solvent that creates the non-drying property. Print it on a coated paper and it will not dry; print it on an absorbent uncoated paper and it will set quickly, more by capillary-action absorption rate than oxidation. A relief printmaker using rubber-based ink needs to bear in mind that this ink was developed and is extensively used by the small offset printer, due to its non-drying qualities. The small offset printer is rapidly being superseded in the competitive marketplace and by the increasing use of digital print. Therefore, the existence and availability of rubber-based inks will not be long-lived. Given the very heavy deposit that some relief printers work with, after several layers of ink have been built up on the print and dried between each layer, it can take a long time for rubber-based ink sitting on a heavy ink deposit to dry.

SINGLE-PIGMENT INKS

The best option for the professional relief printmaker, where quality of materials is more important than the lowest cost, is to use a single-pigment ink. The reasons for this are the same as given in Chapter 5: clarity of colour, better lightfast properties and a cleaner result when mixing colour. It is also much easier over a long period to match a single-pigment ink. If you are trying to replace an ink after ten years, the fact that the ink is manufactured from a single known pigment means that colour consistency and accuracy are likely to be much greater than with an ink mixed from several different sources.

Here is a recipe for a generic artist's single-pigment relief-printing ink:
- 36% pigment content (e.g., 26% coloured pigment, 10% extender pigment)
- 62% linseed stand oil (150–200 poise)
- 1% wax
- 1% manganese driers

Formulation principles include: lower pigment strength compared to litho, so the ink will usually contain a percentage of extender pigment to provide correct body (reducing colour strength by oil only would impair working characteristics); the addition of driers is required because a thicker film weight is put down; wax is used to aid rub resistance of the thicker film; and the inks need to be relatively high tack, due to the increased film weight.

WATER-WASHABLE RELIEF INK

A radical revolution in ink use for printmakers over the last two decades has centred on water-washable inks. These are traditional oil-based inks that have been created so that they emulsify with water when it comes to cleaning up. Known as water-washables or Safe Wash, these inks are cleaned up with soap and water. Do not confuse them with acrylic-based inks that can be cleaned up with water. Unlike water-washables, acrylic inks do not offer any long-term environmental gain to the printmaker.

Traditional oil-based ink, on the other hand, is biodegradable. Made from linseed oil, a natural sustainable product made from the flax plant, a simple ink will have possibly a small proportion of magnesium carbonate, or talc, and perhaps some wax, all readily occurring products that are chemically inert. Therefore, to be able to clean up with water, instead of solvent, means no health and safety problems for the user. Pigment, which is in all inks, may not be particularly environmentally sound (see Chapter 2).

Opinions are still not settled on the environmental impact of either solvent-based or water-based inks; each has its advantages and problems. Health and safety and environmental precautions to reduce the potential negative effects are therefore vital. Scrape up as much ink as possible before cleaning. When you clean, use a premixed container of soap and water, and try and clean up as much of the residue with a rag or paper that can be disposed of in a bin rather than down the sink. Then do a final clean with fresh soap and water.

WATER-BASED RELIEF INKS

Water-based inks, often termed 'block-printing' inks, may give the impression of simplicity. In truth, water-based block-printing inks require skilled formulation to hold the pigment in suspension without it settling out. The formulation may variously contain water, pigment and combinations of alcohol, hydrocarbon, silica, additional wetting agents, waxes, anti-foaming agents, pH regulators, biocides and fungicides and other preservatives. The quality of such inks is improving, but generally the printed image achievable will be less defined than when using oil-based equivalents as the water-based inks travel further along the paper lumens, giving a more feathered appearance. Unlike oil-based inks that dry slowly until they are inert, water-based inks can be re-wetted and more easily marked when handled carelessly.

Not all water-based relief inks are cheap or of low quality, although it is true to say that they can be made more cheaply if required. Their rapid drying

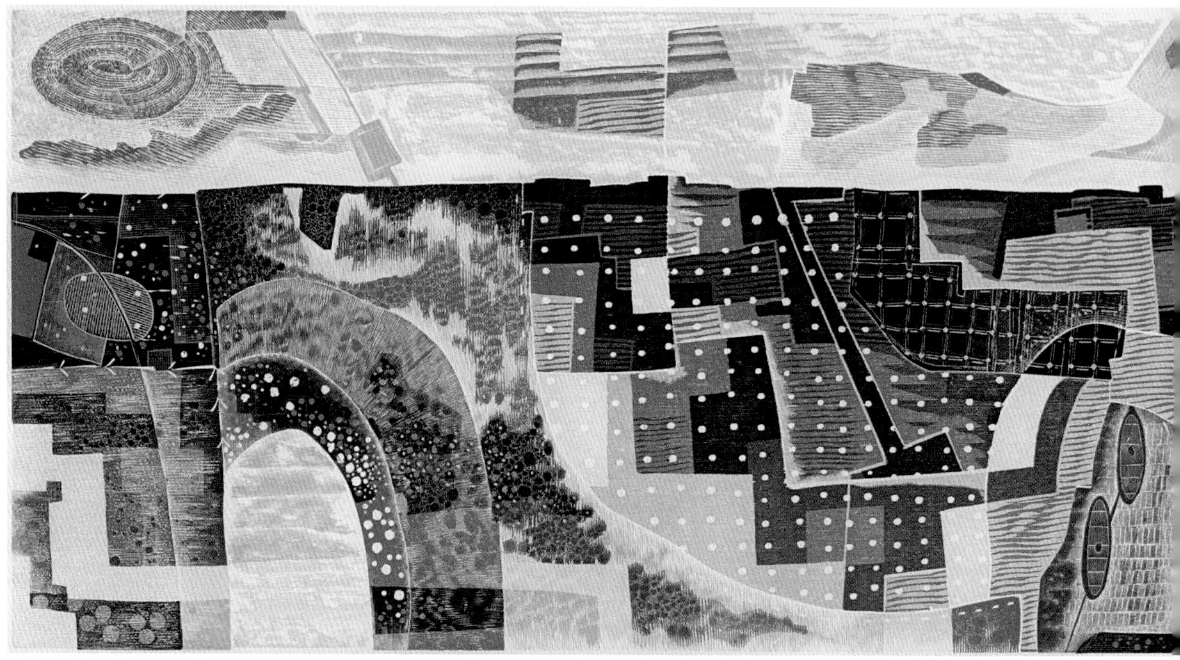

▲ Neil Bousfield *Blue Coast,* 2021. Woodcut and engraving, 16 x 32 cm.
Photo: Neil Bousfield
© Neil Bousfield

characteristics and the ease with which they can be cleaned have made them an obvious choice for the crossover area between printmaking and crafting.

MODIFYING WATER-BASED RELIEF INKS

The modifiers available for water-based ink have different functions. Most water-based systems are of lower viscosity and tack; nonetheless, some ink manufacturers will provide a compatible drying retarder that can extend the drying time so that the ink remains open for longer on the slab, roller and plate. Some water-based formulations can be extended with the direct addition of controlled quantities of water.

When water-based inks are printed, the paper 'consumes' a disproportionate amount of the water available compared to the binder and pigment. If the printmaker does not clean the printing plate but rolls fresh ink over the top, the water-based ink can, in some conditions, become progressively harder to work with. Ideally, it is helpful if water-based inks that have been on an ink slab are not returned to the ink pot, as they can initiate the drying process.

COLOUR IN RELIEF-PRINT INK

One of the factors to remember when printing a relief print is the depth of ink deposit. Most ink manufacturers would be astonished by the sheer quantity of ink and thickness of film deposit used in the majority of prints, and drying times do not relate to the properties the relief printer requires of the ink. The standard methods for checking colour in ink are either to do a drawdown with a palette knife or to undertake a dab test with a finger. Both methods can be accurate, unless you are rolling a relief plate with a very heavy deposit of colour, in which case the film you are printing with can be three or four times the film weight of a drawdown or dab test.

This is not a problem for the relief printer unless he or she wants to recreate a colour or complain to the ink manufacturer. Then a method must be devised to replicate the depth and strength of the ink deposit. Try doing a drawdown with an additional piece of paper under each edge of the knife, keeping a gully in the middle for the ink – this will give you a controlled colour deposit – and then experiment with different thicknesses of paper to give a better colour match and density of colour to your prints.

TACK

Ink tack presents the biggest problem for relief printers; if the consistency is not correct then a thicker deposit of ink can feather and squelch on the print. This is often a particular problem when using an ink not developed for relief printing, such as a rubber-based ink. It pays to remember that all inks are thixotropic to some extent, so try working the ink with a palette knife on the slab for a while before printing, especially if you are using it straight from the tin. This will enable you to gauge its properties more accurately.

CASE STUDIES

Tom Hück

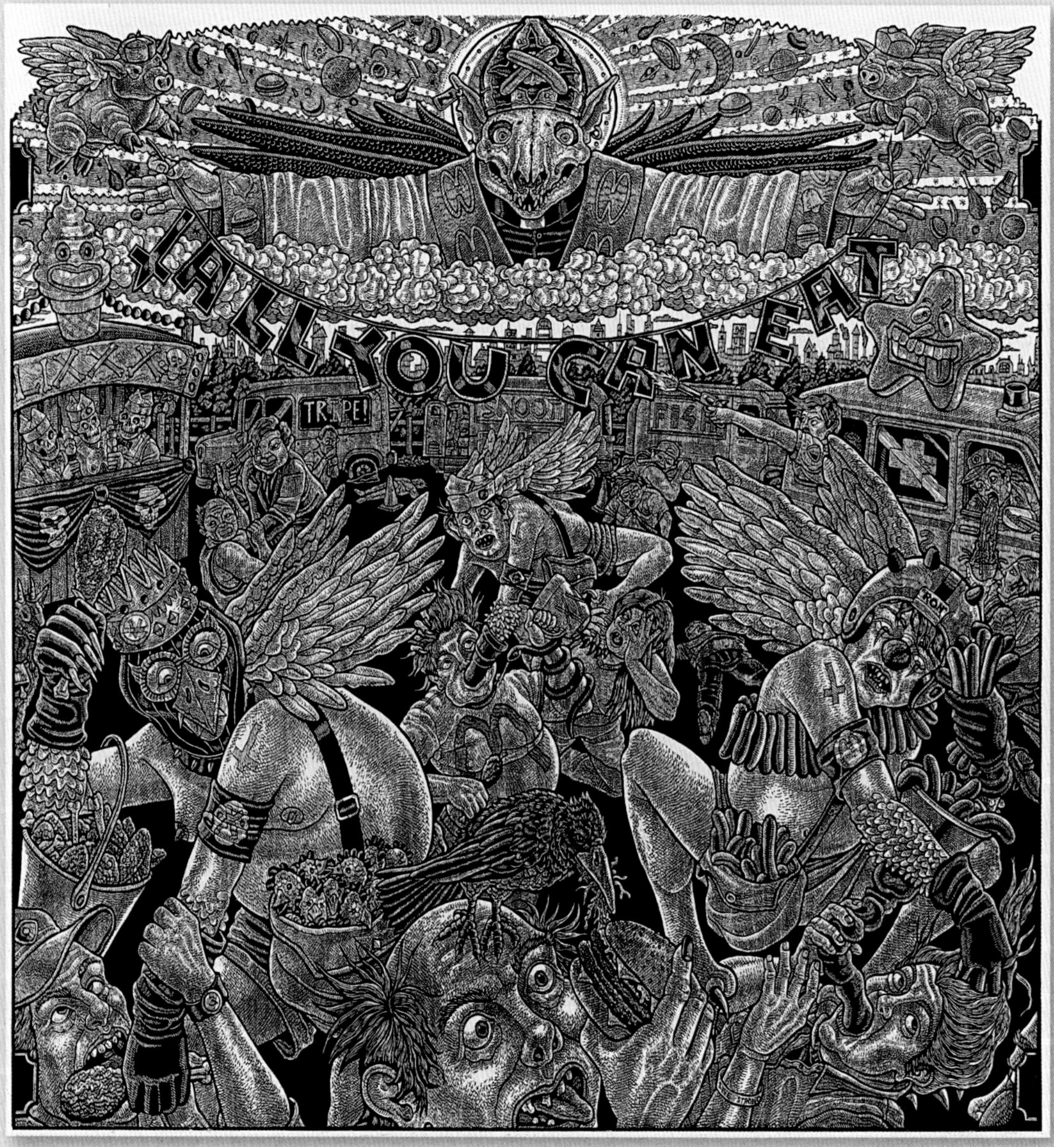

▲ Tom Hück *The Feast of Lord Aporkalyptus*, 2022. Woodcut from *A Monkey Mountain Kronikl*e, 117 x 122 cm. Published by Evil Prints USA & Peacock Visual Arts Aberdeen, Scotland, UK. Photo: Tom Hück © Tom Hück

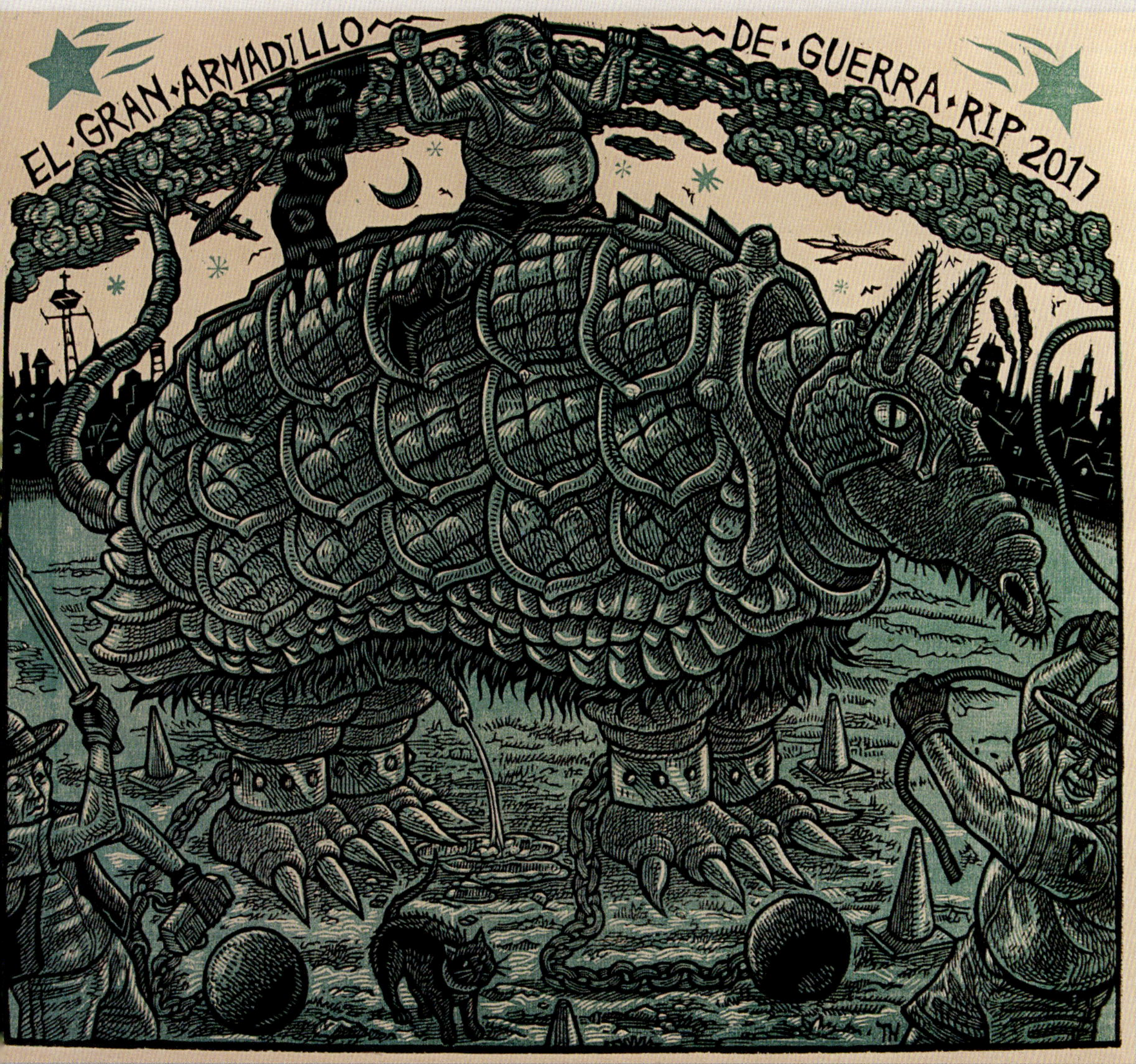

▲ Tom Hück *The Great War-madillo*, 2017. **Woodcut, 40 x 46 cm. Published by University of Nebraska-Omaha.** Photo: Tom Hück © Tom Hück

'When I first started out in the mid nineties, I used what was affordable, then slowly graduated into more top-of-the-line inks such as those by Daniel Smith and Graphic Chemical & Ink. Inks like anything from Charbonnel were completely out of my budget. My favourite back then was Daniel Smith Relief Black #79. This, of course, became unavailable because Daniel Smith went out of business. It was a good, medium stiff ink that was easily modified to my own preference with magnesium carbonate. The addition of mag really stiffened the ink, which is what is needed when printing from extremely shallow cuts like I make. As an aside, there was an ink made by Charbonnel called Typographic Black Luxe RSA, which I was able to use straight from the can with no modifiers needed. Of course, this ink was also discontinued because, apparently, I was the only person in the Western Hemisphere that used it.

Around 2013–14, I was approached by Gamblin Artists Colours to create my own signature ink. This was great, because I was jumping around between inks and modifiers for a number of years prior. Working with the folks at Gamblin, we came up with a blue/black that is extremely stiff, specifically formulated for intense detail and shallow cuts made on woodblocks and linoleum. It's called "Tom Hück's Outlaw Black", and it has become quite popular; it's all I use now for my blocks when printing in straight black and white.

I tend to not "geek out" too much about materials and processes, although I have my moments like anyone else. When I find something that works, I stick with it, preferring to spend my time coming up with concepts and executing them in print and worrying about the art first.'

The Feast of Lord Aporkalyptus, 2022

Woodcut from *A Monkey Mountain Kronikle* by Tom Hück.
Image size: 117 x 122 cm.
Published by Evil Prints USA & Peacock Visual Arts Aberdeen, Scotland UK.
Edition of 30.

The Great War-madillo, 2017

Tom Hück, woodcut.
Image size: 40 x 46 cm.
Published by University of Nebraska-Omaha.
Edition of 40.

'Both of these images have an extreme amount of detail, which is achieved by cutting very shallow into the wood. We used Tom Hück's Outlaw Black on both. When printing the larger blocks, the ink is modified with straight linseed oil for easier coverage of the block when rolling them up. For the *War-madillo* print, which is a chiaroscuro woodcut, we used Handschy litho inks. I like using Handschy for colours because I feel that they give consistent vibrancy when mixing transparent base with them for my two-tone prints.'

Tom Huck, also spelled Hück, (born 1971), is an American printmaker best known for his large-scale satirical woodcuts. He lives and works in St. Louis, Missouri, where he runs his own press, Evil Prints. He is a regular contributor to *BLAB!* of Fantagraphics Books. His work is influenced by Albrecht Dürer, José Guadalupe Posada, R. Crumb and Honoré Daumier. Huck's woodcut prints are included in numerous public and private collections, including the Metropolitan Museum of Art, Whitney Museum of American Art, Library of Congress, Spencer Museum of Art, Nelson Atkins Museum of Art, Saint Louis Art Museum, Milwaukee Art Museum, Minneapolis Institute of Art, Art Institute of Chicago, Fogg Art Museum, Michael C. Carlos Museum and New York Public Library.

Anne Desmet

'For wood engraving, oil-based ink is essential because, as the blocks are engraved on the end-grain rather than along the plank, water-based inks would tend to soak into the wood causing it to swell up and the finely engraved marks to disappear. Also, because wood engraving tends to result in blocks with very finely cut details, the ink used needs to be stiff enough not to fill in those tiny details, yet flexible enough to be rolled out to a completely even, smooth, thin layer on the inking slab and on the block.

I use T N Lawrence's Letterpress Relief Printing Black (oil-based), of which the "Carbon Black" shade of black is my favourite. For colour printing, I like T N Lawrence's oil-based Relief Printing range of colours and its Extender for making colours more transparent/subtler. I also like Graphic Chemical & Ink's oil-based Relief Printing range of coloured inks.

The T N Lawrence inks come in tubes rather than tins, which is much more practical for a wood-engraving printer because printing these blocks requires only tiny quantities of ink, and the ink therefore remains in perfect condition in the tubes between printings. Relief-printing ink in tins too readily develops a hard layer at the top once the tin has been opened, making it difficult to use for subsequent printings without hard bits of ink getting onto the inking slab. For printing in black, I marginally prefer the T N Lawrence Letterpress range of oil-based relief-printing inks because it seems to be just fractionally stiffer than the regular relief-printing range. If printing a small edition (of, say, no more than 25 prints), I don't think there would be any discernible difference between the two ranges of black ink. But as soon as you're printing more than about 25 prints, the relief-printing black can tend to start to fill in the finest marks slightly, whereas the Letterpress black stays just a bit stiffer for a bit longer, enabling me to print 40 or 50 prints without any problems. Also, the relief-printing range has only one "colour" of black, whereas the Letterpress range has four of five different blacks providing a range of warmer or cooler shades. I like having the choice of blacks as well as preferring the way the Letterpress ink handles over a larger edition.

The T N Lawrence coloured inks come in a wide range of colours and are readily mixable to make new hues. The pale honey-coloured oil-based extender (which, like the inks, also comes in convenient metal tubes) mixes with the colours really well to extend the colours and increase their transparency/luminosity. The colours also seem to be respectably lightfast, though I've noticed that the very palest cream tones can fade a bit if exposed to too much sunlight.

I like Graphic Chemical & Ink's coloured inks very much too. The colours are very vivid and the red and white in

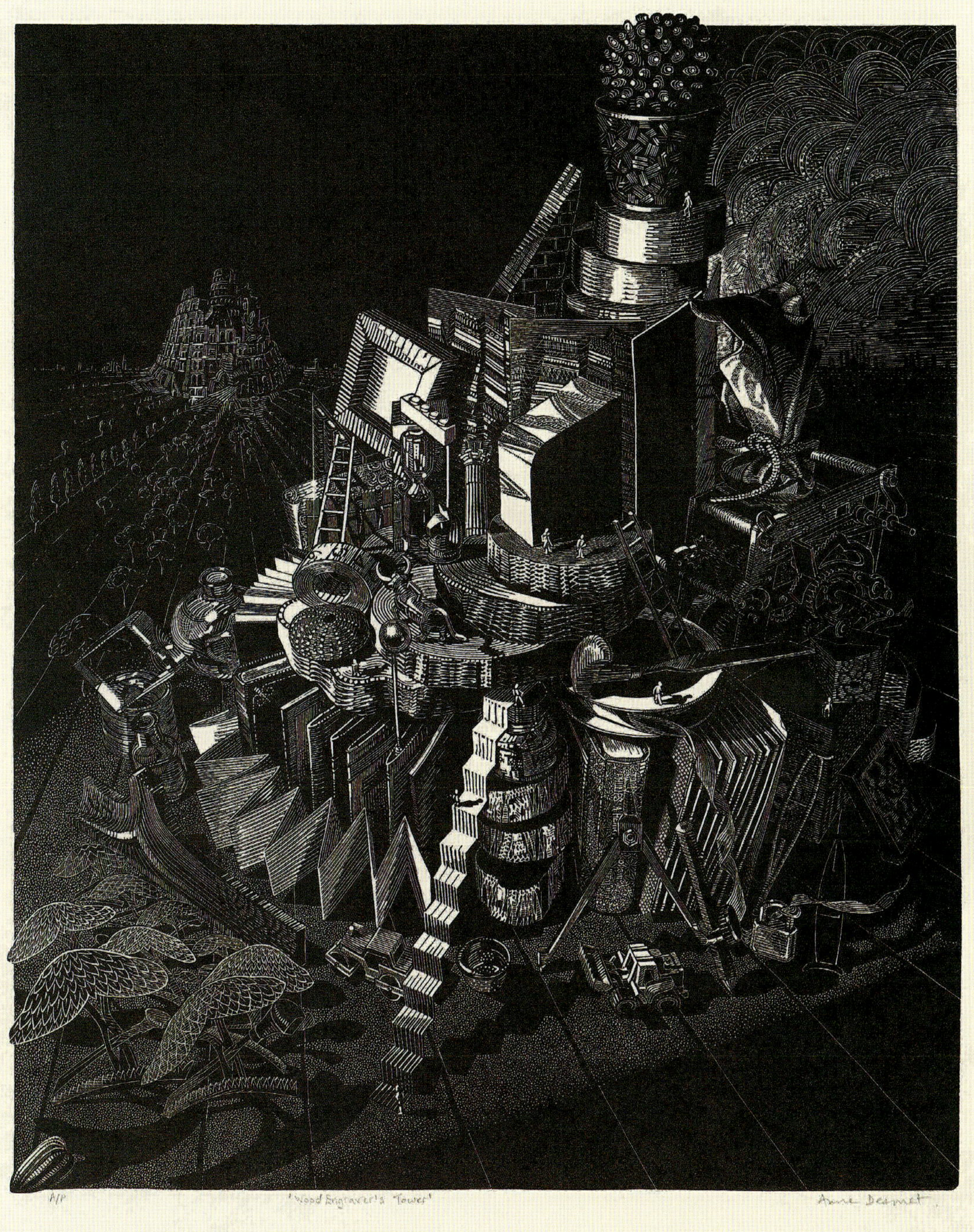

▲ **Anne Desmet** *Wood Engraver's Tower*, **2020. Wood engraving (on boxwood block), 30.3 x 25.2 cm.** Photo: Anne Desmet © Anne Desmet

that ink range don't seem to dry up on the ink slab quite so readily as do the T N Lawrence's inks so, occasionally, I use those instead of T N Lawrence's.'

Wood Engraver's Tower, 2020

Wood engraving on boxwood block.
Image size: 30.3 x 25.2 cm.
Edition size: 45 on ivory-toned Japanese Gampi Vellum paper.
Edition printed by the artist at I. M. Imprimit, Hackney, London: 20 & 21 February, 2020.

'This print involved a single printing of one colour. I used carbon black from the T N Lawrence oil-based Letterpress Relief Printing ink range. It was printed by me on a large Albion relief-printing press at I. M. Imprimit, the editioning studio of Ian Mortimer OBE, in Hackney, London.

The block for this engraving was given to the Society of Wood Engravers (SWE) by the artist George Tute. He bought it some 30 years ago and donated it to the SWE in 2019 to be used to mark the Society's centenary in 2020. The SWE gave it to me to use for a commission, from Manchester Metropolitan University Special Collections Library, to create an engraving celebrating 100 years of the SWE, and also to celebrate the Special Collections Library itself. I interpreted this brief by creating a variation of a Babel Tower – an ongoing theme of mine. *Wood Engraver's Tower* is composed of items in my home which seemed to have relevance to a library, and to the history and contemporary usage of wood engraving; it also includes some autobiographic references. I created a still-life model in my studio as the detailed structure for the foreground tower and made photographic studies of this model, which became the basis of this engraving.

The engraving is designed to be read from the bottom-left corner upwards. In that corner is a sunflower seedcase to acknowledge George Tute's spectacular sunflower engravings. The paper-cut-out trees recall Eric Gill's SWE logo of 1921. A glass egg-timer recalls a motif in *Madman's Drum* (1930), a novel in wood engravings by US artist Lynd Ward (1905–85). The egg-timer and inside mechanism of a mantel clock suggest time passing and the time it takes to engrave a block. A tiny blank canvas indicates that this composition is not about painting but about another art form. The wooden chess piece (knight) alludes to similarities between wood engraving and chess because each "move" in both has to be carefully planned. The engraving tool denotes the technique, the compass and pencil the measured drawing which engraving can involve. The fabric "dolly" recreates an old-fashioned inking dabber for printing blocks prior to the invention of rollers. Several planed blocks are stacked up as elements of the tower. They represent the "stuff" of engraving and recall

engravings and engraved marks by artists Monica Poole (1921–2003) and Gertrude Hermes (1901–83).

Amongst very many other references, the tiny seashell, padlock, plastic bull and potted cactus all refer to engravings by other leading wood engravers, past and present. The tape measure suggests the tiny scale of many engravings and gives a key to the real size of elements in my tower. A LEGO® brick denotes tower building as do the tiny steamroller and digger truck. Open and closed books indicate a library. The tiny ladders reinforce the idea of a building with many levels that could be explored. The pair of crutches is an autobiographical element, while the Babel Tower in the background is derived from Pieter Bruegel the Elder's painting (of c.1563) in the Kunsthistorisches Museum, Vienna.'

British Museum – Blue Sky, 2023

Wood engraving (on lemonwood block).
Image size: 17.4 x 24.8 cm, with linocut and stencil printing.
Edition size: 35 on Zerkall extra smooth white hot-pressed paper.
Edition printed by the artist at her home studio in Hackney, London, February 2023.

'This print involved six printings. It was printed by me in my home studio on my small cast-iron Albion hand printing relief press (made in 1859 and in full working order). First, the woodblock was printed in an extended Payne's Grey ink (T N Lawrence relief-printing ink plus T N Lawrence extender, as described above). Then, a lino block was printed over the first printing. This was in a slightly darker shade of the same grey (i.e., a ratio of a bit more grey ink and a bit less extender than I'd used for the key block). Then another lino block was printed over these printings. That block was inked in a sky blue (a mix of mid-blue ink with a tiny touch of magenta, plus extender) fading to a pale transparent cream blend using T N Lawrence relief-printing inks plus extender as before. Then, three small stencils were used to add all the black details on the print (actually a very dark grey using the same Payne's Grey ink as previously, with a tiny touch of Letterpress Carbon Black added) plus the darker blue reflections in the window areas of the print. The T N Lawrence inks provided me with the subtle shifts of tone and colour that I wanted for this print and created the light and luminosity in the image that I was looking for.

This is a substantial reworking of a woodblock I engraved in 2004–5 and from which I had already printed a series of four engravings showing the Great Court of the British Museum at different times of day and night, and in different light conditions. The engraving was developed from my own photographs and sketches on site. For this

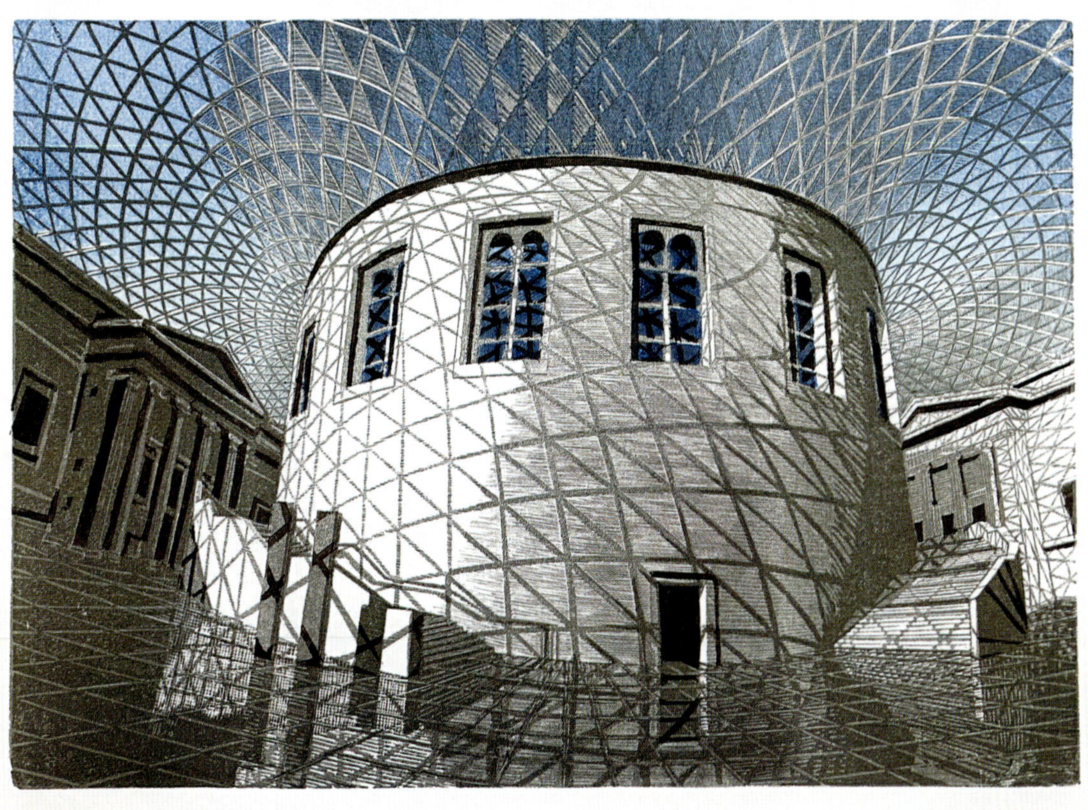

▲ **Anne Desmet** *British Museum – Blue Sky*, **2023. Wood engraving (on lemonwood block), with linocut and stencil printing, 17.4 x 24.8 cm.** Photo: Anne Desmet © Anne Desmet

new version of the same image, I cut two lino blocks to create extra layers of printed colour, overprinting a mid-grey printing of the key block (the wood engraving). I also added extra tiny details (in blue and black inks) in the windows using paper stencils, which I printed with my index finger. The finished work is intended to show the museum's Great Court under a vivid blue sky, and the way in which the dramatic steel and glass roof architecture creates its own subtly modulated variations of tone and light. The entire series was inspired by my interest in Claude Monet's wonderful paintings of Rouen Cathedral at different times of day and in different light and weather conditions.'

Anne Desmet RA was born and raised in Liverpool. She has BFA and MA Fine Art degrees from Oxford University, Postgrad. Dip. in Printmaking from Central School of Art, London, and in 2018 was elected Honorary Fellow of Worcester College, Oxford University, for 'distinction in the world of art'. She is only the third wood engraver ever elected to membership of the Royal Academy of Arts (RA). She exhibits widely, has won over 40 awards (including the Rome Scholarship in Printmaking and awards in Brazil, Britain, Bulgaria, Canada, Finland, Italy, Russia and USA) and has works in museum collections worldwide. The Ashmolean Museum, V&A and Whitworth Art Gallery have significant holdings of her works. Over 40 solo shows include museum retrospectives in the UK and Moscow. Commissions include engravings for the British Museum; National Gallery; British Library; V&A; Sotheby's and the Royal Mint. Desmet is author of seven published books on printmaking and drawing and was Editor of *Printmaking Today* magazine (1998–2013). She lives and works in London and curated an historic exhibition, *Scene through Wood: A Century of Modern Wood Engraving*, for the Ashmolean Museum (2020) and toured the UK until 2023. www.annedesmet.com Instagram: @anne_desmet

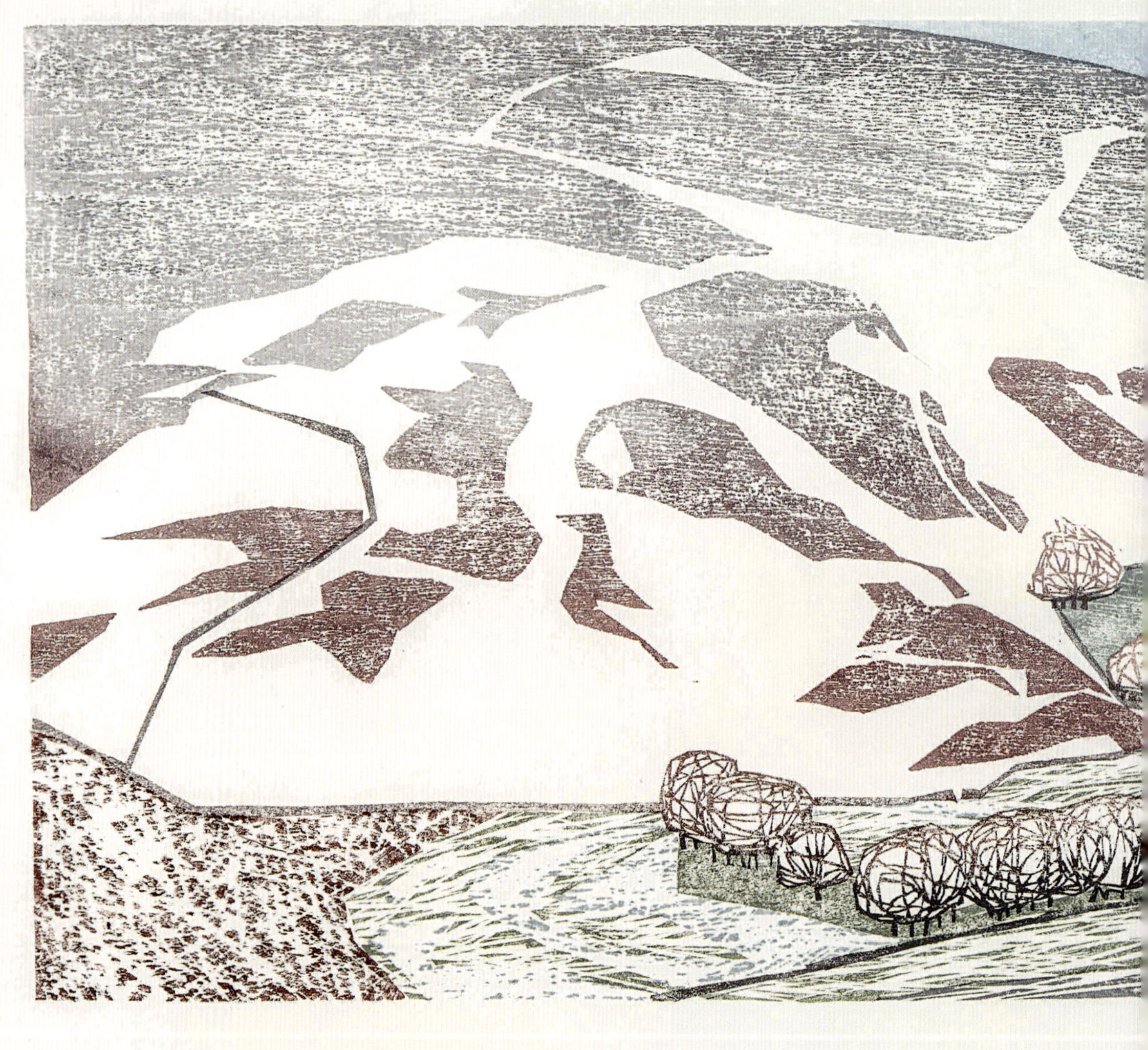

Anne specialises in wood engraving, linocut, lithography, original digital prints and mixed-media collage. Her collages are made from multiple fragments cut from sample printings of her engraving and lino blocks and other materials such as pen/pencil drawing, gold leaf and street map fragments. These are glued to diverse surfaces including archival card, painted wood, seashells, mirrored and convex glass, ceramic tiles and bowls, stones and roofing slate. Her subject matter pulls in two directions: one is topographical yet subject to metamorphoses; the other is concerned with intuitive architectural fantasies, urban myths and histories of urban destruction and regeneration such as the biblical Tower of Babel. Desmet aims to suggest the timeless solidity that architectural forms can convey, along with their visual manifestations of human aspiration, humour, hubris and folly, as well as their impermanence and vulnerability.

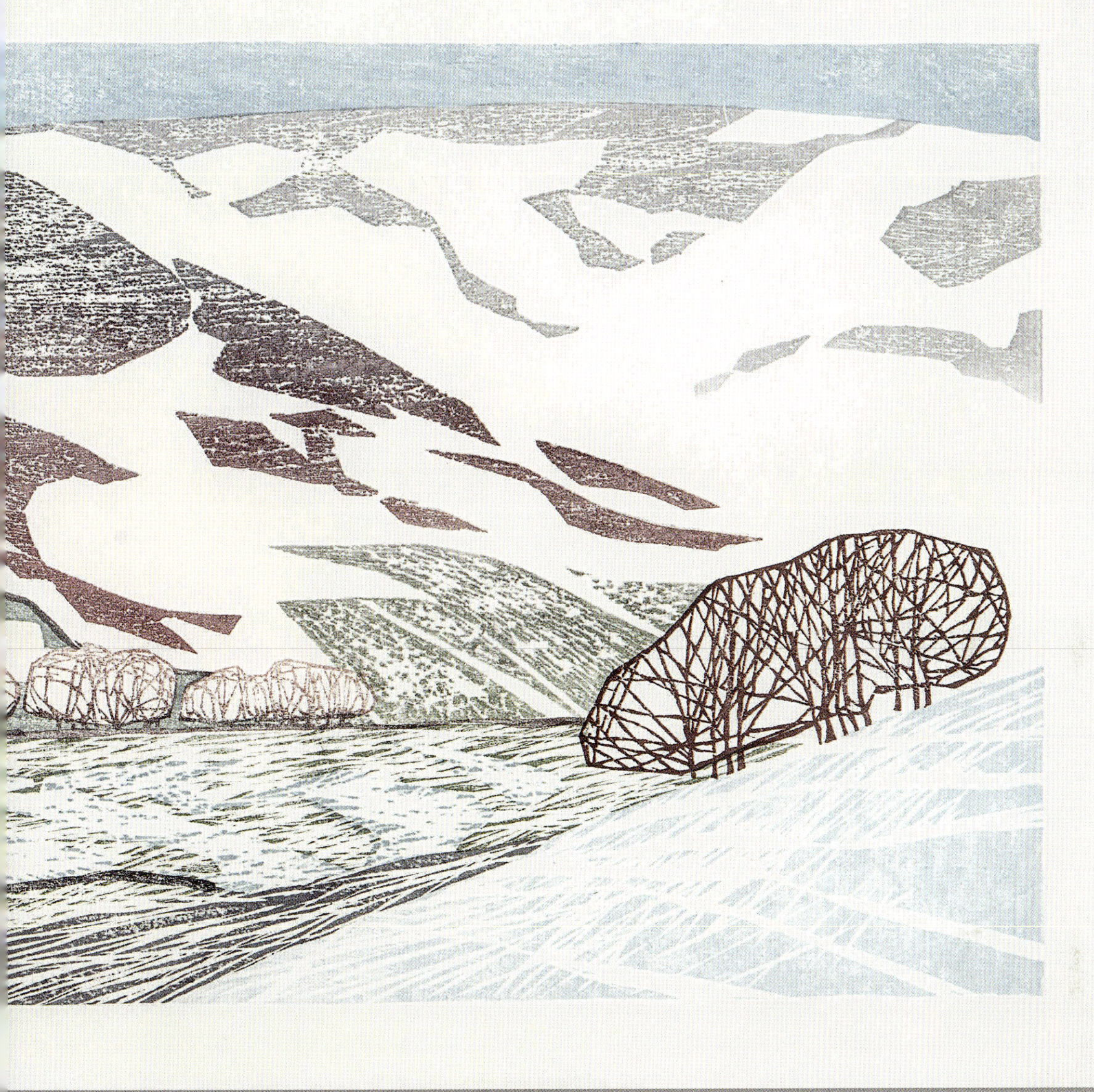

Laura Boswell

'I work with professional quality watercolours when printing *mokuhanga* and combine them with rice paste to create a printing medium. I prefer to use the Holbein brand of watercolours whenever possible. *Mokuhanga* printing requires that liquid colour is blended with rice paste directly onto the block using animal-hair brushes. Holbein watercolours are very rich in pigment and very smooth, which means they dilute well and are consistent in use. They require very little stirring while printing to keep

▲ Laura Boswell *Snow on the Moors*, 2020. Woodcut, 47.5 x 190 cm. Photo: Laura Boswell © Laura Boswell Printmaker

the colour evenly dispersed in the mixing pot, keeping the colour uniform across the edition. There is a very wide range of colours available, especially natural organic shades, which are my preferred palette and are easily sourced in Japan where I buy most of my *mokuhanga* supplies. In addition, I use a good-quality liquid sumi ink

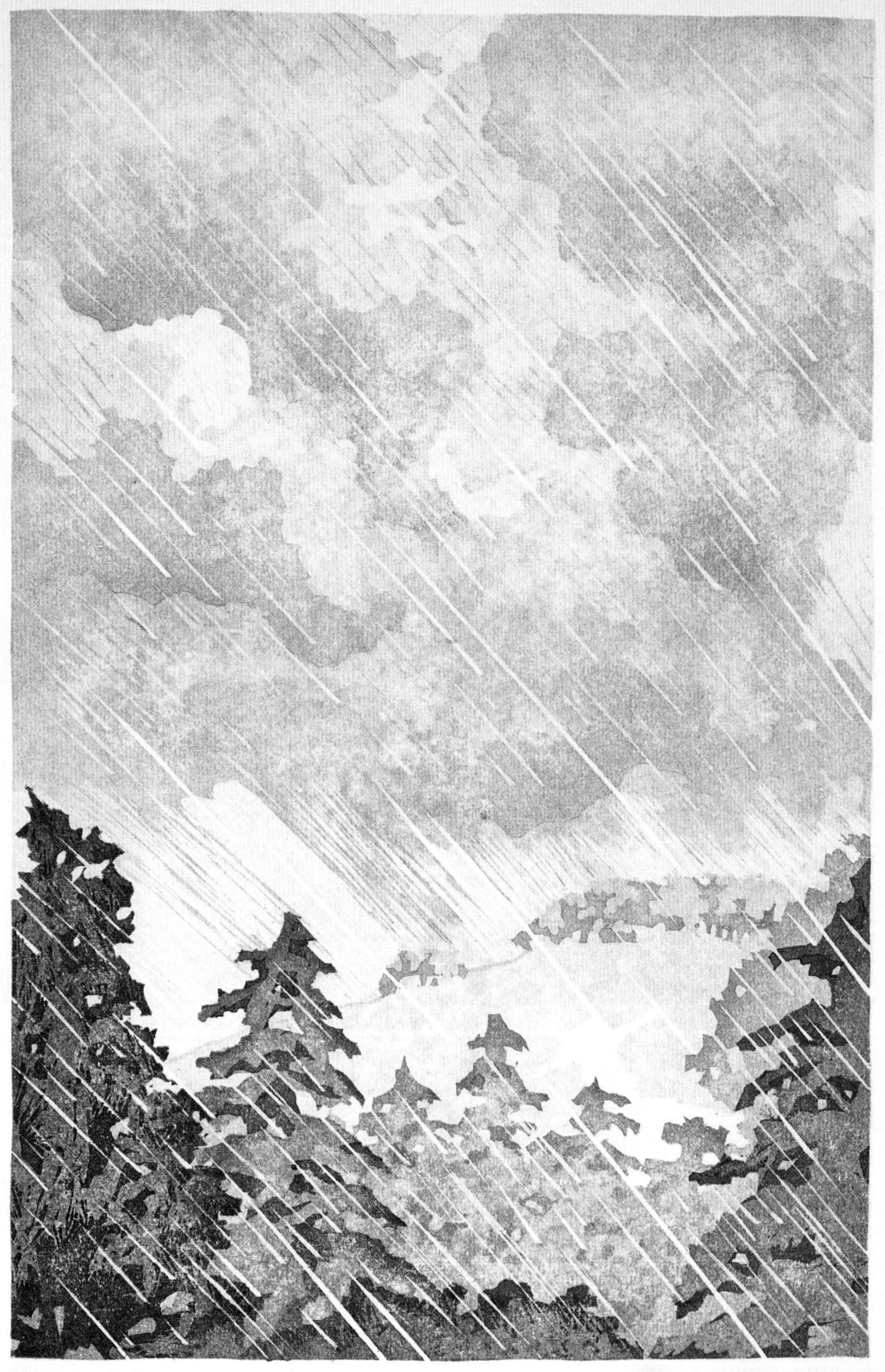

also sourced from Japan. Sumi is important in *mokuhanga* printing, both to provide the dense black required for the key block printing of traditional Japanese prints and for colour mixing. Sumi adds depth and richness to colour mixes.'

Snow on the Moors, 2020

Edition of 20.
Image size: 47.5 x 190 cm.

'*Snow on the Moors* is a multi-block print. The blocks are cut from Shina plywood and printed onto Shiramine *washi* paper using traditional *kento* registration. The Shina plywood has been wire brushed in places to raise the grain to create texture. It is printed with watercolour and sumi ink, both combined with rice paste (nori) on the block during printing in the traditional manner.

Holbein watercolours are used throughout. The print is made up of four basic colours: neutral grey made from diluted sumi ink, perylene maroon, perylene green and Prussian blue, which are then mixed in various combinations to give variations of colour. The sumi is added to all the colours to enrich them and to give a natural feel. There are six blocks in total. The dense pigment in the Holbein watercolours is especially important for the printing of the fine detail of the trees and in the cut textures. A weaker pigment would be likely to require extra printing to build up colour, which would risk losing registration or flooding delicate carving and textures. The smooth and consistent texture of the paints allows for the traditional *bokashi* shading technique to be applied successfully in demandingly small spaces. Please see the transition of the trees in the centre of the image from deep red-grey to red across a centimetre or so of fine detail.'

◀ **Laura Boswell *Twelve Views: Heavy Rain, Whiteleaf Cross*, 2015. Multiblock print, 25 x 39 cm**
Photo: Laura Boswell © Laura Boswell Printmaker

Twelve Views: Heavy Rain, Whiteleaf Cross, 2015

Edition of 17.
Image size: 25 x 39 cm.

'*Twelve Views: Heavy Rain, Whiteleaf Cross* is a reduction print cut from a single sheet of Shina plywood and printed onto Fabriano Rosaspina paper using traditional *kento* registration. The print is both cut and printed as the print edition is produced. The block is gradually cut away as each layer is printed, working from light to dark shades. The print is part of a series of 12 views of Buckinghamshire created in 2015, and is printed with watercolour combined with sumi ink and rice paste (*nori*).

This print is entirely printed in sumi ink with the addition of some Holbein Shadow Green and Prussian Blue. It is reduction printed, which is unusual for *mokuhanga*. It is possible here because the entire image is made in shades of the same colour (tints of grey), which allows for layering the print, working from light to dark shades without the colours becoming muddy or confused. The sumi ink in the print gives more complexity than a simple black watercolour pigment, resulting in a much livelier and subtle result.'

Laura Boswell is a printmaker based on the west coast of Scotland. Her work is an exploration of space, scale and light in a wild landscape. Her travels and residencies in Japan, studying traditional Japanese printmaking, have had a profound effect on her approach to printmaking. Laura's prints have their foundation in observational drawing and photography but are not direct geographic representations. They are a result of her response to the location, the season and the weather, with the final drawings done in the studio. Laura uses a variety of materials to draw onto the blocks and the prints rely on precise cutting of her drawn and painted lines and marks. Laura experiments constantly with a mix of linocut, *mokuhanga* (Japanese woodblock) and Western woodblock.

Laura is an associate member of the Royal Society of Painter-Printmakers. Her book, *Making Japanese Woodblock Prints*, was published by Crowood Press in 2019. Her second book, *Linocut and Reduction Printing: Design and Techniques*, came out in 2022. Laura's prints feature in national collections including The House of Lords, the National Library of Wales and Buckinghamshire County Museum. She also has prints in the Nagasawa Art Park collection and the MI-Lab Print Collection in Japan.

CHAPTER

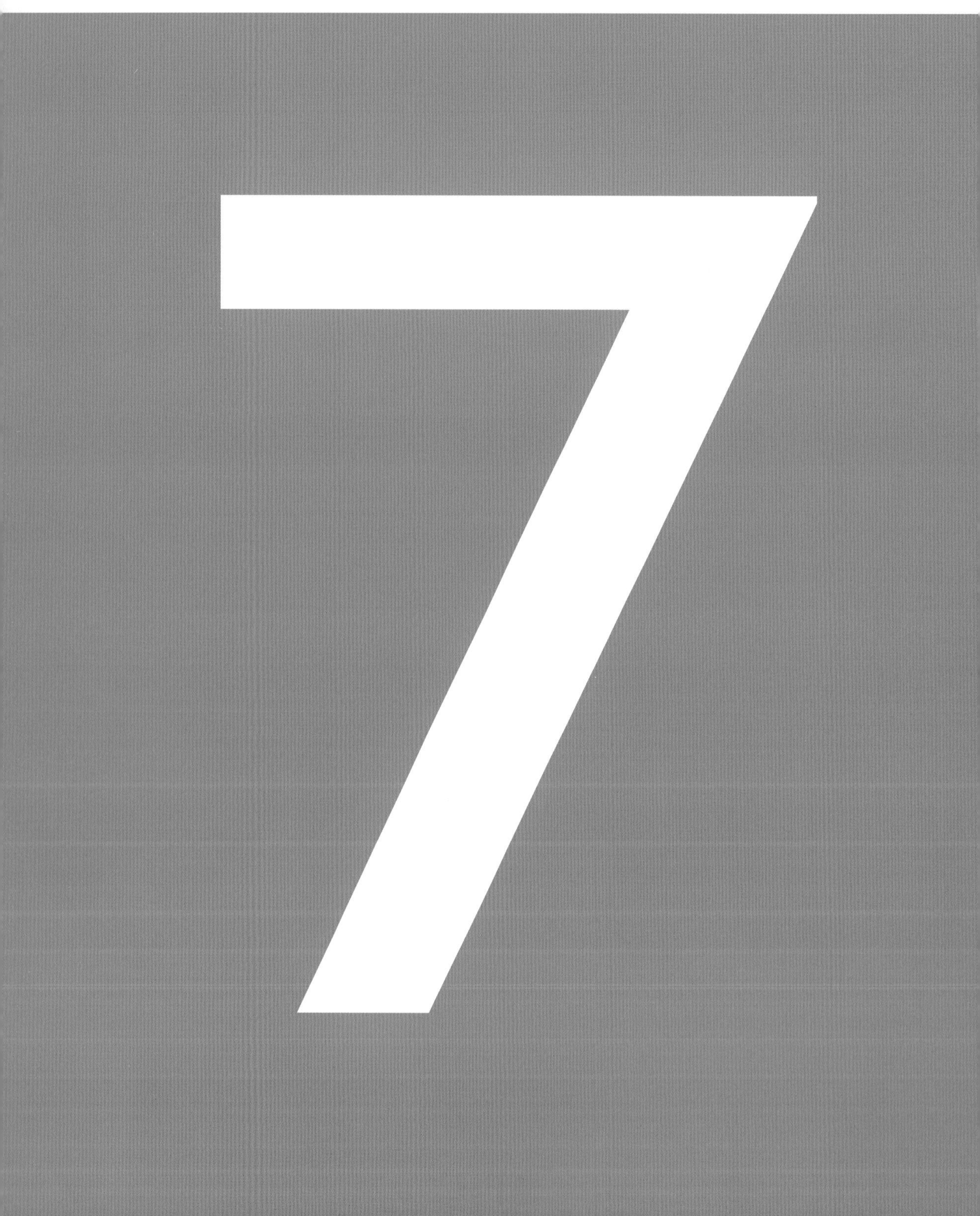

INK FOR SCREEN-PRINTING

This chapter discusses solvent- and water-based inks; the section on water-based inks also covers acrylic ink for graphic printing and artists' water-based ink developed for textile printing. It then covers how they are constructed, why each has its merits and what the future may hold.

The changes to screen-printing since the 1990s are primarily due to the diminishing role that screen-printing plays in the graphic art industry and the ubiquitous rise of wide-format inkjet printing, which has almost completely overtaken any role that screen-printing previously had in the graphic arts. This has changed significantly over the last 20 years and, consequently, the primary manufacturers of ink are no longer the large companies that made ink for the commercial graphic art market.

In the water-based arena, the manufacturers and suppliers for artists and printmakers who screen-print tend to be small and specialist, primarily catering to either artists or, increasingly, to the T-shirt printing and textile trades. There are a few companies, including TW Graphics in the United States and Sico Screen Inks in Belgium, who still make commercial screen-printing inks for industry. More commonly, the manufacturers are companies like Speedball, Daler-Rowney and Lascaux, who cater to artists, or Hunt the Moon and Wicked Printing Stuff, who cater mainly to the T-shirt fabric trade. The traditional manufacturers of solvent ink, such as Sericol in the UK, Sun Chemical in Europe and Nazdar in the USA, still cater for the industrial and commercial screen-print industry.

Over a period of nearly 60 years, from the initial development of screen-printing in the US in the early part of the twentieth century until the 1960s, screen-print inks were solvent based and were akin to household gloss paint.

Most textbooks on printing up until the 1970s almost completely ignore screen-printing's place in the canon of print. Letterpress was the dominant form of printing, followed by gravure and lithography. This is not surprising, as screen-printing was rarely seen as a serious printing process, but rather as a means for printing point-of-sale materials or banners. Because it was not taken seriously, the process was non-unionised, and an industry to support this new technique with supplies was slow to grow.

From the mid 1960s, new thin film inks were introduced that still used hydrocarbons – in this case ethyl hydroxyethyl cellulose (EHEC). Screen-printing ink changed drastically as awareness of the impacts on the user's health grew, and many artists moved over to inks that use an acrylic polymer, or hydroxypropyl cellulose (HPC), as the vehicle, thus enabling the ink to be cleaned up with water rather than a hydrocarbon solvent.

These inks are very different in formulation to the equivalent relief-printing acrylic inks, so require a slightly different approach to their use. The volumes of ink used, the amount of water or solvent for cleaning, and the amount of waste generated are invariably far greater than when creating an equivalent relief print. More recently some younger screen printers have started using dye-based textile inks to print with. Currently it is hard to evaluate the permanence of these inks on paper, due in part to the lack of heat setting that is required on fabric to make them permanent.

In the last few years, attitudes to health and safety and the environment have come to the fore in new ways. While the acrylic water-based screen-printing inks that replaced the traditional solvent-based inks were far healthier for the user, and complied with contemporary health and safety legislation, we now know that, if not treated properly, they can create microparticles in the waste water systems that are extremely harmful to the environment.

There is much that can be done to mitigate these harmful impacts, but research is lacking, and there is much confusion about which are the best solutions. The first question is one of environmental life cycle, from manufacture to disposal, and whether it is better to continue to use acrylic water-based inks, or to consider the possibility that solvent-based inks have a smaller environmental footprint. Currently, not enough data exists on which to base a truly informed decision. Therefore, in the light of health and safety legislation and health of the user, it is probably best to keep using the current water-based inks, but mitigate the problems and reduce the environmental impact as much as possible (see p.164).

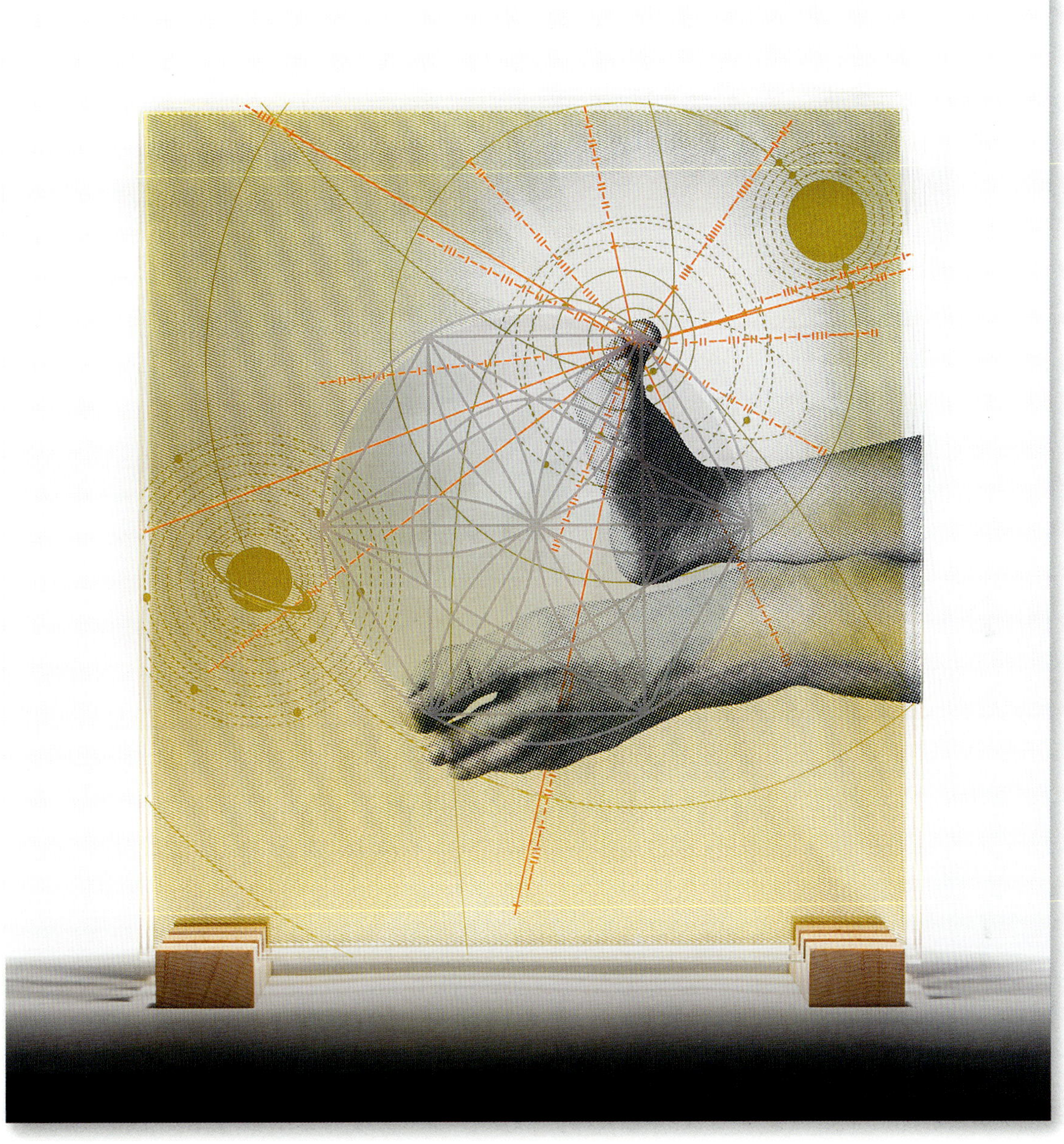

▲ Jennifer Gover
Escape Velocity, **2018.**
Screenprint on acrylic
panels, 30 x 34 x 16 cm.
Photo: Michael Garner ©
Jennifer Gover

SOLVENT-BASED INKS

Unlike ink used for the other printmaking processes, solvent-based inks are not formulated just from traditional linseed oils and pigment, although the older formulations of screen-print inks still contain linseed oils. John Stephens, in his book *Screen Process Printing*,[51] describes several typical commercial paper-and-board inks used by artists.

Synthetic, thin film inks first came into use in the 1960s and were partially responsible for the heyday of screen-printing in the years that followed, and the boom of Pop Art. These inks tend to be formulated around cellulose ethers, in particular EHEC. A typical ink formulation for thin film ink, according to Stephens, is as follows (an example of an ink with this type of formulation would be Sericol's Tristar range):

Constituent	%	Function
Pale Scarlet Chrome	15.00	pigment
Calcium 4b	3.00	pigment
China clay	23.00	extender
High-viscosity EHEC	6.00	resin
Pentaester gum	10.00	resin
White spirit	30.00	solvent/diluents
Aromatic hydrocarbon (160–180°C)	10.00	solvent
Propylene – glycol monomethylether	3.00	flow additive

Long-oil alkyd inks have replaced the original oil-based gloss inks that were similar to traditional oil-based paint. These inks still retain elements of traditional oil ink within their construction. Stephens again lists a typical ink (an example of this type of formulation would be the Supergloss inks that Sericol used to make):

Constituent	%	Function
Titanium dioxide	14.00	pigment
Phthalocyanine beta blue	5.00	pigment
Calcium carbonate	20.80	extender
Long-oil linseed alkyd	40.00	resin
Mixed naphthenate	1.00	drier
White spirit	19.00	solvent
Methyl ethyl ketoxime	0.20	anti-skinning additive

Note: here the linseed oil content of 40%, although substantially modified as an alkyd, gives these inks a gloss appearance and slow-drying properties

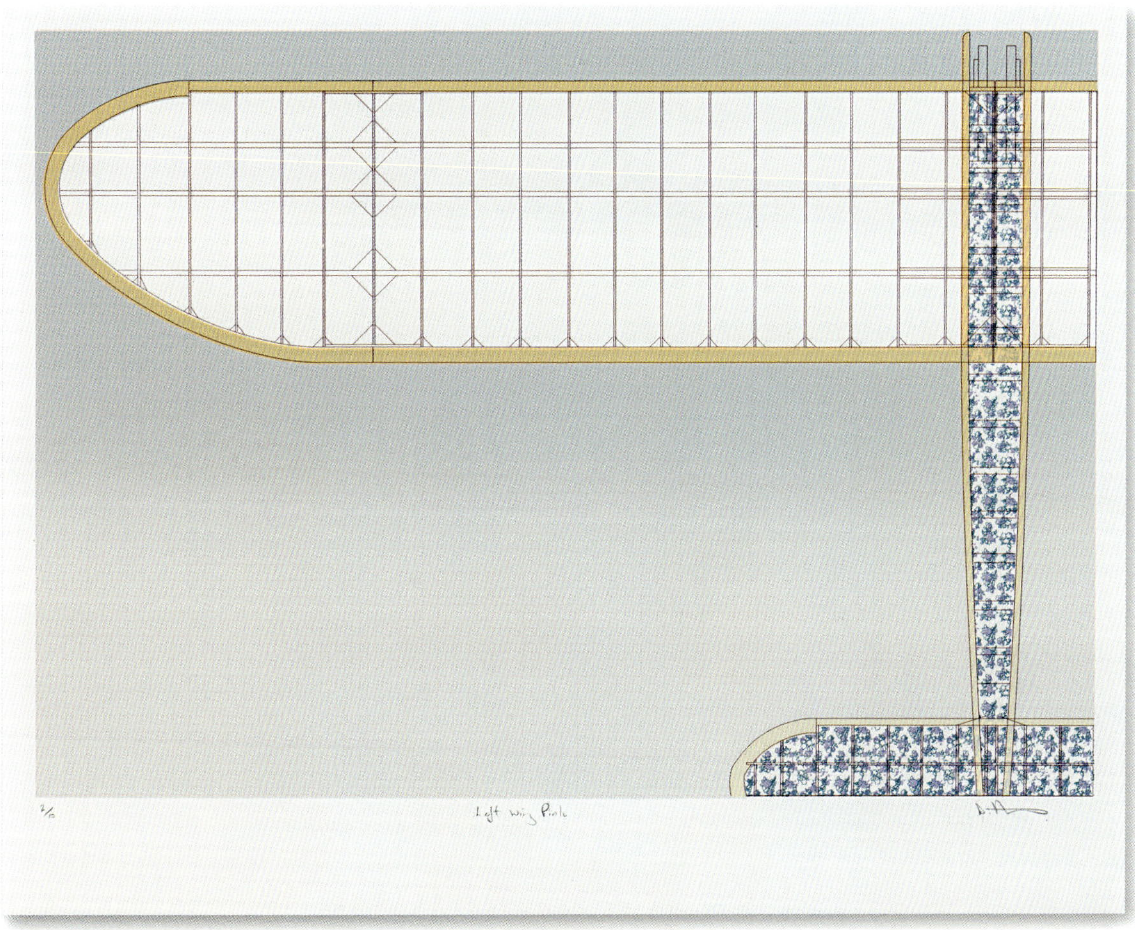

▲ Stephen Hoskins
Left Wing, 2016.
Screenprint, 56 x 76 cm.
Photo: Jo Hounsome
© Stephen Hoskins

(up to 12 hours), which make them feel as if they belong to the same family as a traditional oil-bound etching or lithographic ink. These types of paper-and-board ink are slowly disappearing as UV-curable water-based inks take over the commercial paper-and-board screen-print market. The longer-term future of screen-print paper-and-board inks may well be in jeopardy, as this market has already been eroded by wide-format digital print.

WATER-BASED INKS

Since 1990, artists have gradually moved away from the norms of the commercial industry and developed their own, now distinct, brand of screen-printing using water-based inks. Some of the long-established collaborative studios in the UK, such as Coriander and Advanced Graphics, still use oil-based inks. Other studios, such as Jealous Gallery, Print Studio and K2 Screen, use a mixture of both water-based and solvent-based depending on the requirements of

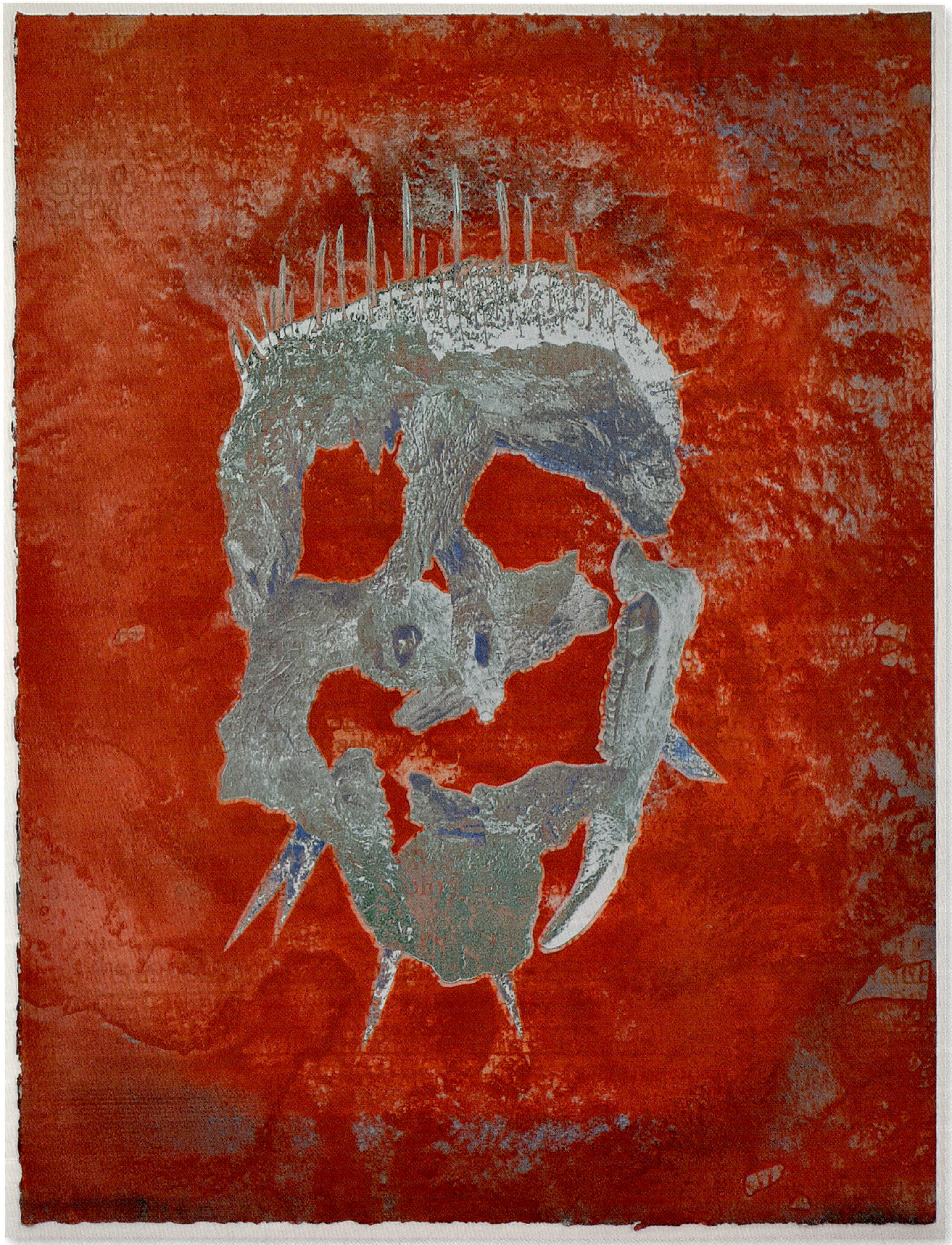

▲ **Justin Diggle** *Aspect Recognition 111*, **2023. Laser-engraved screenprint, 56 x 76 cm.**
Photo: Justin Diggle © Justin Diggle

the job. All the art schools and public-access workshops, such as Edinburgh Printmakers, Glasgow Print Studio and the now-closed London Print Studios, use water-based inks.

Although the term 'water-based' is in everyday general use by artists, it is, in fact, a misnomer. The acrylic inks are, in fact, not water-based but water-miscible. What's the difference? It means that the acrylic polymer is mixed with a solvent that is emulsified with the water content, much like mayonnaise, whereas a water-based ink would be similar to artists' Indian ink or a Japanese sumi ink. This is an important distinction, as it helps us understand why one does not add water to a water-based screen-printing ink.

Almost all water-based screen-print inks and bases are prepared in order to be press-ready. The addition of water can actually cause problems, as the water can go off and develop bacteria in the ink, which causes the ink to agglomerate and harden, thus creating small, hard bits in the ink, which will clog the screen and prevent clean, easy printing. If this happens, throw away the offending ink and clean up extremely well. This agglomeration can rapidly spread to other pots of ink from contaminated palette knives or adding ink from a pot that has previously gone off.

Water-based inks used by artists fall into four categories:

1. Acrylic paints for artists: these are mixed with a screen-printing medium to make them suitable for printing;
2. Industrial inks developed for the screen-printing paper-and-board industry: these are produced by the traditional solvent ink manufacturers, and are mostly in their infancy, having not yet received a great deal of interest from potential developers;
3. Premixed inks specifically developed for screen-printing use by small-scale manufacturers with the specialist user in mind;
4. Textile inks mixed with a binder: these inks have existed for many years, but are not normally considered for printmaking for two reasons: first, dye is used rather than pigment, which makes the colour very fugitive; second, as these inks are intended for use on cloth, there has been little incentive to reduce the water content, resulting in a marked tendency to buckle paper.

A previous book by Stephen Hoskins, *Water-based Screenprinting*, specifically covered water-based ink. Since that publication was written, over 20 years ago, printmakers and art schools have settled on the use of water-based ink and the discipline has matured somewhat. Everybody now has their favourite brand or combination of brands. Generally, prints in exhibitions have gone back to being labelled simply 'screen print', rather than 'water-based screen print', which was the case at one point.

Textile water-based screen inks have become more common for use on paper, particularly for the craft and hobby end of the market, which has expanded rapidly in recent years.

In terms of water-based inks for paper and board, there do not seem to be any notable new entrants in the market, the main contenders still being TW Graphics, Speedball and Aquaset for purpose-made ink for screen prints, with Lascaux, Daler-Rowney and Golden making screen-printing clear bases to which you add their own standard acrylic paint.

Adams[52] gives a formula for a typical acrylic gel-based ink:

Constituent	Proportion (%)
Organic pigment (in presscake form with 50% water)	20–50
If in organic pigment (dry)	40–60
Solution resin (30% w/v)	5–10
Base additive (amine or ammonia)	0.5–1
Emulsion resin (30% w/v)	30–50
Water	5–10
Co-solvent (alcohols)	0–20
Additives	1–7

These acrylic gels are acidic, and the addition of amines or ammonia keeps them soluble. The addition of more acid upsets this balance, which is why screens are often cleaned with a mild alkali before printing; this prevents the balance being destroyed and allows the polymer to harden and dry in the screen. This happens because the diazo or styrene-butadiene (SBS) polymer emulsions used for making direct photo stencils are naturally acidic; therefore, if the emulsion is not washed off thoroughly before printing, the acidity can affect the pH balance of the ink.

Most of the acrylic inks can be re-wetted by the addition of an alkali solution. If your ink has hardened on the screen, then the addition of an alkali may be enough to soften and remove it.

A water-based textile ink for screen-printing differs very little from a standard water-based ink. For paper, the real difference may occur in the colour, which can be, but is not always, dye rather than pigment.

A typical formula consists of:

Constituent	Proportion (%)
Water	11
Dispersant agent	3
Defoamer	1
Propylene glycol	3
Antiseptic	1
Titanium dioxide	31
Acrylic polymer emulsion	44
Rheology agent	5
Polyurethane (PU) thickener	1

The Titanium white in this case is the colour. The proportions may vary depending on the intensity of the pigment. This example is for a pigmented textile ink.

COLOUR FOR WATER-BASED INKS

Colour tends to be added to screen-printing bases in one of three forms.

First, as an addition to a manufacturer's proprietary acrylic paint system. This is the case with screen-printing systems from Daler-Rowney, Golden, Liquitex and Lascaux. All offer a screen-print base to which their individual acrylic paints can be added to create the colour, usually in a proportion of up to 50 per cent. These systems have very slow drying times in the screen and are therefore usually very easy to print. The downside can be a slightly dull or chalky appearance to the colour due to the fillers added to the paint systems, especially if using cheaper acrylic paint. To combat this and increase colour intensity, some manufacturers, such as Lascuax, offer specialist, more concentrated screen print pigments.

Second, colour is added as a pigment-base or colour-tint, such as in TW Graphics' ink systems. Here, the colour tends to be much more intense and can be very translucent or opaque dependent on the base used. Colour pigment is added into a base in concentrations of up to a maximum of 30 per cent. TW's system comes with a clear base, gloss base or white base. The downside is that these systems can dry very quickly and need to be handled by an experienced printer. Some of the colour bases can be extremely expensive to buy at the outset, but will last for a long time.

Third, colour is premixed with the base and the ink is used straight from the pot, such as with ink systems from companies such as Speedball, Nazdar and Sico.

Colour quality varies hugely across the range of inks available and does not generally bear any relation to ease of printing. Colour quality is one of the most subjective areas, along with the overall quality of an individual ink range.

SAFE CLEANING OF SCREENS AND INK

In the past, the easiest way to clean the screen was to put it in the sink and wash the ink down the drain. I previously recommended a triple trap under the sink to remove the ink sludge, but this practice is no longer acceptable. There are several ways to avoid putting acrylic down the sink: first, after printing, scrape all the colour from your screen, squeegee and palette knife either back into the pot of colour or into a sludge pot; next, wipe the palette knife and squeegee with a paper cloth or old newspaper and dispose of it into the bin. Clean the screen and the tools with a sponge and a bucket of water, or a series of cleaning rags. The screen can stay in the bed if you are printing another colour. If the screen does not clean easily with a sponge and water, it can be sprayed with a mild alkali to loosen the ink. Ideally, the bucket of water can be used several times, greatly reducing the amount of water used in the process.

Zea Mays Printmaking studio in Florence, Massachusetts, has an extremely good guide on flocculating the acrylic in the cleaning bucket in order to avoid throwing any acrylic down the drain. Fundamentally, the water needs to become more acidic, with a pH of around 5.4, to make the acrylic cross link. By adding a flocculent, the acrylic clumps together in the bucket and the water can then be strained through a filter paper, such as a large coffee filter. The resultant water will then be free of micro-particles.

Disposal of the remaining, old ink is more complicated depending where you live. Some authorities will just dispose of old acrylic ink in landfill, while others will convert old paint and other rubbish into Refuse Derived Fuel (RDF), which is then burnt to create power. Additionally, Golden has an advisory sheet on its website giving detailed advice for the safe disposal of acrylic paint rinse water.[53]

In the interest of balance and to inform the debate, the case studies for this chapter are split between a water-based acrylic studio that removes all of the solids before disposing of the ink, and an editioning studio that still uses traditional oil-based ink.

▶ **Stephen Hoskins** *French Peacocks*, **2017. Screen print, handmade paper and carbon fibre rod, 38 x 28 cm.** Photo: Jo Hounsome © Stephen Hoskins

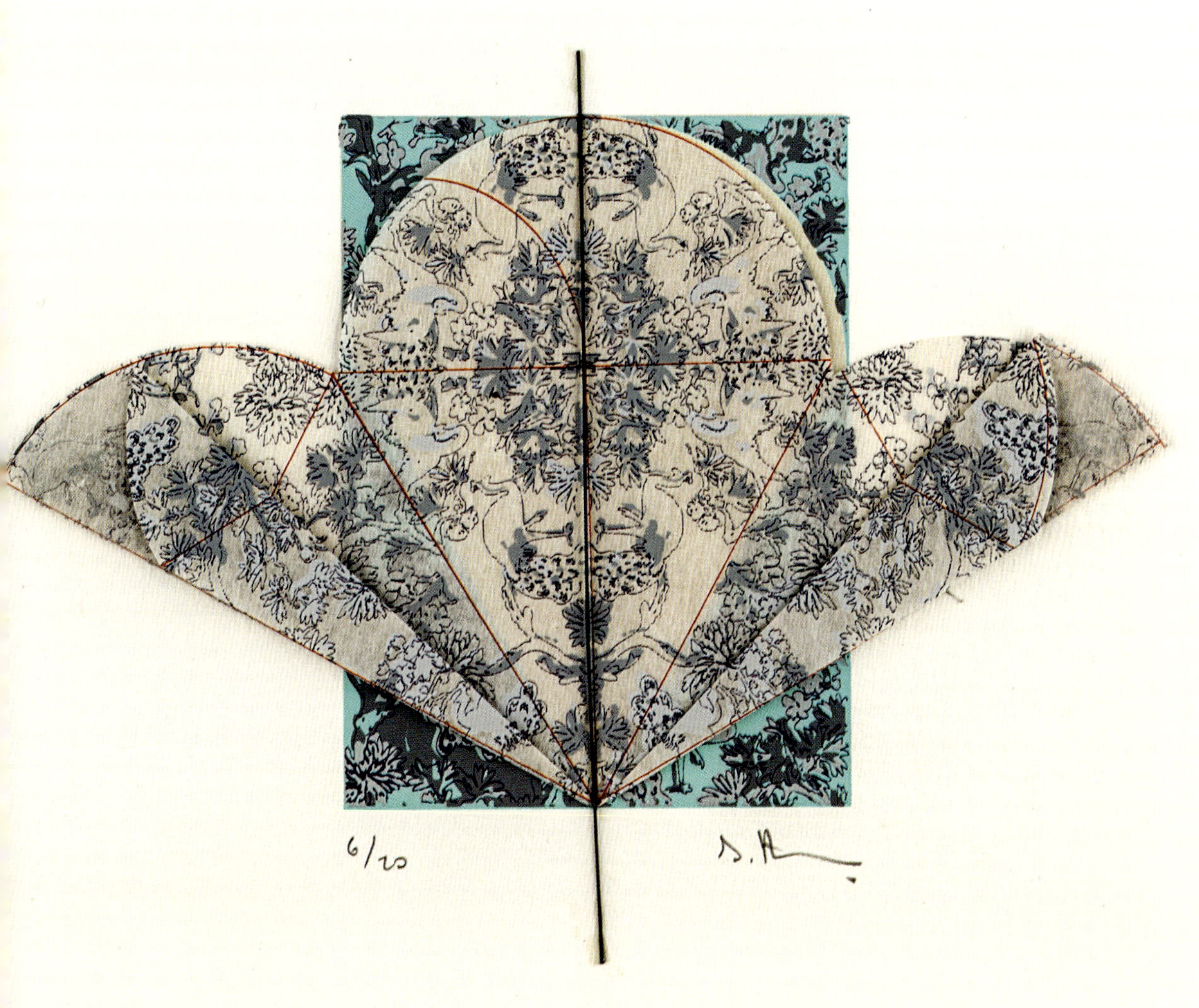

6/20   S. H.

CASE STUDIES

Artizan Editions

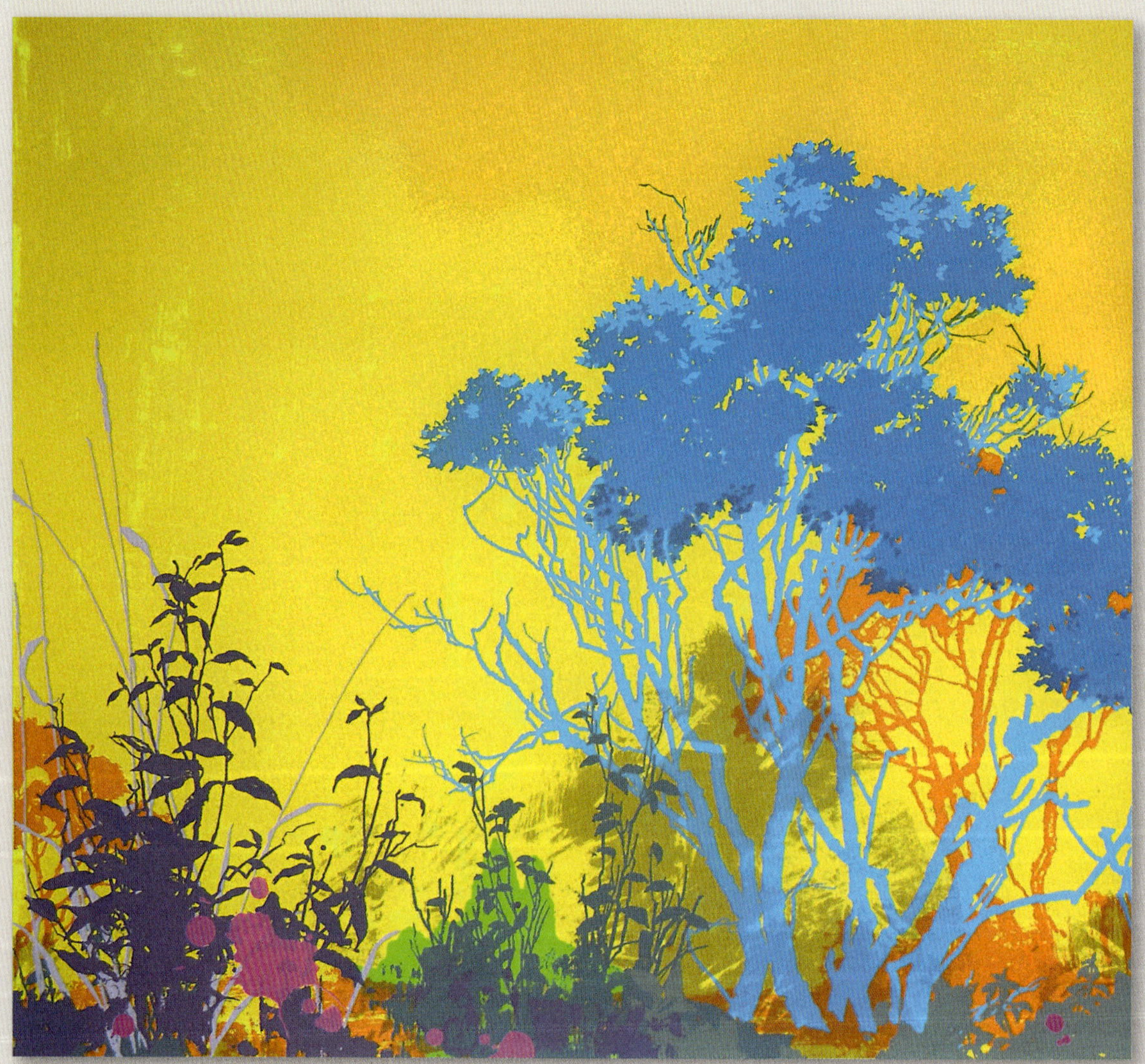

▲ Henrik Simonsen *Yellow light*, 2016. Screen print, 90 x 80 cm.
Photo: Sally Gimpson © Henrik Simonsen

Artizan Editions was formed in 1994 by experienced printer and technician Sally Gimson, who identified a need for another accomplished, accessible and expert workshop able to advise, promote, guide and collaborate with professional, established artists in the production of high-quality and affordable original serigraphs. Artizan Editions gained a widespread reputation for creative collaborations with leading artists, including the internationally acclaimed painter, Bridget Riley, whose colour compositions lent themselves naturally to the crisp, visually strident and colourful medium of screen print. Gimson is definite in her preference for craftsmanship, authenticity of medium and uniqueness of expression. A mutually fruitful accord between the creative, conceptual and technical aspects that go to make a clear and convincing screen print is at the heart of all Artizan Edition prints. Sally explains more below.

HENRIK SIMONSEN

'*Yellow Light* is an 18-colour screen print on Bockingford 300 gsm HP paper, supplied by John Purcell Paper.

All the 16 stencils were hand painted by the artist, either on a drafting or a TrueGrain film, using acrylic black paint and India ink.

The first three yellows, from lemon to golden, are made from Apollo Colours S31050 HV extender base with the addition of universal tinters from Sericol and Apollo. In recent years I have used Zest-it Oil Paint Dilutant from J & T Blackman as a thinner. As this is made from aliphatic hydrocarbon and orange terpenes, it not only extends drying time for the ink but reduces fumes, is non-toxic, non-flammable and environmentally friendly. The fourth colour, lime green, has a tiny amount of Ad Colour Art Jet Extra Opaque White. This has the best opacity I have found in an ink. A transparent orange is followed by four blues made with the opaque white, universal tinters, thinners and some Apollo R146 gel retarder. This product is invaluable on hot days to reduce blocking in on the screen. The tenth colour was a transparent grey/violet, creating a shadowing, followed by five opaque mixes of warm grey, grey/blue, light mauve, violet and blue/violet. It took three printings through the same screen to achieve the magenta. An initial light opaque pink was overprinted twice with a pure magenta to give the colour its lift and strength.'

Henrik S. Simonsen was born in 1974, in Denmark, and has worked with Artizan Editions for over two decades. Simonsen says himself that he enjoys making something original in print because 'it's a much more interesting way of working as you are not trying to make a print look like a painting.' On the use of colour, Henrik remarks, 'Each colour brings its own personality and atmosphere; change a colour in a piece and you change every colour and all their internal relationships. Colour changes everything.'

Simonsen graduated from Sotheby's Institute of Art, London and Montclair University, New Jersey. His successful solo shows include The Royal Opera House, and his work has been commissioned for a public museum collection in Belgium. He shows regularly in Copenhagen and consistently with Findlay Galleries in New York and Palm Beach.

BRIAN RICE

'The *Pavilion Series* screenprints were created as a collection of 41 unique images. Starting with three different background areas, various horizontal framed shapes and a collection of dot patterns designed by the artist formed the basis of the works. The creative process was aided by Brian Rice's in-depth knowledge of printmaking, the colour choices and selections, being driven by Brian in collaboration with the printmaker.

For *Pavilion II*, we used a mixture of fine pumice powder from Intaglio Printmaker, an oil process base – Quattro Plus HQ – from Sun Chemical, which seemed to have a lower odour than the comparable Tristar product, plus thinner, mixed to a thick consistency and printed through a 77T mesh. This made a very matt, rough background colour grey, which was then overprinted with a blue border using the same ink structure and mesh. The central black oblong was made with carborundum powder from T N Lawrence & Sons, Hove, mixed with a base medium, printed through a 16T mesh. This created a thick, shiny texture which took over two days to dry.

Light magenta-coloured dots over the blue border were again made with pumice and base medium, printed through a 16T mesh, and you can see the ridged grid pattern of the mesh if you look closely. Finally, the white dots were printed using Ad Colours Art Jet Extra Opaque White, a truly opaque colour, which, as the ink dried, cracked like crazy paving over the rough carborundum surface – a slightly unexpected but happy result.

The colours are all made using Sericol Universal Tinters, which I have always found to be the cleanest, most intense pigments to use. I have favoured oil-based inks because of the colour depth and intensity they bring, along with good opacity when required. The paper size is 40 x 50 cm on Bockingford 300/400 gsm paper.'

Painter and printmaker Brian Rice studied at Yeovil School of Art followed by Goldsmiths.

He continued to establish himself in the 60s art movements, living and working in London from 1962

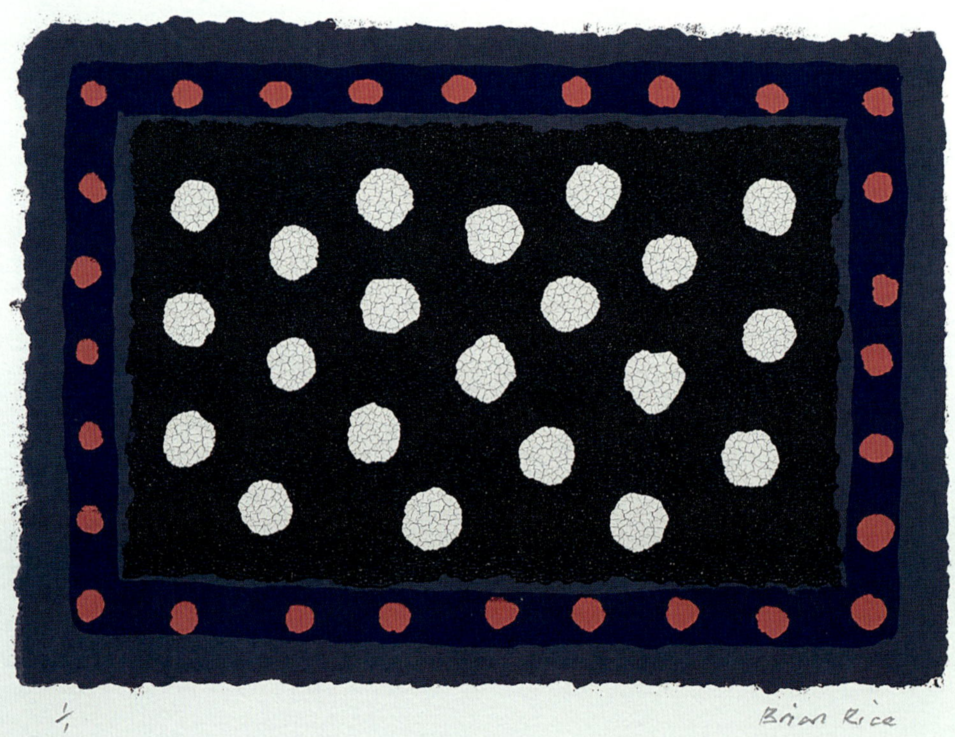

to 1978, where he produced non-representational prints and paintings, including his *Japanese Series*, strengthening both the conviction of his work and his reputation.

In 1978, Rice rejected London and its art scene. Buying a 50-acre farm in West Dorset, he immersed himself in farming, his only remaining contact with the art world for a period being his teaching of printmaking and drawing at Brighton Polytechnic where he taught for more than 32 years.

Rice was chairman of the Printmakers Council of Great Britain between 1974 and 1977. He has had over 40 solo exhibitions and around 200 group exhibitions. His works are in many collections worldwide, particularly in both private and public ones in the USA. His work is also housed within the collections at the Tate Gallery and the V&A.

▲ **Brian Rice** *Pavilion II*, 2009. Screenprint, 40 x 50 cm. Photo: Robin Hannagan-Jones, Fabled Ltd © Artizan Editions

Always an unconventional printmaker, Rice's association from 2006 with the publishing/printing house Artizan Editions encouraged a series of works where the primacy of experiment is apparent, and the freedom of process brought much creative pleasure to both artist and workshop in their making. It is at times only through collaboration that an artist can truly thrive and fully achieve their desired result.

Zea Mays Printmaking

Zea Mays Printmaking (ZMP) is a professional printmaking studio, located in Western Massachusetts. Since its founding in 2000, ZMP's mission has been to provide a space and community to learn, create and promote prints made with the safest processes available. Zea Mays Printmaking collaborates with artists, studios and schools around the world to share innovations in non-toxic and sustainable printmaking.

The 6,000 square-foot, state-of-the-art printmaking facilities provide studio access for over 100 artist members, residencies, workshops, internships, exhibitions and educational programmes.

'In 2019, ZMP began a research project dedicated to finding a safe way to dispose of acrylic screen-printing ink after cleaning screens with a sponge and water and keeping the inky water in a bucket. The research concluded in 2022. In a printmaking studio, artists produce large amounts of

▼ **Richard Turnbull** *Liverpool Composite*, **2023. Screen print, 28 x 38 cm.** Photo: Richard Turnbull © Richard Turnbull

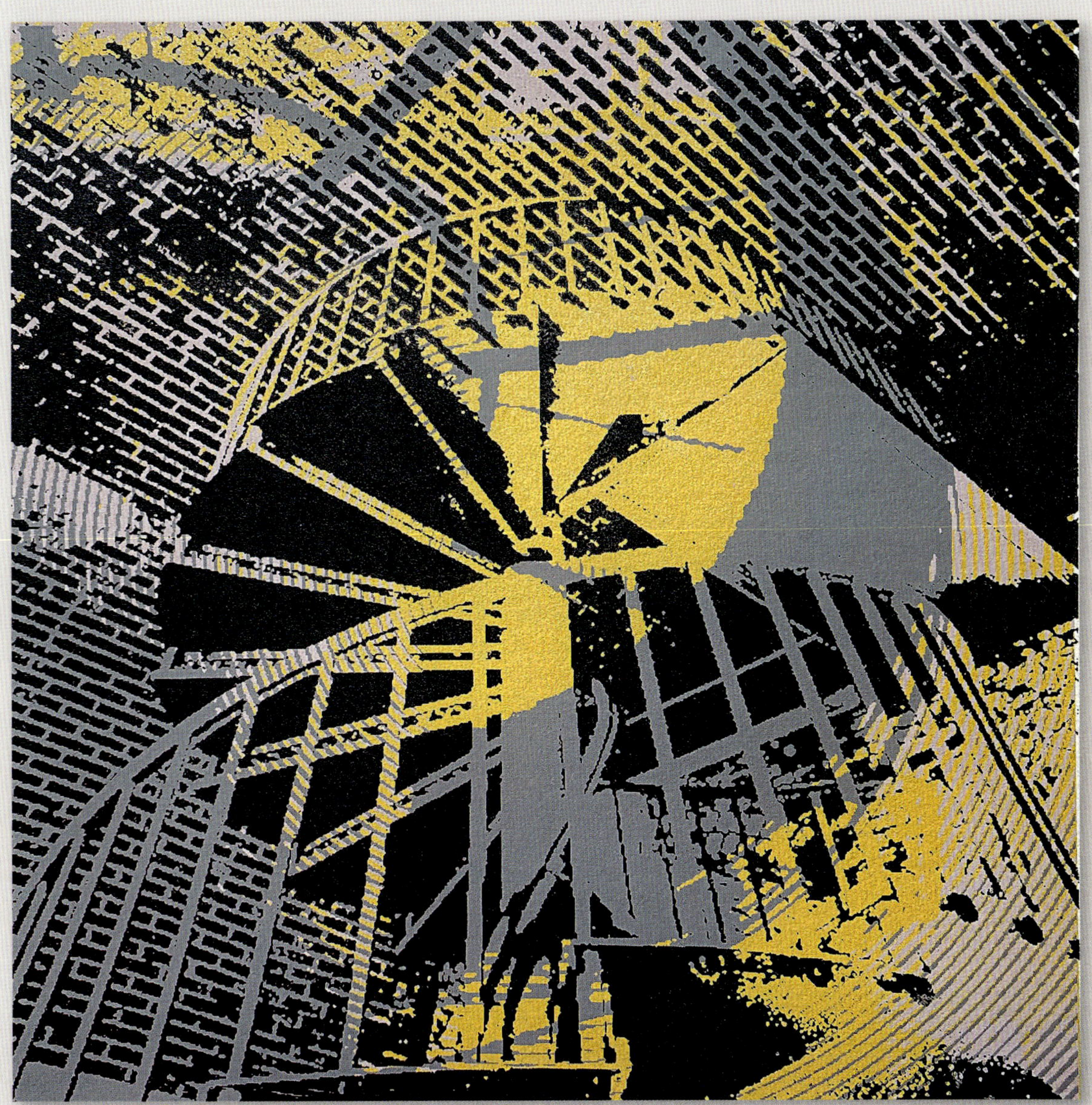

wastewater containing acrylic particles, which have proven to be toxic to humans and the environment. When this waste is washed straight into the drain, these particles are released into the water system, where they can cause harm. Flocculation is a process used widely in water treatment 'in which colloids come out of suspension in the form of floc or flake, either spontaneously or due to the addition of a clarifying agent.'[54]

Zea Mays Printmaking aims to define a practical method for flocculating and filtering out acrylic particles to create clean, pH-neutral wastewater before disposal. Researchers Catherine Aiello and Lydia Giangregorio began with online research into existing studio flocculation systems and drew from previous experiments at Zea Mays by Olivia Arau McSweeney, Pace Knowles-Donnelly and Margo Temple. Researchers tested combinations of aluminium potassium sulphate (alum), calcium hydroxide (lime) and sodium carbonate (soda ash) as flocculants. They conducted a series of experiments isolating variables including order, combination and concentration of chemical additives, time and filtration techniques, defined a recipe, and constructed a filtration system where the task of flocculation and filtering are shared between the user and shop monitor. Additionally, they noted the need for defined best practices when working in acrylic mediums to increase the success and ease of this flocculation system.[55]

RICHARD TURNBULL

Liverpool Composite, 2023

Silkscreen.
Image size: 20 x 20 cm.
Paper size: 28 x 38 cm.

'I made this print of various overlaid motifs of the crypt of Metropolitan Cathedral in Liverpool, UK, from photos I took in the summer of 2023. I used Photoshop to manipulate the images and then printed four separate layers on acetate that I in turn exposed on screens in the screen-printing studio at Zea Mays Printmaking. The initial layer is a gold square which tends to read as yellow, and subsequent layers were printed in a light pinkish-violet, grey and black mixed with a little silver. I almost always mix my colours with white because I prefer opacity to transparency in most of my work. I use Speedball inks (mixed with a small amount of Golden silkscreen base) almost exclusively because they behave consistently over a long period of time and don't dry up in their containers. I've experimented in the past with Jacquard inks (deep colours

but a relatively short shelf life) and metallic pigments in powder form (potentially hazardous to the respiratory tract), but tend to stick with Speedball, in part because they also seem to flocculate very cleanly.'

Reykjavik Composite, 2023

Silkscreen.
Image size: 15 x 20 cm.
Print size: 28 x 38 cm.

'This print was made from various photos taken of Reykjavik streets and architecture in the summer of 2023. I like creating composite images by juxtaposing objects and scenes that would not normally occur together. In this case, I used a photo of an industrial space, manipulated and separated into three layers and then turned on its side, as the background for a subsequent layer of street construction and a somewhat anomalous large billboard with a human head. There are actually five layers/colours here, printed in sequence: first, a gold rectangle, then light grey, pink, darker grey, and finally, silvery-black. All the inks are Speedball, mixed with a small amount of Golden silkscreen base (for fluidity) and white (for opacity).'

Rich Turnbull is a New York- and Western Massachusetts-based printmaker, book artist and experimental photographer. He has a BA in History from Cornell University and an MA and PhD in Art History from the Institute of Fine Arts, New York University. He teaches art history at the Fashion Institute of Technology in New York and lectures at the Metropolitan Museum of Art. His work is in various private collections, and he regularly exhibits nationally and internationally. He has curated a number of recent printmaking and artist's book exhibitions at Zea Mays Printmaking in Florence, MA, and the Manhattan Graphics Center in New York.

▶ **Richard Turnbull** *Reykavik Composite*, **2023. Screen print, 28 x 38 cm.** Photo: Richard Turnbull © Richard Turnbull

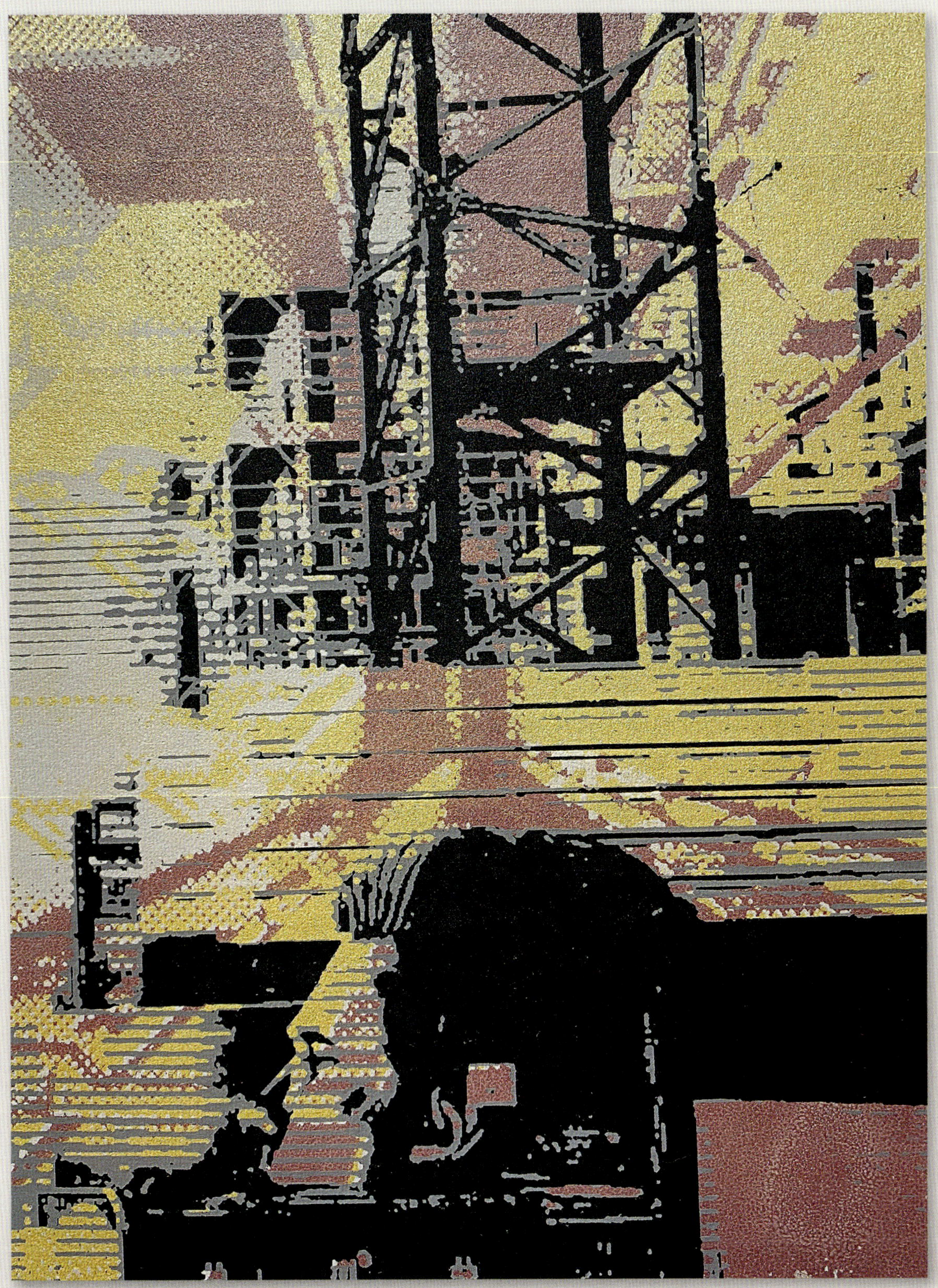

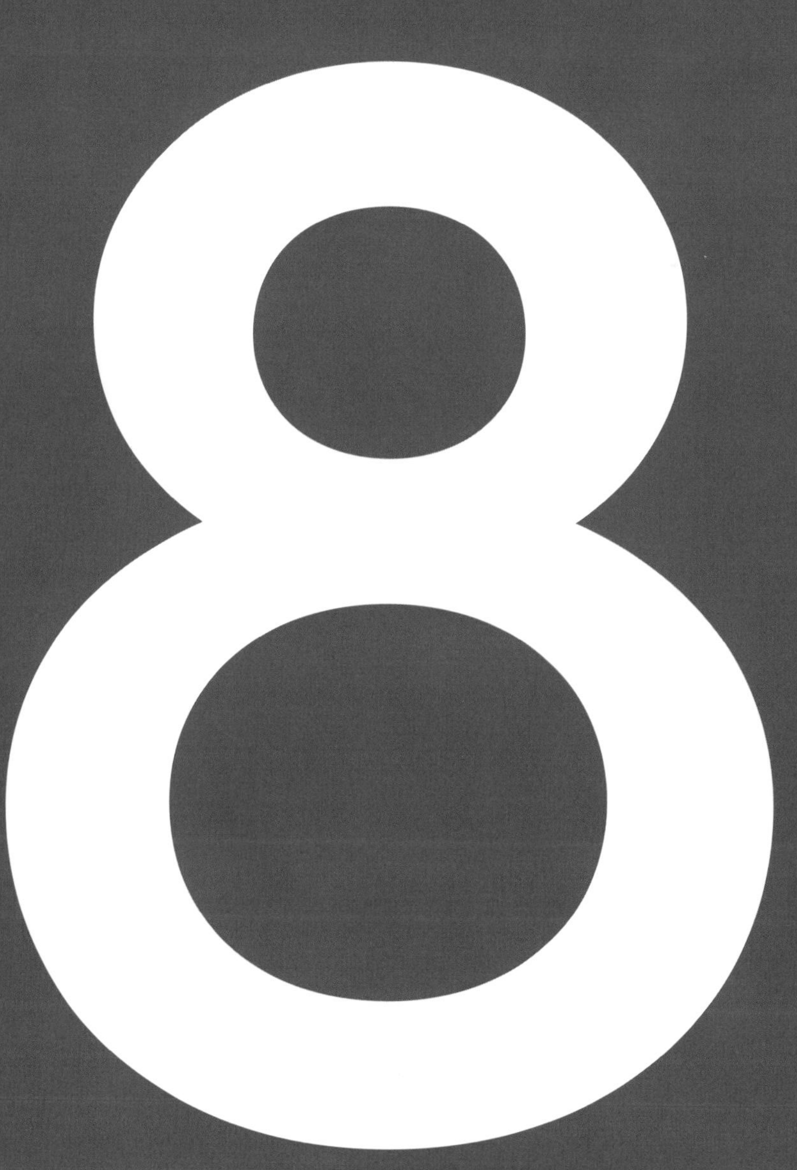

CHAPTER

8

INKJET PRINTING

In the last 20 years, inkjet has become a staple of the printmakers' armoury. It is used extensively, not only in its own right as a method of producing artists' prints, but also as the primary means of creating photographic negatives and positives used to create printing matrices in most of the traditional printmaking processes. The rise of its influence was extremely swift, and names as diverse as Wolfgang Tillmans, Richard Hamilton and Lesley Dill have all made digital prints an integral part of their printmaking practice.

BACKGROUND

There are two primary categories of inkjet printing: continuous and drop-on-demand. By far the most common is drop-on-demand; these printers use printhead nozzles that each eject a single drop of ink only when activated. Drop-on-demand is divided into two subcategories: piezo-electronic and thermal. Piezo-electronic uses an electrical current that swells the ink and forces it through the inkjet head under pressure. This sort of printer is typical of Epson, who are the main producers of piezo printers in wide format. Roland and Mimaki also make printers that use piezo technology. Thermal technology relies upon the ink being heated and the drop being forced through the nozzle as it vaporises. The main manufacturers of printers using thermal technology are HP and Canon.

CONTINUOUS INKJET

Continuous inkjet printers generate a steady stream of ink, deflecting drops electronically onto the printing medium. This is the oldest inkjet technology, used in high-speed production lines to print small characters on product surfaces. The continuous flow makes image resolution difficult to control, and

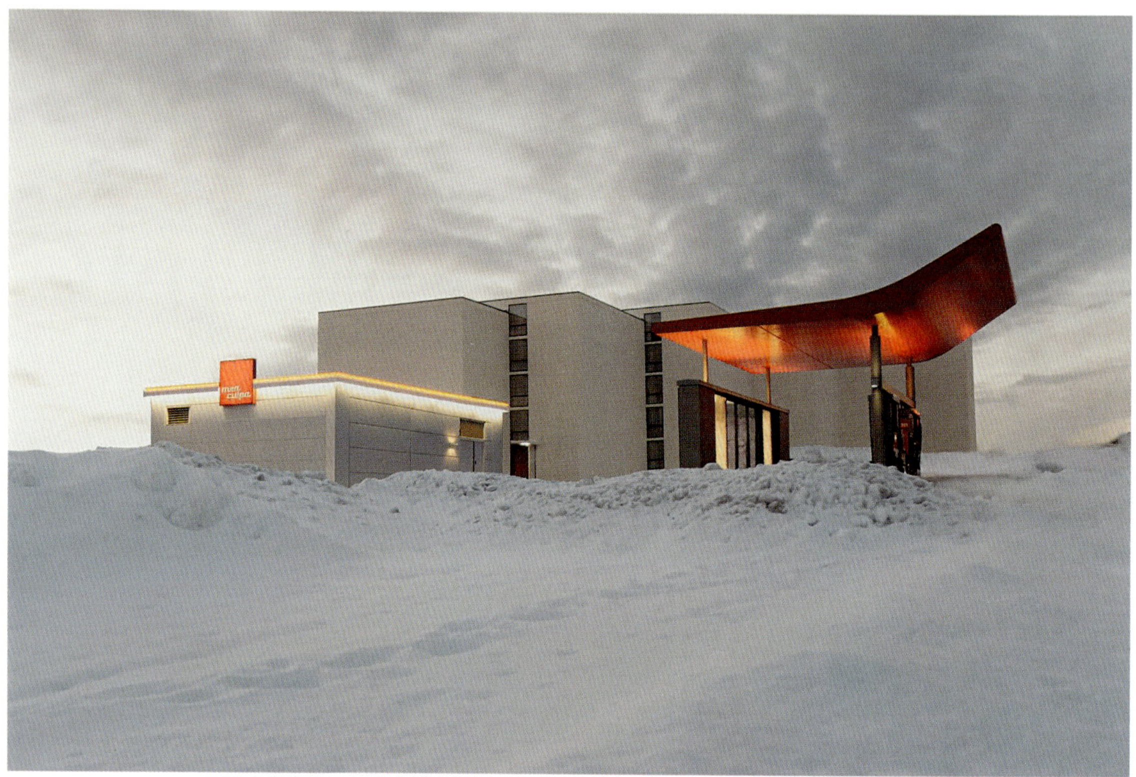

▲ Carolyn Bunt *Station to Station (Once there were mountain)*, 2013. **Pigmented inkjet, 56 x 76 cm.** Photo: Paul Laidler © CFPR, UWE, Bristol

the complex ink-circulation system must be maintained. The process usually requires solvent-based inks, which are dependent on the correct liquidity and must have a strong surface tension to avoid the splashing of the ink dots and the development of minute satellite droplets, which influence the shape of each printed droplet.

However, this variation and subtle surface, which creates a near-continuous-tone appearance, was the very characteristic that first drew artists to inkjet printing. Among the first continuous inkjet printers was the Iris printer from Scitex, but its huge cost and troublesome maintenance actually inhibited the initial popularity of wide-format inkjet for artists. The Scitex Iris printer dominated the early years of inkjet printing, and it still holds a particularly soft and beautiful quality, but the very high cost and temperamental nature of the printers meant they died out in the competition from Epson, HP and Canon.

DROP-ON-DEMAND INKJET

Drop-on-demand inkjet printers use printhead nozzles that each eject a single drop of ink only when activated. Thermal and piezoelectric are the two most common drop-on-demand inkjet technologies. They work by using a discrete electrical signal, or waveform, to fire individual drops from each nozzle of every printhead. Generally, they need far less maintenance and are more economical than continuous inkjet printers. Economies of scale have also vastly reduced the costs of drop-on-demand printhead technology. The inks tend to be water-based, although the introduction of solvent-based mediums for outdoor display graphics is a growing trend.

THERMAL INKJET

Thermal inkjet printers use heat to generate vapour bubbles, ejecting small drops of ink through nozzles and placing them on a surface to form text or images. Its advantages are: high printhead-operating frequency, excellent system reliability and highly controlled ink drop placement. Integrated electronics mean fewer electrical connections, faster operation and good colour resolution. Originally developed for desktop printers, their disadvantage is that the heads need to be replaced more frequently than in piezo printers.

PIEZOELECTRIC

Piezoelectric printing technology – commonly called piezo – pumps ink through nozzles using pressure. The printhead regulates the ink by means of an electrical current passed through a material that swells to force ink onto the paper. Piezo print speeds are slower.

SOLVENT AND LATEX PRINTERS

Since the publication of the first edition of this book, there have been significant developments in the field of inkjet printing, with the introduction of both UV-cured and solvent printers from companies such as Roland DG and Mimaki. UV-cured and solvent printers come in both wide-format and flat-bed versions. Solvent inks can be useful to the artist for several reasons: first, they print on a wider variety of substrates without losing colour intensity, and can be more durable in an outdoor environment; second, they can print onto really lightweight papers and tissues; third, white ink often comes as standard with these printers, which means you can print onto dark-coloured substrates. Inks are improving in terms of their environmental impact.

HP now manufactures what it calls a 'latex printer', which uses a large quantity of water – up to 65 per cent – rather than other solvents in its ink. This ink is a resin in suspension, and other manufacturers make a similar ink. The advantage of latex printers is that you get many of the benefits of the solvent printers with a lot less smell.

It is now possible to obtain pigment ink for all these inkjet technologies, and the early problems of fading and fugitive ink can be surmounted by using a good-quality pigment-ink manufacturer's own ink, rather than a cheap substitute. The old adage, 'you get what you pay for', applies across the board with almost any ink that you buy. Investing in good-quality artists' ink of any type is almost always the best long-term investment.

RISOGRAPHIC PRINTING

Risographic printers made by the Riso Kagaku Corporation in Japan have become very popular as a digital alternative to screen-printing in recent years. Riso is not a new technology, and is primarily based on the mimeograph printing first invented by Thomas Edison in 1876. The first commercial machine, produced in collaboration with the A.B. Dick company, was launched in 1887. A.B Dick went on to dominate the office duplicator market throughout the twentieth century.

It is a very popular process, used by many illustrators, graphic artists and printmakers. The current technology uses a rice bran-based oil in its inks in order to be more environmentally friendly. The process works best when using the branded inks from the Risograph company, although third-party inks are available and some are very good. However, as with all inks for digital printing processes it pays to match the ink to the machinery and the paper you are using. You are more likely to get a better result using the manufacturer's own brand of ink.

INK

Initially, ink for the inkjet printer was based on dye, which was perfectly reasonable, given the extremely fine dot size printed by a single printhead. The initial conception of these printers was as proofing machines for commercial litho; a matched print or pre-production proof needs only to be used for a few weeks before being discarded. The problems occurred when artists and photographers, who were seduced by the wider colour gamut that could be printed, took up the technology; the wide colour range was much greater than anything produced by commercial lithography. The quality of surface of the early Iris prints was also far more seductive than a standard four-colour lithographic print. The dye-based ink, however, was very fugitive and many of the

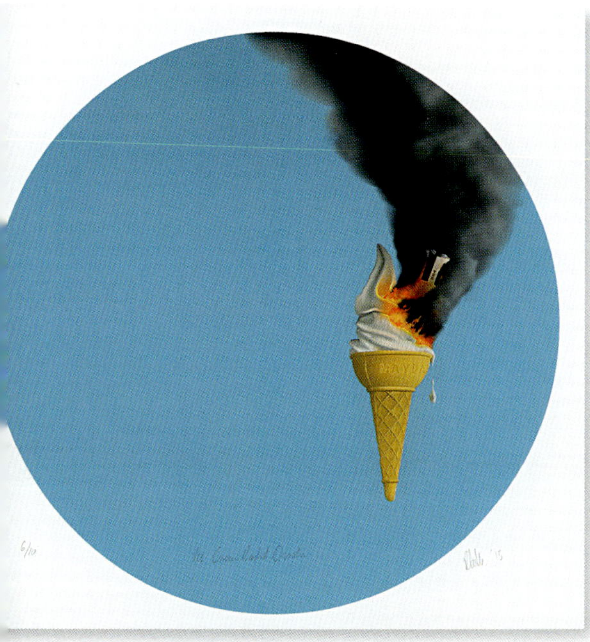

▲ **Richard Falle** *Ice Cream Rocket Disaster,* **2013. Pigmented inkjet, 56 x 76 cm.** Photo: Paul Laidler © CFPR, UWE, Bristol

early prints faded very quickly. Depending on the paper stock used, in some cases the prints faded in a matter of weeks rather than years.

To counteract this problem and, in the case of the larger manufacturers, to service the demand for large-format prints that could be displayed outdoors, pigment-ink sets began to be available. Initially for artists, these were manufactured by small companies such as Lyson, and were available for the Iris printers. As the market grew and the drop-on-demand printers manufactured by Epson took over due to the greatly reduced capital cost of the machine, a wider range of pigmented ink then became available. Unfortunately, at this point, exaggerated claims of lifespan exacerbated the confusion and uncertainty in the marketplace.

Fortunately for the printmaker, the confusion has now settled. Pigmented inks are now relatively stable, although it is not possible to predict stability unless one is aware of the particular combination of ink and paper. However, some generalisations may be made. First, always use pigmented ink. The colour gamut may not be quite as wide as the dye-based inks but it is much greater than any photographic colour gamut that you could obtain before inkjet appeared on the market. To make the best of this range you need to consider the paper profile you are using when you print. Much confusion exists about ICC (International Color Consortium) profiles for wide format, and this book is not the forum to deal with that problem.

However, it is sufficient to say that for artists' use, the most important profile is optimising the ink-and-paper combination, rather than trying to create an artificial profile optimised to a particular RIP (raster image processor – see p.201) designed for commercial-workflow requirements.

If you need a very simple solution for printing intense colour, try printing with the colour gamut setting on 'saturation' rather than 'perceptual'. This will put more ink on the paper and create an image with a greater contrast, though it will do little for the overall balance and quality of your image.

In tests undertaken in the past at the Centre for Print Research and by Wilhelm Imaging Research, both the Epson and HP inks seem to have similar lightfast characteristics. We did not make the same tests for the Lysonic pigmented sets, but circumstantial evidence seems to suggest that these inks have similar lightfast properties to the other pigmented sets.

Keep a close watch on the paper-and-ink combinations. Inks tend to be optimised for certain paper types and vice versa, so most of the coated paper for artists, such as Somerset Enhanced and Hahnemühle Digital FineArt Papers, are optimised for use with pigmented-ink sets. Uncoated, traditional artists' mould-made papers such as those made by Somerset, Arches, Hahnemühle and Fabriano tend to perform well in lightfast tests, both for dye-based and pigment inks, but the look of the print is much more subdued because the ink sinks into the paper surface. It is this characteristic that makes the paper-and-ink combination more resistant to fading.

The construction of the ink is based on very fine particles suspended in an aqueous solution. The liquidity of the water-based ink can create problems when trying to build intense colour; only a small amount of colour needs to be put onto the paper before bleeding or cockling of the paper occurs. This is a problem with any inkjet printing, as the most obvious characteristic of inkjet is also its limitation: it is only possible to put the print through the printer once in registration. Therefore, the density of colour obtainable is very restricted.

However, there are two mitigating factors for the inkjet printer that compensate for only being able to pass the paper through the printer once. The first is that due to eight-bit processing, it is possible to build upon a single dot of colour. The same dot can be printed up to four times in one pass. This allows for much greater tonal variation in the mid- to dark-tone sections of a print. The second factor is the greater gamut or colour range available from an inkjet printer. The CMYK inks of an inkjet printer are much more intense than a standard litho CMYK set, thus allowing a greater range of brighter colour to be printed.

In recent years, in terms of pigmented ink, most manufacturers offer a 10–12-colour ink set that includes cyan, magenta, yellow and black (CMYK), and red, green and blue (RGB). Other inks offered can include a light CMYK set, the addition of orange and a range of greys and blacks. Two factors explain why the trend has been to introduce light cyan and magenta into the colour sets before introducing an orange or green. Inkjet can print bright colour well, but has a greater problem rendering the lighter tertiary colours and flesh tones. Inkjet is still based on printing a dot structure, even though this is softened using error diffusion and stochastic algorithms (see p.201). In the light-tone areas, where the dots are widely spaced to create pale tone, it is easier to see the structure of the dots. Introducing a light cyan and magenta enables the light areas to use more dots to produce these lighter tones, thus creating a much smoother tone change from light to dark.

CASE STUDY

Stephen Hoskins

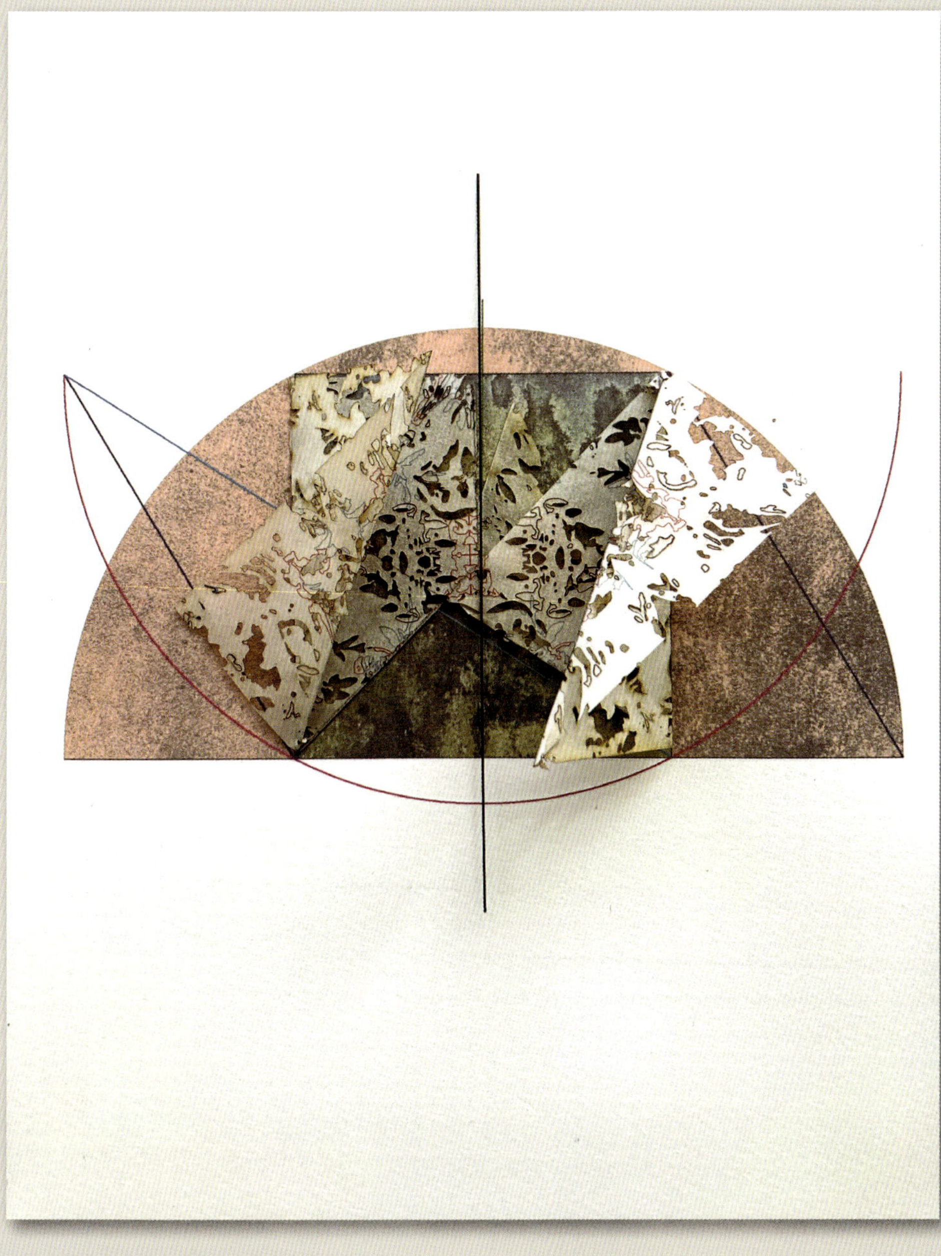

◄ Stephen Hoskins *Golden Section, Aribica*, 2013. Pigmented inkjet and laser cut handmade paper, 28 x 38 cm. Photo: Stephen Hoskins © Stephen Hoskins

Golden Section, Arabica, 2013

Inkjet print on Saunders 400 gsm paper, with laser cut, inkjet printed, handmade arabica and a carbon fibre rod. Edition of 20. Printed on 400 gsm Saunders with a Canon imagePROGRAF PRO-300 using Canon own-brand inks: the pigment-based Lucia Pro PFI-300 series. This is a 10-ink colour set that consists of: black, medium black, cyan, magenta, yellow, photo cyan, photo magenta, grey and chroma optimiser.

'I use this printer and ink set for two main reasons. The first is that this is a relatively affordable printer that will print 13 inches (32.5 cm) wide paper and pretty much any length. It will also feed up to 400 gsm paper. This means I can print on artists' papers such as Somerset, Saunders and Arches. I find that the pigmented inks give a pretty good intensity and coverage on these papers, without having to resort to the specialist inkjet coated versions.

The second reason is that the ink set is pigmented. From my research and collaboration with both HP and Canon in the early part of this century, pigmented ink is always the choice for the professional artist. To be honest, currently there is little to choose between the major manufacturers in terms of quality and lightfastness of their pigmented, UV or Latex ink sets. It becomes a matter of personal preference.

For photo cyan and magenta, one needs to read pale cyan and pale magenta, as these help the rendering of skin tones in photographs. Likewise, the grey helps this and lighter tones generally. The chroma optimiser is there primarily to make sure the surface appearance after printing on a gloss paper, looks even and consistent, without the bronzing and shine that sometimes comes with inkjet ink on glossy paper.

The cartridges only contain 14.4 ml of ink and a full set costs around £150. I find that I can print several editions from one set, which does not make the cost expensive per print, while I am achieving good-quality archival quality prints.

I always make my files in RGB Adobe 1998. In essence, all these printers take RGB files and then convert them at the last stage. I want the widest gamut possible out of the colour set; therefore, I do not use a RIP. A RIP is great if you want to match a colour from a supplied specification or sample, but it will always restrict the colour space available. I send my RGB files directly and then proof from the print in exactly the same way I would for a screen print or a litho. I am not concerned with reproduction, only the final original image I am creating.'

Lilienthal Feathers, 2013

Inkjet on Japanese handmade paper, screen print on plywood, 31 gsm Japanese paper, glass fibre rod.

'The central inkjet sections are printed on Sekishu Shi 31 gsm Japanese paper on a roll, using a Roland VersaUV LEC-300A. This is a solvent printer that uses eco-solvent UV ink. The printer prints with a CMYK, plus white, plus gloss ink set. Because the printer has UV solvent inks, it is just possible to print 31 gsm paper, but with extreme care, to avoid smashing the print heads. The advantage of a solvent ink set on such lightweight absorbent paper is that a much crisper and intense lay down of colour can be achieved without making the paper too wet and soggy. I like to be able to mix processes within one artwork (print). I use the Japanese paper because it wraps well around the balsa wood structure of the artwork.

The feathered sections of the work are screen-printed on plywood first, and then laser cut and assembled. I use TW1000 series water-based inks. I first encountered them in the mid 1990s in Los Angeles and was impressed with the colour, plus they use a clear base and a white base, with an extra opaque white to add to the base. Therefore, one can easily mix transparent or opaque intense colour. Also, TW make the best overprint gloss I have found in any water-based ink. The intense colour is added to the printing base and, although the colour is expensive to buy in the first place, it lasts a very long time. I have had some of my pots of colour for over 20 years. It is not an easy ink to print. It performs very like a solvent-based ink in that it dries very quickly in the screen if you do not keep the ink moving across the screen, as it is fairly self-solvent. I clean up with Mr Muscle® kitchen cleaner, but any mild alkaline cleaner will do. It means I can clean the screen in situ with a rag and then throw the rag away once fully saturated, rather than putting the acrylic ink down the drain. I dry and rotate my rags so that I get the most use out of them before disposal.'

Stephen Hoskins has been a practising printmaker for over 40 years, and is a firm advocate of traditional craft skills and the unsung societies that represent them. His work is an attempt to highlight those skills in a different context and show the art world that an appreciation of skill and aesthetics still have a place in contemporary society. His obsession with kites and aeroplanes is an appreciation of those unsung skills that are often hidden from mainstream society.

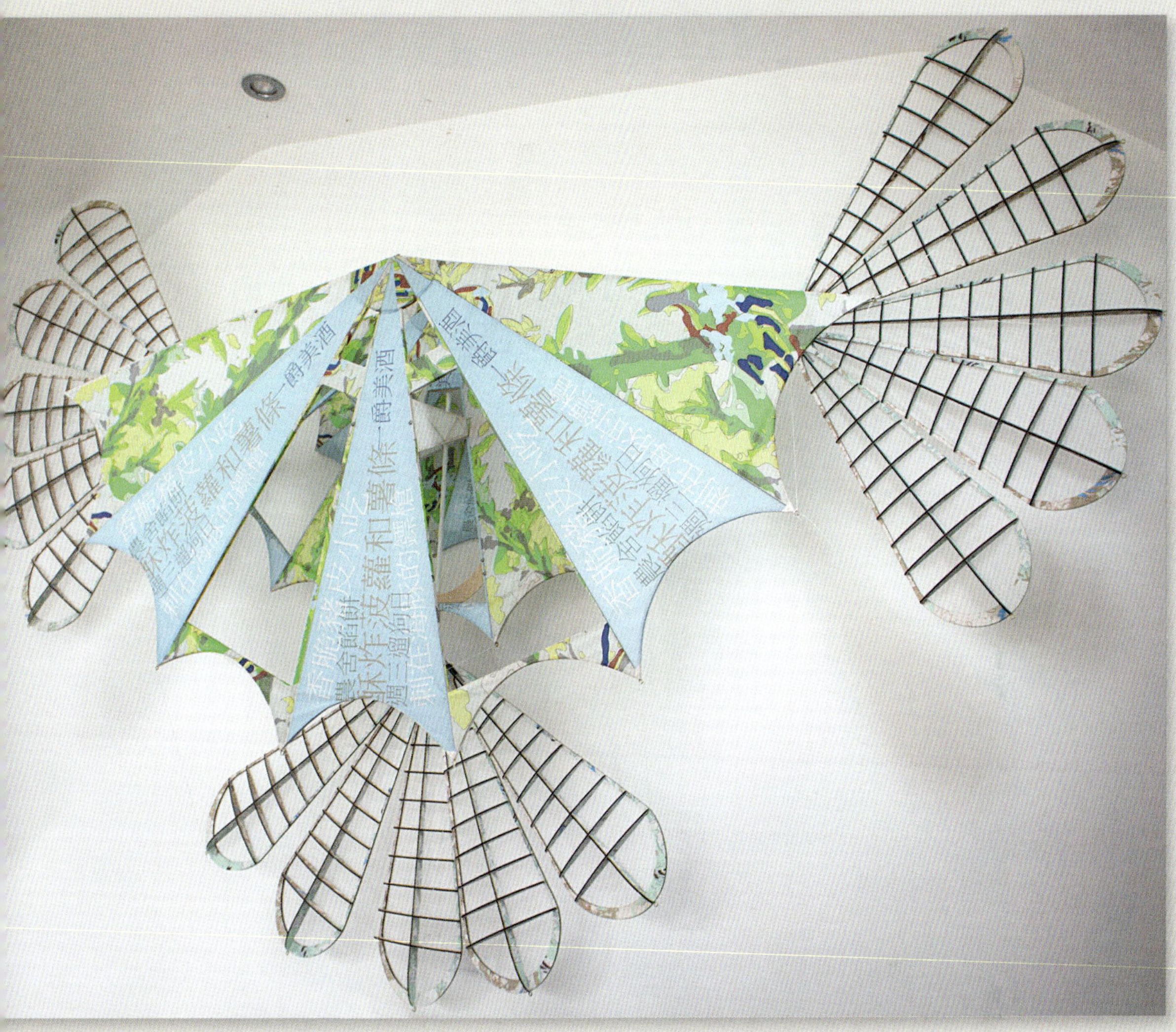

Stephen recently had a solo exhibition, *Flights of Fancy: Prints That Fly*, in Hong Kong. He has exhibited at the Krakow Biennale *Behind the Curtain* Exhibition, the *Original Print* Exhibition at the Bankside Gallery, London, The Royal Academy, London and at the London Original Print Fair. He undertook a residency at the Frans Masereel Centrum in Belgium in August, 2016 following a previous residency in 2014. His work is held in many collections worldwide, including the V&A, and the Tate, London, and corporate collections including Microsoft and Lloyds TSB.

▲ **Stephen Hoskins *Lilienthal Feathers*, 2013. Solvent inkjet, screen-printed plywood, balsa wood and handmade paper, 240 x 180 cm.** Photo: Stephen Hoskins © Stephen Hoskins

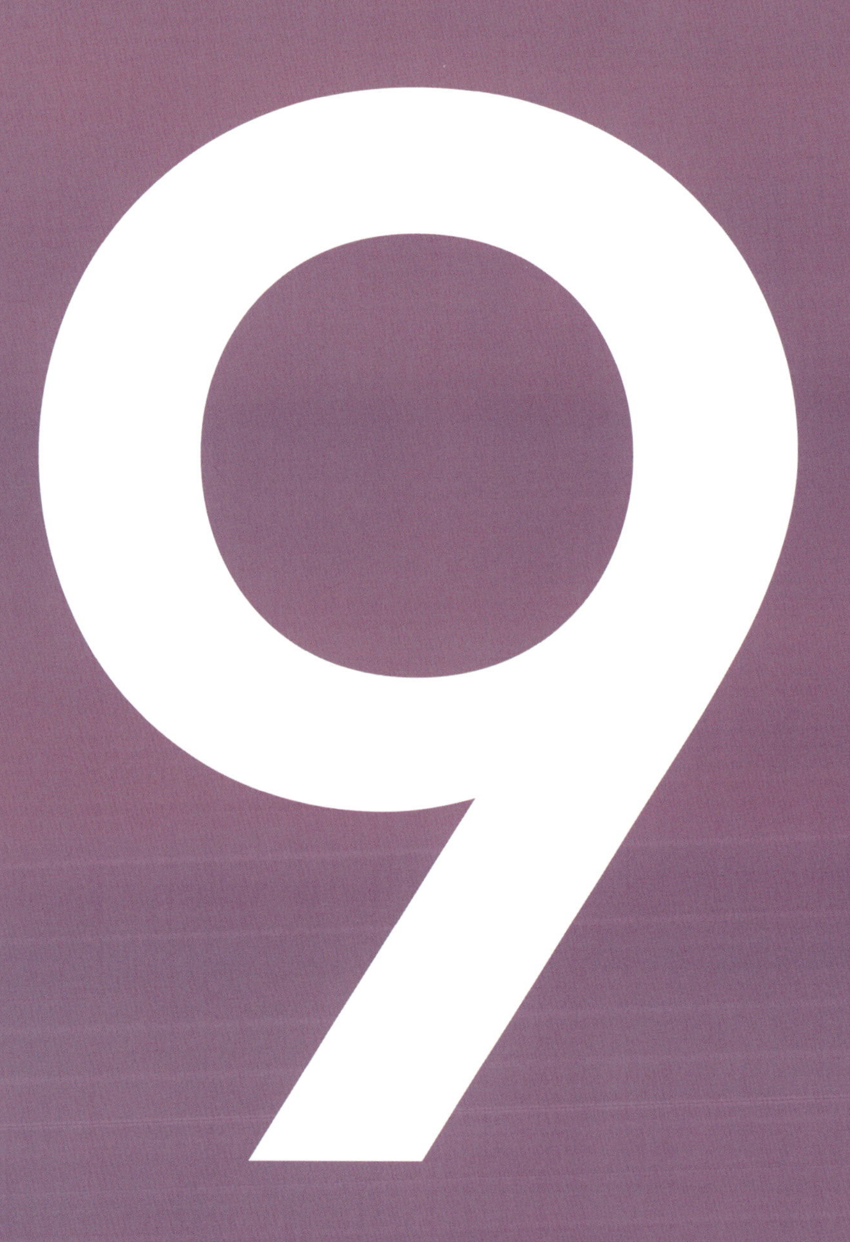

CHAPTER
9

HEALTH, SAFETY AND THE ENVIRONMENT:
The future of printmaking inks

Historically, print studios have not always been the safest of places to work. The potential for injury from moving parts, heavy lithographic stones, corrosive and poisonous chemicals, and poor ventilation made for grim statistics right up until the latter part of the twentieth century. While immeasurably improved, even today printmaking studios are on occasion still to be found in less than ideal situations, including poorly ventilated basements below pavement level, perhaps because of the space required and the weight of machinery.

Nonetheless, significant improvements in understanding and practice have been made in recent decades, with greater awareness of regulatory affairs, legal requirements and a desire to improve standards of housekeeping.

While different countries and regions will have their own unique regulations in place, there is international agreement that an understanding of the hierarchy of controls is a useful way to gauge and manage the risks in any working environment. It is rightly said that there are no such things as safe chemicals, just safe ways of handling them. Chemicals and processes that constitute a danger are still used in the printmaking studio, although they may accurately still be classified as 'without known hazard'. Similarly, a chemical may be classified as non-toxic, but that does not mean it is without danger when incorrectly used. This is true in our lives outside the studio where the deaths in the USA from water (generally seen as 'harmless'), are more than 3,500 per year through drowning.[56] Dwarfing this figure are the number of alcohol-related deaths, estimated at around 140,000 per annum in the USA alone.

Sourcing reliable figures for printmaking injuries and health impacts is almost impossible, but to give some context, the commercial printing sector of the 1970s was so strongly linked with injury through inadequate training, non-existent or overridden guarding, chemical poisoning and certain cancers associated with composing lead type and proximity to heavy metals used in ink production that many companies struggled to find insurers willing to underwrite the risk. Now, nearly all the small number of reported injuries are equipment- rather than chemical-related.

The hierarchy of control requires those using the studio to ask the first and obvious question about any and every chemical: 'Do we have to use it?' When it comes to the matter of ink, the answer is 'yes', but there is an element of choice here, as a range of possible ink types are available. However, it is inaccurate to suggest that water-based (or, more accurately, water-containing) inks are inherently safer than oil-based alternatives. There are environmental and health and safety advantages and disadvantages to both.

The replacement of heavy metal pigments has thankfully been completed by previous generations, and some of the most harmful of solvents are no longer available, so a level of elimination and substitution is complete.

Hierarchy of controls

Most effective	Elimination – physically remove the hazard and stop the process.
	Substitution – replace the hazard with something less harmful.
	Engineering controls – isolate people from the hazard.
	Administrative controls – change the way people work.
Least effective	PPE alone – protect the user with personal protective equipment.

For most studios, attention should be focused on the middle area of the hierarchy diagram, putting controls in place (ventilation, for example), changing working practices (with tidy working routines), and with the provision of PPE when required.

PRACTICAL STEPS TO KEEP A STUDIO SAFE

An obvious area to start with is the control of solvent vapour. The working environment is very important. A very large, well-ventilated studio space with a single person using a small amount of solvent is going to be very different to a small basement with many people using liberal amounts of solvent. Air flow should be uninterrupted with good ventilation throughout the studio. For those who find the smell of turpentine or mineral spirit objectionable, an organic vapour mask will be needed. The solvent particle is so small that it will pass through a standard face mask. Lids should be put back on all materials, and containers – especially those decanted in the studio for distribution to the workstations – should all be clearly labelled with a label that won't easily come off. Where products are decanted into non-standard containers, these should be suitable for the product and purpose.

For the care of the environment, water-based formulations should be treated with the same caution as any other chemical. Water itself is a solvent, and formulations contain biocides and fungicides to prevent bacterial growth, which can present an irritant to the user and are harmful for the environment. Acrylic formulations are essentially microplastics and should be disposed of

▼ **Health and safety suit.**
Photo: Jo Hounsome Photography © Cranfield Colours

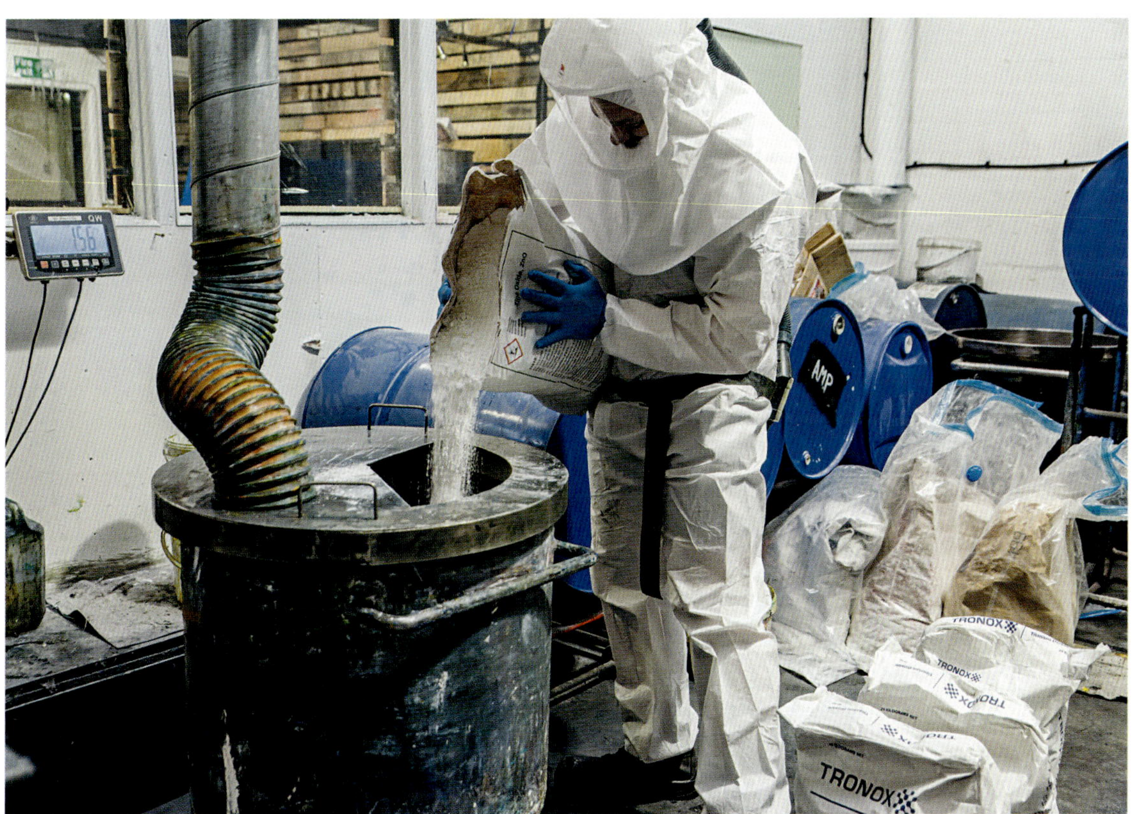

in accordance with local instructions. Plastic filtration procedures should be in place for washing up acrylic inks (see p.164).

One of the most common issues faced in today's studios, where risks have largely been reduced to an acceptable level, is that of skin irritation or dermatitis. Any solvent, including hand soap, will remove sebum – the skin's natural greasy protection. We have access to copious amounts of very hot water that would be unimaginable to our forebears. The constant washing of hands in hot water exposes the skin to other chemicals that may otherwise be entirely innocuous and not generally associated with sensitisation, causing contact dermatitis.

Contact dermatitis can be prevented by: washing hands less frequently using cold or lukewarm water; wearing protective clothing or gloves to shield from substances that cause irritation; and applying a barrier cream at the start of the working day and after each hand washing to help protect and moisturise the skin. Regularly applying moisturising lotions can help restore the skin's outermost layer and keep skin supple.

Perhaps the most important task of those responsible for their own health and that of others in the studio is education. It is good to have a healthy respect and caution when using chemicals, especially for the first time, without instilling an attitude of fear. Reading the label is not always a natural desire, but it is important. It is essential that we educate ourselves and never assume that we know the risks – formulations may change over time.

Not all vegetable-derived solvents (while providing a useful function in the studio) should be treated as being entirely without risk. The pleasant odour alone does not tell us all we need to know. Some solvents labelled as studio safe may be a blend of citrus oils and a hydrocarbon, and this will only be evident from the label. Even if entirely citrus based, if the solvent has the power to remove oil-based ink, it will also remove the skin's natural protection. It's what solvents do!

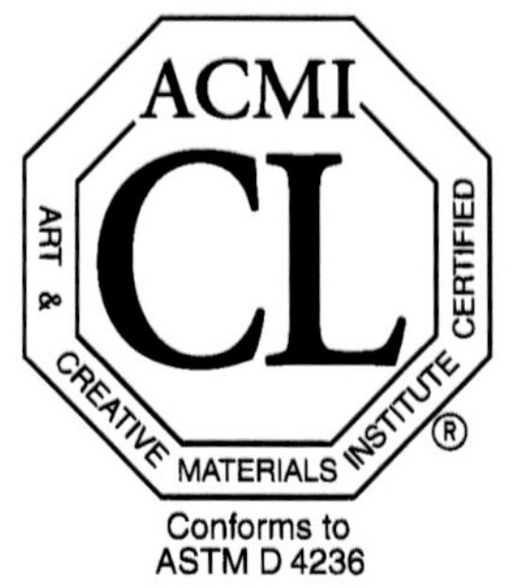

CL Seal

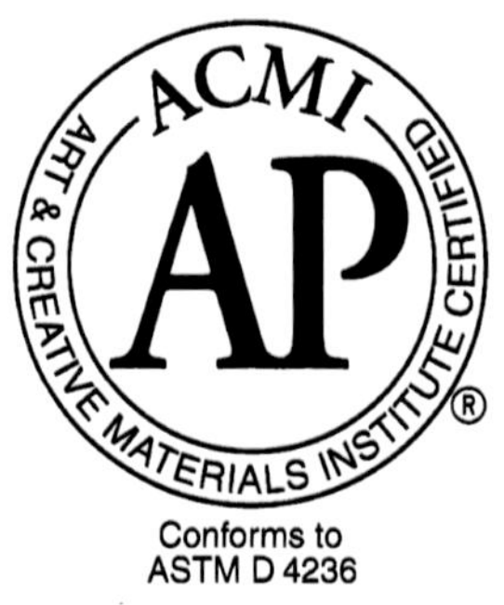

AP Seal

IMPROVED LABELLING

Today, printmakers can use inks that are clearly labelled and supported by harmonised hazard symbols and material safety data sheets (MSDS). These are obtainable by law from any supplier or manufacturer, and should be kept and read. It is possible for the user to make informed choices. Further assurance and guidance is provided by such bodies as the ACMI in the USA, which provides a clear logo that interprets compliance to US regulatory affairs to give the internationally recognised symbols for Approved Product (AP) and Cautionary Labelling (CL).

The CL logo informs the user that, while approved for use, greater caution is required with such products. This may be because of hydrocarbon content, or because the formulation contains an earth pigment where it is impossible to rule out the presence of certain trace element contamination, e.g., from heavy metals naturally found in the earth.

UNDERSTANDING RISKS TO THE BODY

There are four ways that a substance can enter the body and cause harm:
- Ingestion (eating)
- Respiration (breathing)
- Through the skin
- Via the eye

The effect of a toxic material could be of two kinds: acute or chronic. A good example of the difference between the two would be the effects of alcohol. The acute effect is the sense of euphoria, dizziness and the headache the following morning. The chronic effects would be liver damage and the socio-economic and domestic impact of alcohol.

Chemical hazards as encountered in everyday life and in the studio may present an acute, chronic or combined risk, and an understanding of this science is important so that each substance is handled correctly.

It is worth remembering that chemically inert substances may not be without hazards. Any dust is combustible, and any explosion will be harmful to the printmaker, whatever it says on the label of the tin! Dust is also a respiratory hazard, even if the compound itself, now in micronised-form floating in the atmosphere, is not otherwise classified as a hazard.

This is why good housekeeping is essential in the studio: keeping lids on all products when not in use; keeping used rags in a container with a closed airtight lid; listing the products used; and taking actions based on the potency of the material and the length of time we are exposed to it.

HAZARD LABELS

Understanding hazard symbols is important. Pictograms, now internationally harmonised and recognised, should be evident on any chemical that is classified as presenting a possible hazard.

Printmakers should take special care when using chemicals that may still be in the cupboard of an older studio after many years. These older chemicals are

International hazard labels

Skull and crossbones

The skull and crossbones symbol is the most extreme of the classifications. Such products should not be found in any printmaking studio. They will prove fatal if taken into the body.

Exploding heart

The exploding heart tells the user of significant damage to organs or affects that are long term/chronic. The label should indicate what the risk is and how it might be mitigated.

Corrosive

The hazard warning showing a chemical being poured onto a human hand and onto an unspecified surface tells us of the corrosive nature of the chemical.

Environmentally damaging

Flammable

The flame symbol warns of flammable products, while the exploding bomb symbol warns of explosive chemicals.

Irritant/general hazard

This exclamation mark is the lowest level of warning but should still be taken seriously. It is a general hazard symbol that indicates the presence of substances dangerous to health, which may cause irritation, dizziness or allergic reactions.

more likely to contain substances that would not be used today *and* they were produced at a time before the warnings (both in text and pictograms) were widely and internationally adopted!

INTERNATIONAL REGULATORY AFFAIRS AND LABEL ANOMALIES

While toxicology is an exact science, the interpretation of regulatory consequences, legislation and guidelines differ around the world and are not always uniformly informative or helpful. Some countries may use terms such as 'may be harmful' until proof is supplied that the product does not present a risk. With some small product lines that are for specific use, there may be insufficient sales to justify the very high costs of toxicological testing and certification. In California, for example, the risk of possible litigation means that very many compounds seen as low or no risk elsewhere carry warnings.

Great strides have been made in European countries, with proposals to establish poison centres so that if anyone is exposed to a chemical and needs medical attention, medics will be able to contact a national poison centre quoting the product reference to receive full disclosure of the risks, potency and suggested treatment.

THE USE OF THE TERM 'NON-TOXIC' IN PRINTMAKING

Generally, terms such as 'non-toxic' can be unhelpful when applied to chemicals or compounds, as they are used in a context that may either mitigate or aggravate any health or safety risk. To this end, the truism that 'there is no such thing as safe chemicals, just a safe way of handling them' is helpful.

Analysis of the life cycle of oil-based printmaking inks highlights their surprisingly low impact on the environment. The growing awareness of environmental impact of microplastics and biocides on the environment has somewhat clouded the reputation of acrylic and some water-based inks, and concerns both the formulations and the plastic packaging.

A similar sense of unease surrounds the widespread dependence on vegetable oils such as soya that are generally farmed in a more aggressive or corporate manner than the smaller linseed sector. Soya production is highly mechanised and requires extensive irrigation. The term 'oil-based' is therefore so broad as to be almost meaningless, and individual printmakers will want to research so as to make their own informed choice.

The printmaker now has access to a safer environment with lower risk alternatives for a wide range of studio chemicals, and there really should be few, if any, circumstances where the average studio environment has any chemical labelled with the exploding heart symbol.

Given that the need for highly toxic chemicals has largely been eliminated from the printmaking studio, printmakers may be tempted to show less care or respect for non-toxic products that may nonetheless still carry a risk to either the environment or to the user. Health and safety in the workplace is a major issue for printmakers, especially those in colleges and universities. Control of Substances Hazardous to Health (COSHH) regulations and risk assessments are a major consideration of any studio in the twenty-first century.

COSHH

A COSHH assessment concentrates on the hazards and risks from hazardous substances in the workplace, which a studio most definitely is. The UK legislation UK is directed at workplaces rather than private homes or individual studios. However, the motivation behind COSHH is useful for everyone as it encourages an awareness that health hazards are not limited to substances labelled 'hazardous'. Some harmful substances can be produced by the processes we use, for example, wood dust from the preparation of woodblocks.

Some problems for COSHH and its users relate to the volatile organic compounds (VOCs) such as turps substitute, which is used to clean up oil-based inks. These solvents in high concentrations have been proven hazardous to health. Some overreaction and confusion has arisen about the use and abuse of such substances. The measurement of hazard ratings for solvents relates to parts per million (ppm) in the atmosphere. Therefore, if a workshop has good housekeeping practices, is large and well-ventilated and only uses a small amount of solvent to clean up at the end of the day, the ppm count will be very low. If, on the other hand, the workshop is in a small, enclosed space with poor ventilation and lax housekeeping, with open cans and liberal use of solvent, the ppm count can be very high. The ventilation of a space is the most important issue, with good housekeeping a close second.

The careful handling of waste printmaking ink and its correct disposal remain at the heart of good housekeeping. For example, if, when cleaning up the ink at the end of printing, all the surplus ink is scraped up and put onto paper or a rag, and then placed in a bin, then cleaning takes less solvent and there is less potential for ink residues to enter the water table through disposal in the waste system.

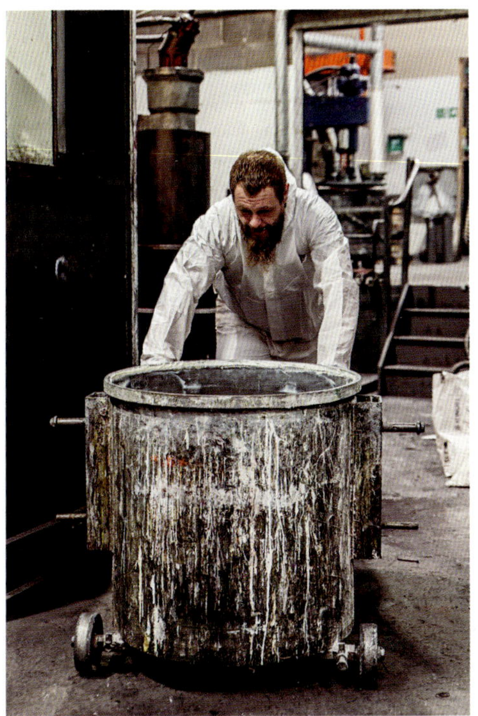

Most users of printmaking ink will be fully aware that, for financial reasons alone, wasting ink is a bad idea. The printmaker will therefore want most of the ink to leave the studio on paper as a work of art, rather than via the dustbin. Through careful storage and use, the contents of most tubes and tins will be thoroughly exhausted, and may be considered emptied packaging, which can be processed through the usual household waste channels.

Concerning the cleaning of ink knives, rollers etc., remnants should never be simply flushed down the sink, even for water-miscible inks, including acrylic. Instead, take a paper towel or old newspaper, wipe the item as clean as possible and dispose of the waste through the usual channels. Ink can be retained in a suitable airtight tin or jar and can be used to make some wonderful grey shade.

▲ **Good overalls.**
Photo: Jo Hounsome
Photography © Cranfield
Colours

MATERIAL SAFETY DATA SHEETS

It is the legal duty of all manufacturers to supply those in the retail chain with a safety data sheet (SDS), sometimes referred to as a material safety data sheet (MSDS). The manufacturer is not obliged to divulge the detail of the formulation, as that would compromise their commercial position or reveal the manufacturing process. Instead, the MSDS will contain information on the potential hazards (health, fire, reactivity and environmental) and how to work safely with the chemical product. It is a logical and essential starting point for the development of a complete health and safety policy for the studio. The MSDS also contains information on the use, storage, handling and emergency procedures related to the hazards of the material. It is intended to outline the hazards of the product, how to use the product safely, what to expect if the recommendations are not followed, how to recognise symptoms of overexposure, and what to do if such incidents occur.

RISK ASSESSMENTS

Helpful developments in the field of health and safety include the development of risk assessments that take into account the likely exposure scenarios. These encourage greater consideration of the chemical in question in its common usage. For example, it may be deemed preferable to use a slightly stronger and more effective solvent than a solvent of lower potency if the stronger solvent will decrease the quantity required and reduce the length of time needed.

The length of exposure to chemicals, the competence and experience of the user and the general environment are all variables, so it follows that the risks will not be uniform. To ensure a right approach to health and safety, the printmaker and those responsible for a shared space will want to use information provided by the product labels, MSDS sheets and COSHH assessments to conduct a risk assessment. This will include environmental and mechanical risks, and requires checking whether devices and machines are adequately guarded, and chemicals that could present any kind of hazard (including slip hazards) are marked and in suitable containers.

WHAT ARE THE CURRENT ENVIRONMENTAL ISSUES?

This issue is subject to more misinformation than almost any other in the field of printmaking. There is tension between safe working practices, ease of use for the practitioner and the long-term health of the environment. These factors are not always compatible. Take the example of professional etching ink that we looked at in Chapter 4. This contains carbon black pigment and linseed oil. Carbon black is usually created by burning oil or gas, and linseed oil occurs naturally in the linseed plant. Therefore, this particular ink is safe to use and not harmful to the environment. Carbon is inert and linseed oil is sustainable. However, coloured inks of any form are never simple in environmental terms; inks made from heavy metals and similar compounds are now non-existent, but other coloured pigments are not necessarily 'healthy' in environmental terms and are still manufactured as products of the huge petrochemical industry. The individual will always have to make certain compromises between their ideals, their aesthetics and their environment if specific qualities of colour are required.

The careful handling of waste printmaking ink and its correct disposal remain at the heart of good housekeeping and is a factor in better environmental disposal of ink. Preventing or minimising waste in the first place requires good housekeeping: replacing the caps on tubes and the protective film and lids on tins, and avoiding the unforgivable crime of plunging the ink knife deeply into the tin of ink.

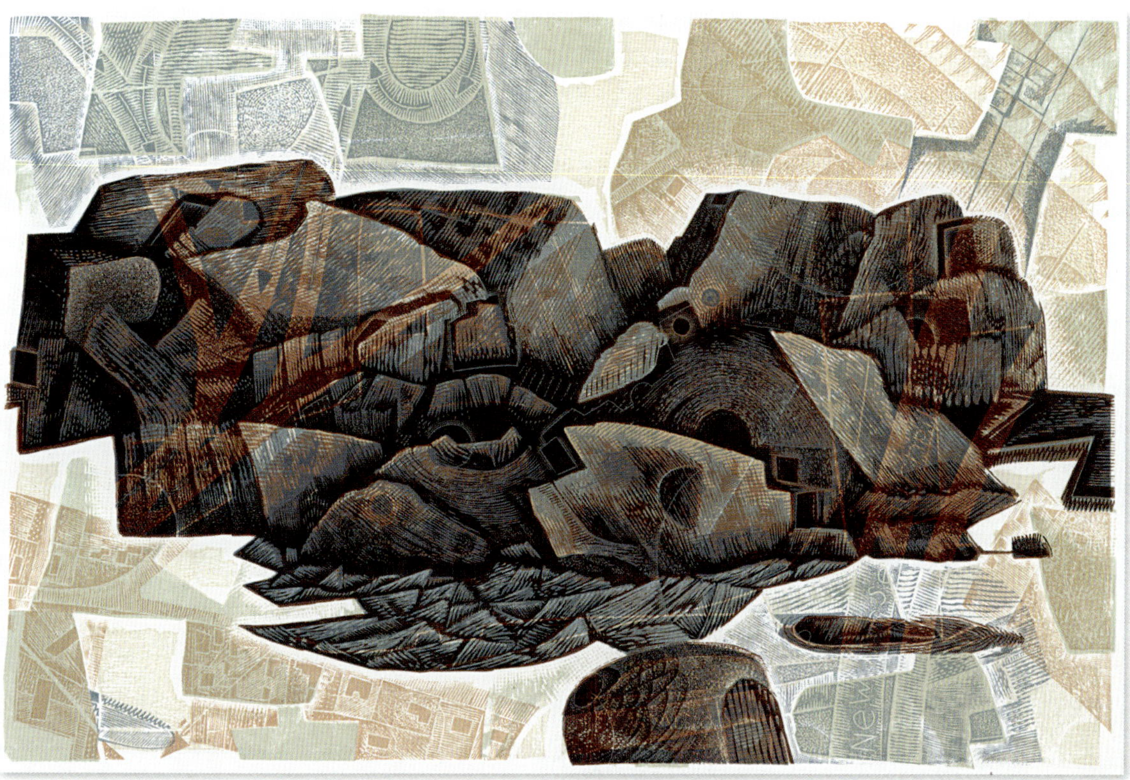

▲ Neil Bousfield *New Jersey Turnpike*, 2022. **Reduction engraving and woodcut, 12.5 x 19 cm.** Photo: Neil Bousfield © Neil Bousfield

LIFE CYCLE ANALYSIS

A life cycle analysis is a study of the environmental impact of a product or process in the context of its entire life history. Printmaking inks themselves have a positive effect on society, mental health and the economy. They provide employment and economic benefits, and contribute enormously to well-being. The packaging is also found to be effective and proportionate.

By prolonging the life of artists' products by using high-quality ingredients and protective packaging, the ink maker is able to contribute to a cycle that provides aesthetically appealing works of art that have value and will be retained by the printmaker or purchaser, thereby saving resources from both an environmental and an economic perspective when compared with cheaper, disposable art forms such as commercially reproduced posters and prints.

CONCLUSION

We hope that the second edition of this book will remain of use to printmakers for a number of years, not for our own benefit, but with the understanding that the discipline of printmaking has not abandoned its roots for the glamour of new technology. We are heartened to see that the growth of the internet has had a positive effect on spreading the discipline.

We also hope that practitioners will not just abandon old methods as health and safety legislation and attitudes evolve. Although there is good reason for considering the health and safety aspects of the product you are using, materials and methods have not developed over very long periods of time without being effective at the job for which they were created. We hope we have described the processes by which ink is manufactured and thereby put the manufacture into context in terms of the different qualities and performances printmakers require from their inks.

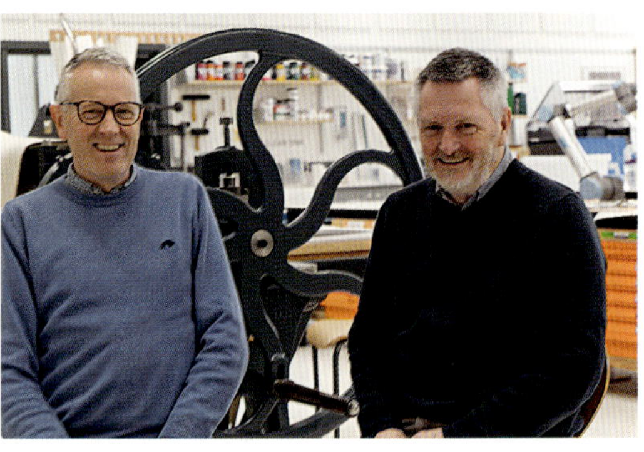

▲ **Authors: Stephen Hoskins and Michael Craine.** Photo: Frank Menger

It is our wish that this book should provide some insight regarding how and why a particular ink may perform a specific task, and, if it doesn't perform as you hoped, why the manufacturer may have been unaware of your particular and personal requirements.

To cope with the changes that are currently taking place in the world of print, artists have to retain a firm grasp on the historic context of their materials, but they must also understand that rapid change is inevitable. In addition to the potential of mixing new and old technologies to obtain a greater vocabulary for print, there are some exciting opportunities for new materials within traditional print manufacture, such as synthetic resins, new polymer bonds and replacements for traditional linseed oils. These changes need to be carefully evaluated, while also keeping in mind that if a new product performs better at the task required, and is stable and reasonably lightfast, there is every reason to embrace new technology, especially if it means creating a healthier environment in which to work.

The discipline of printmaking, even given its recent expansion in global terms, is tiny when compared with other arts. We demand very specialised products and materials and, therefore, as a discipline we need to remember

that the specialist manufacturers and suppliers are also tiny companies, often with fewer than 15 employees. Without the full support of the community those companies and suppliers are vulnerable and could easily cease to exist.

Fortunately, the rush to embrace healthier products with almost evangelical zeal has slowed recently, and printmakers are more reasonably assessing their materials. Water-based screen inks made sense for the majority of users, as the traditional product was definitely not very healthy, but they are now due for reappraisal as the traditional product may, in the long term, be less harmful to the environment. Many of the other, 'healthier' replacements offered little advantage to the professional printmaker. At the Centre for Print Research, we have tried to appraise products in the light of their historic context; beyond this is the quest for the best possible quality.

If the content and conception of the idea is of the highest quality, then there is no point in using inferior-quality products. There is a need for a printmaking knowledge and skills resource; this should not be a dead repository, but a store that functions in a living working environment where historical knowledge is evaluated against new knowledge.

It is only by building on the proven foundations of our shared past and by utilising the best of today's technology that printmaking, in all its great variety, can be assured of an equally exciting future.

▼ Miniature prints from the annual UWE Bristol staff and student miniature print exhibition © CFPR

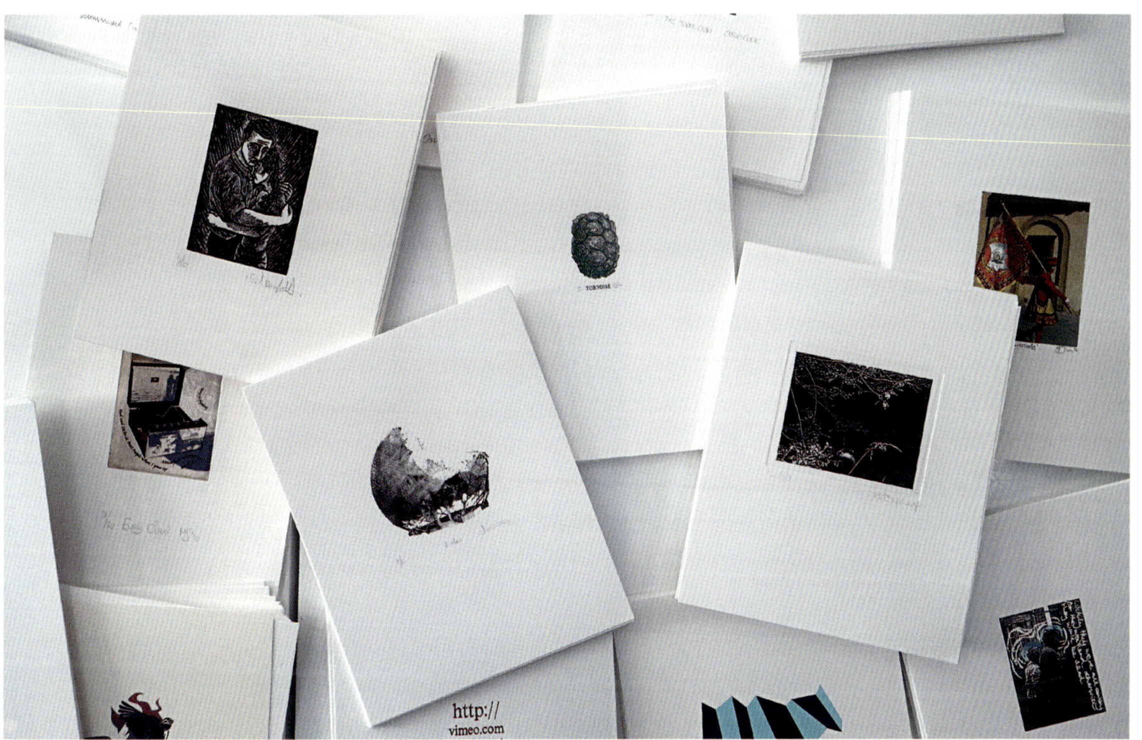

RESEARCH ISSUES

There is a lack of a substantial, focused literature about printmaking inks. Therefore, a significant and essential part of the work on this book has been original research, necessary to extend the basis of knowledge of ink as part of the printing process. There are several underlying assumptions underpinning this research and the validity of the statements in this book.

All research for a practical subject – in this case, creative development in the art, design and craft of fine print – is often based on a simple pattern of discovery and research through looking, reading, doing, using, experimenting and experience. Results of research by printmakers are often inherent in their work, but are not always recorded in any other way. Yet the methodology for new development in the visual arts, either in terms of incremental improvements or innovative developments, is well tested in the training and educational programmes for professional practitioners.

As one works on the creation of a print, or any other visual product, problems often appear which will require further work to solve. For the most part, this means honing practice, but searching for solutions often also involves seeking examples or literature that might provide answers. This is where a methodological research problem crops up. How can one be sure that the literature or work chosen holds the right answer? Often, reference material can be random, based on ease of availability. Source material can be too extensive to filter through, and at some point choices must be made to limit the range, based on assumptions which might lead to less successful choices. This abundance of material is certainly the case for print-based research. The wealth of materials available worldwide is staggering. On the other hand, as is the case when narrowing research to the subject of ink, source material is not very readily available and requires a search for new insights based on scant or difficult-to-obtain material. That, too, poses philosophical problems about how sure one can be that the new insight is actually valid.

In either case, one can base their experiments on insight gained from

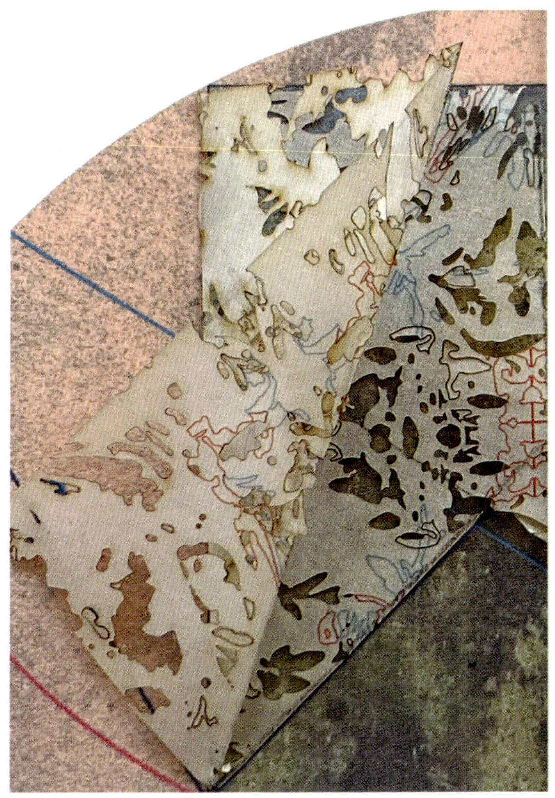

▲ Detail of *Golden Section, Aribica*, 2013. Pigmented inkjet and laser cut handmade paper, 28 x 38 cm.
Photo: Stephen Hoskins
© Stephen Hoskins

others or one can ignore the literature and start to experiment until something acceptable occurs. Many professional artists and designers try their experiments in a systematic fashion; others believe in random tryouts. This implies that there are at least three main approaches to professional relevant research:

- looking at examples done by others and comparing these with own work;
- reading how others have done relevant work and trying things out;
- seeking new ideas and solutions, regardless of previous experiences.

The first method is essential for quality control and quality improvement, for looking at how ink is bonded to the paper and assessing if this enhances or detracts from the visual quality of the image.

The second method is useful to extend one's experience and maintain professional standards. It can confirm existing or generate new ideas for a practitioner. However, it seldom leads to innovation, since it is philosophically based on using information that is, in principle, already known and available to the profession. Its strengths lie, therefore, in finding ways for incremental improvements.

The third method is more radical. It is, however, unlikely to lead to anything useful for others unless the person who follows it has the knowledge and experience to recognise in the results that something new has occurred. Thus results of free experimentation can generate fun and satisfactory results, but also lead often to useless work. Only deep understanding from experience and from the literature can generate the insight to recognise if such free experimental work leads to outcomes that were previously unknown and are worth sharing with the profession. Free experimentation is, in principle if not in practice, random since it builds on availability of knowledge, materials, techniques and talent. A dearth of those, and chances diminish that something useful will occur. Increase the volume of available research resources – talent, knowledge and infrastructure – and chances for success will increase.

This study, like many in this field, is founded on a combination of methods based on these three principles for the development of professional practice.

Combining them is done by seeking to compensate for possible weaknesses in each approach and adding other research methods to emphasise the advantages inherent in each available research tool or researcher.

Reporting on the outcome of research is twofold. Above all, for printmaking, results count in the finished work exhibited for peer evaluation and for commercial fortune in the marketplace. This does not indicate whether research was based on observation, a review of ideas created by others or levels of personal experimentation. Publishing written reviews of research does this, and also requires outlining insights and assumptions before more profound statements can be given as facts.

The first chapter of this book, for example, is mainly based on available literature that emphasises ink usage in the wider remit of print practice. This approach allows for gathering scant and scattered information about ink by drawing it into a more easily accessible arena focused on the historical developments of mark making, writing, drawing, photography and printing in terms of the relationship with the materials and techniques that underpin these processes. The subsequent chapters are based more on reports of experience with ink, which have been gathered worldwide from major studios, manufacturers and individual artists, as well as from in-house experience gained through our own experiments.

The framework for selecting information from all these practice-based sources is based on years of involvement in building national and international networks for fine print. Contacts have been established through participation in exhibitions of work for peer evaluation, conferences and presentations, as well as through conference and course organisation by our research teams in Bristol. Ideas gathered in these ways have been systematically tested through different research project settings by different fine-print researchers. This has neutralised any unwitting bias towards any particular material or procedure. Research projects were either curiosity-driven or based on conditions defined by grants gained in a competitive tendering process within the research communities of the UK, the EU and agencies in the US and South Africa.

GLOSSARY OF TERMS, TECHNIQUES AND MATERIALS

Agglomerates
Primary particles and aggregates joined at the corners and edges in a looser type of arrangement than found in aggregates.

Aggregates
Collections of primary particles that are attached to each other at their surface or crystal faces and show a tightly packed structure.

à la poupée
A method of putting several inks on one or more etching plates using folded pieces of scrim known as dollies (*poupées* in French). This name refers to the small, doll-like shape created when a piece of scrim is loosely rolled and then folded in half and secured with a band of tape wound around it. These dabbers are used selectively, one for each colour, to apply ink to the plate.

Algorithm
A procedure or formula for solving a problem, used within computer code to enable a calculation or process to occur.

ASTM standards
Performance or chemical standards for industrial materials and components set by the ASTM (American Society of Testing and Materials).
www.astm.org

Calcine
To reduce to a powder or to a friable state, as volatile components are expelled by means of heat and so, usually, to produce disintegration, such as carbonic acid from limestone.

CMYK
Cyan, magenta, yellow and keyline (black). Cyan, magenta and yellow are the subtractive primaries identified as the opposites to red, green and blue (the additive primaries). The keyline colour that holds these together has always been the black plate.

COSHH
Control of Substances Hazardous to Health. UK government legislation concerning the use of chemicals in the workplace. Two useful websites for further reference are: www.hse.gov.uk and www.hse.gov.uk/coshh/essentials/index.htm

Densitometer
An instrument for measuring the density of black in a print. A densitometer works by measuring the amount of light reflected by a printed substrate – this is transferred to a logarithmic scale where 0 = 100% reflectance (or white), 0.3 = 50% reflectance (or mid-grey), 2.0 = 10% reflectance (looking black), and 3.0 = 1% reflectance (very intense black). A densitometer is also used to measure the density of a negative or a positive for printing.

Dyes
Colour additives that are soluble in the medium in which they are used.

Easy Wipe
A proprietary additive made by Graphic Chemical for adding to etching ink to make the plate wipe cleanly, and to assist in ease of printing.

Flocculates
Primary particle aggregates and agglomerates generally arranged in a fairly open structure. They may be broken down easily under shear, but will form again when such shear forces are removed and the dispersion is allowed to stand undisturbed.

Frankfurt black
A carbon pigment known as vine black, particularly favoured by etchers until the early 1960s. It was made by burning the lees or sediment left at the bottom of a wine vat. The reason for its popularity was due to its granular structure, as opposed to the light and fluffy nature of lampblack pigment, so it was easier to wipe from an etching plate. It is also recorded as being made from burnt vine twigs, with additives such as burnt sheep's bones and burnt peach stones.

Friability
Tendency to crack, lack of flexibility.

Lake colours
Lake pigments are derived from colours that are laked
– bonded chemically to a colourless, insoluble salt that
acts as its own mordant – which turns the dye into an
insoluble pigment. Among the more common mordants
used in laked pigments are chalk (calcium carbonate)
and alum (aluminium potassium sulphate – used to lake
pigments since the Roman era).

Lampblack
The creation of this black for printing has a long and
well-documented history; Bloy devoted a chapter to
it and Fertel gave a detailed description of how it is
made. Lampblack was created by gathering the carbon
from the smoke given off by burning oil. The methods
of doing this are many, and a few examples have been
illustrated in this book.

Lumen (fibres)
The hollow channel running the length of natural
fibres. The lumen originally carried sap through a plant
but once these fibres are incorporated in paper, they
provide absorbency for printmaking ink.

Lumens (light)
A unit of measurement for visible light emanating from
a light source. With the development of energy efficient
lighting, the Lumen is increasingly helpful where
traditional values such as wattage are no longer directly
linked with the brightness of a bulb.

MSDS
Materials Safety Data Sheets. The American Health and
Safety in the Workplace Standards, the equivalent of the
UK COSHH.

Muller
A pestle of stone or glass, flat at the bottom, used for
grinding ink or colour pigment.

Particle size
The size of particles of pigment measured in microns.
This is important in printing as particle size can have a
large influence on how an ink will print.

Pick
The term used to describe the pulling away of fibres
from the surface of the paper by the ink during printing.
Defined by the Wax Pick Test, which is important in
checking surface strength that could affect linting
and picking. Sticks of special wax of varying adhesive
strengths (made by Dennison and rated 2A to 26A) are
melted and applied to a sheet, then pulled off when
cool. The result is reported as the highest number wax
that does not disturb the surface of the sheet. This test
should not be attempted on loosely felted papers or on
coated papers containing thermoplastic resins. While
the Wax Pick Test is still widely used in the industry, its
limited application has led to the use of other devices,
particularly on coated papers (www.legionpaper.com).

Pigment
The definition of a pigment proposed by the Color
Pigment Manufacturers' Association is: 'Pigments are
colored, black, white or fluorescent particulate organic
and inorganic solids which usually are insoluble and
essentially physically and chemically unaffected by the
vehicle or substrate in which they are incorporated.
They alter appearance by selective absorption and/
or by scattering light. Pigments are usually dispersed
in a vehicle or substrates for application. Pigments
retain a crystal or particulate structure throughout the
coloration process.'

Pigments are divided into two broad categories:
organic and inorganic. The organic pigments are
generally brighter and more intense than the inorganic
ones. On the other hand, the inorganic pigments exhibit
better stability than organic ones.

Pigment wetting
Describes the process whereby the medium covers the
surface of each pigment particle, hence wetting the
pigment.

Poise
The European system of measuring viscosity in
printing oils, ranging from 1 for the very thinnest and
most watery through to 700 for the thick and viscous
varnishes with a toffee-like consistency. There is also
a system of micropoise for measuring the viscosity of
liquids such as petrol where 100mP = 1 poise.

Polymers
Polymers can be both naturally occurring and synthetic
substances made up of large molecules known as
'macromolecules'. These are multiples of the basic
chemical unit of monomers or 'mers'. Where polymers
are made up of two or more different monomers, they
are known as 'copolymers'.

ppm
Parts per million. This is a means of describing how much of a substance is contained in a sample, i.e., parts of analyte per million parts of sample.

Rheology
The branch of science that deals with the deformation and flow of matter, especially the non-Newtonian flow of liquids.

RIP
Raster image processor. A device, consisting of hardware or software, that converts vector graphics or text into a raster (bitmapped) image. Raster image processors are used in page printers, phototypesetters and electrostatic plotters. They compute the brightness and colour value of each pixel on the page so that the resulting pattern of pixels recreates the vector graphics and text originally described.

Spectrophotometer
In simple terms, this is a device for measuring and assigning a numeric value to a colour for reproduction purposes. Essential in the creation of profiles for colour management. A more precise definition is: an instrument for measuring the ratio of two values of a radiometric quantity at the same wavelength. Normally, one of these values represents the sample, and the other a reference white.

Squash
Most common in litho, but occurs in all printing. Happens when the print is under pressure during printing and spreads beyond the area defined on the plate for holding the colour.

Stochastic printing
Also known as frequency modulation. A halftoning method that uses smaller dots than conventional halftone and distributes them within the print in random patterns determined by mathematical algorithms, thus reducing the potential for moiré and enabling more colours to be printed.

Undertones
Easier to describe with black ink. The colour that an ink shows when made transparent. Blacks usually have blue or brown undertones when transparent medium is added.

Varnish numbers
The American system of measuring viscosity in printing oils, ranging from #00000 for the very thinnest and most watery through to #10 for the thick and viscous varnishes with a toffee-like consistency.

ACKNOWLEDGMENTS

Michael and Stephen wish to thank all of the artists and studios who agreed to be case studies. Pete Kosowicz and Cornelia Parker, Peter Moseley, Ian Chamberlain, Valpuri Remling, Tamarind Institute, Ellen Berkenblit, Jarvis Boyland, Stephanie Turnbull and The Lemonade Press, Andreas Rüthi, Tom Hück, Anne Desmet, Laura Boswell, Sally Gimpson and Artizan Editions, Henrik Simonsen, Brian Rice, Zea Mays Printmaking and Richard Turnbull. We would also like to thank Neil Bousfield, Justin Diggle and Ivan Durt of the Frans Masereel Centrum for supplying images at short notice and all of the other artists who supplied images for the book. Both authors would particularly like to thank the staff at Cranfield Colours for their help towards this book, and Lauren Mabley for help with the technical illustrations.

Thanks must also go to Editors Jayne Parsons and Sara Simper at Herbert Press for their patience.

Finally, Stephen would particularly like to thank Sandy for all her help and forbearance, whilst writing just one more book!

LIST OF SUPPLIERS

A list of manufacturers and suppliers with a dedicated interest in printmaking. This list can never be exhaustive but is meant as a starting point to those searching for printmaking material manufacturers or those retailers who carry their own brand. Up-to-date lists are available under the 'where to buy' section on many manufacturers' websites.

UK

Cadisch
Cadisch.co.uk
Suppliers of AquaArt screen-printing inks and supplies.

Cranfield Colours Ltd
Cranfield-colours.co.uk
Manufacturers of traditional oil-based and Caligo Safe Wash printmaking inks.

Daler-Rowney
Daler-rowney.com
Manufacturers of System3 screen-printing inks.

Essdee
essdee.co.uk
Supplier of lino, scraperboard, etching tools, lino-printing tools and water-based inks.

Handprinted
Handprinted.co.uk
Supplier of relief and screen-printing ink, varnishes and additives, and provider of training and instruction.

Hawthorn Printmakers
Hawthornprintmaker.com
Supplier of presses, etching, lithography, relief and screen-printing ink, varnishes and additives, including their own brand of ink.

Intaglio Printmaker
intaglioprintmaker.com
Supplier of etching, lithography, relief and screen-printing ink, varnishes and additives, including their own brand of ink.

Jackson's Art Supplies
Jacksonsart.com
Supplier of etching, lithography, relief and screen-printing ink, varnishes and additives, including their own brand of water-based ink.

John Purcell Paper
Johnpurcell.net
UK supplier of TW Graphics screen-printing ink.

SISS Ink and Solvents
inkandsolvents.co.uk
Screen-printing supplies, including Sericol solvent inks and MagnaPrint AquaFlex.

T N Lawrence & Son
Lawrence.co.uk
Supplier of etching, lithography, relief and screen-printing ink, varnishes and additives, including their own brand of ink.

Wicked Printing Stuff
wickedprintingstuff.com
Manufacturers of WPS water-based paper-and-board ink for screen-printing.

EUROPE

Belgium

Sico Screen Inks
Sico-inks.com
Manufacturers of AS Aquaset water-based screen-printing ink.

Denmark

Aart de Vos
Aartdevos.dk
Supplier of printmaking materials.

Finland

Tempera
Tempera.com
Supplier of printmaking materials

France

Joop Stoop
joopstoop.com
Manufacturers of a range of printmaking inks including H2O screen-printing inks.

Lefranc Bourgeois
lefrancbourgeois.com
Owner of the Charbonnel brand of printmaking inks.

Germany

Gerstaecker
Gerstaecker.de
Branches throughout Europe supplying etching, lithography, relief and screen-printing ink, varnishes and additives, including their own brand of ink.

Netherlands

Polymetaal
polymetaal.nl
Manufacturer of presses and supplier of a range of printmaking equipment and supplies.

Norway

KEM
kem.no
Supplier of printmaking materials.

Spain

Grabadonline
grabadonline.com
Supplier of printmaking materials.

Sweden

IB Wahlström
Ibwahlstrom.se
Supplier of printmaking materials.

Switzerland

Lascaux
Lascaux.ch
Manufacturer of water-based screen-printing inks.

AMERICAS

USA

Blick Art Materials
Dickblick.com
Supplier of etching, lithography, relief and screen-printing ink, varnishes and additives, including their own brand of water-based ink.

Gamblin Artists' Colors
gamblincolors.com
Manufacturer of a range of printmaking inks and supplier of printmaking materials.

Hanco
Hancoink.com
Supplier of printmaking materials and the Hanco brand of inks.

Kremer Pigmente
kremer-pigmente.com
Suppliers of dry pigment and mica paste.

McClain's Printmaking Supplies
imcclains.com
Specialist importer and supplier of inks and materials to relief printmakers, including a range of Japanese printmaking materials.

Speedball
Speedballart.com
Manufacturer of a range of printmaking inks and printmaking materials, including water-based screen inks.

Takach Press
shop.takachpress.com
Manufacturer of printing presses and a supplier of a range of printmaking inks.

TW Graphics
Cosmexgraphics.com/tw_color.htm
Manufacturers of TW water-based screen-printing ink.

Brazil

Armazém da Gravura
Armazemdagravura.com.br
Specialist supplier of printmaking materials.

OCEANIA

Australia

Melbourne Etching Supplies
Mes.net.au
Supplier of a range of printmaking inks and ancillary products.

New Zealand

Aotearoa Art Supplies
aotearoaartsupplies.co.nz
Specialist printmaking material supplier

National Art Supplies
naskits.co.nz
Specialist printmaking material supplier.

ASIA

South Korea

Print Art Research Centre (PARC)
parc-printmaking.com
Specialist training centre and supplier of regional and European printmaking materials.

USEFUL WEBSITES

cfpr.uwe.ac.uk
The Centre for Print Research. A listing of all the research we undertake in regard to fine print at the University of the West of England, Bristol.

chemmanagement.ehs.com/9/ebinder
This website allows you to search by chemical name and company name. However, neither of the above MSDS sites are particularly easy to use.

www.cie.co.at
Commission Internationale de L'Eclairage (International Commission on Illumination).

www.eea.europa.eu/help/glossary/eea-glossary
European Environment Agency (EEA) multilingual environmental glossary. A useful source of acronym definitions relating to the environment.

www.gutenberg.de
Gutenburg Museum, Mainz, Germany.

www.handprint.com/HP/WCL/wcolor.html
The most useful website we have found to describe colour for artists. You need to delve a bit under the watercolour section.

www.hse.gov.uk/coshh
UK Government Health and Safety Executive COSHH (Control of Substances Hazardous to Health) information.

www.imprimerie.lyon.fr/en/edito/presentation_musee
Museum of Printing and the Book, Lyon.

www.pra-world.com
The Paint Research Association website contains information regarding the lightfastness of paint and how it is measured.

www.sbf.org.uk
The St Bride Printing Library is one of the specialist public reference libraries of the Corporation of London. Its world-famous collections cover printing and related subjects: paper and binding, graphic design and typography, typefaces and calligraphy, illustration and printmaking, publishing and bookselling, the social and economic aspects of the printing, book, newspaper and magazine trades. The Library's catalogue is available online here: stbridefoundation.soutron.net/Portal/Default/en-GB/Search/SimpleSearch

www.vam.ac.uk/info/national-art-library#search-the-library-catalogue
Victoria and Albert Museum, National Art Library.

BIBLIOGRAPHY

Adams, Irena Zdena, *Exploration of Water-based Inks in Fine Art Screenprinting*, D. Phil Thesis, Faculty of Art and Design, University of Ulster at Belfast, 1998.

Antreasian, Garo Z. and Clinton Adams, *The Tamarind Book of Lithography: Art & Techniques*, Harry N. Abrams Inc., New York, 1972.

Apps, E. A., *Printing Ink Technology*, Leonard Hill (Books) Ltd, London, 1958.

Ball, Philip, *Bright Earth: The Invention of Colour,* Vintage, London, 2008.

Bloy, C. H., *History of Printing Ink, Balls and Rollers, 1440–1850*, The Wynkyn De Worde Society/The Sandstone Press, London/New York, 1967.

Bosse, Abraham, *Traité de manières de gravure en taille-douce,* Paris, 1645, 1745 and Dover Publications, New York, 1982.

Boston, Ray, *The Essential Fleet Street: Its History & Influence*, Blandford, London, 1990.

Carter, Thomas Francis and Luther Carrington Goodrich, *Invention of Printing in China and Its Spread Westward*, 2nd Edition, Ronald Press, New York, 1955.

Chamberlain, Walter, *The Thames and Hudson Manual of Etching and Engraving*, Thames & Hudson, London, 1972.

Christie, Robert, *Colour Chemistry*, Royal Society of Chemistry, London, 2001.

CIE 1931, International Commission on Illumination, *Proceedings of the 8th Session*, Bureau Central de la CIE, Paris, 1931.

Clair, Colin, *A Chronology of Printing*, Praeger, New York, 1969.

Cumming, David, *Handbook of Lithography*, A&C Black, London, 1948.

Dobras, Wolfgang (ed.), *Gutenburg: Man of the Millennium: From a Secret Enterprise to the First Media Revolution,* Exhibition Catalogue, City of Mainz, 2000.

Fertel, Martin Dominique, *La Science pratique de l'imprimerie*, Hachette Livre, Paris, 2018.

Finlay, Victoria, *Colour: Travels Through the Paintbox*, Sceptre, London, 2002.

Gabra, G, and Hany N. Takla (eds), *Christianity and Monasticism in Upper Egypt: Volume 1: Akhmim and Sohag,* American University in Cairo Press, Cairo, 2008, pp.211–224.

Gage, John, *Colour and Culture: Practice and Meaning from Antiquity to Abstraction*, Thames & Hudson, London, 1993.

Gilmour, Pat, *The Mechanised Image: An Historical Perspective on 20th Century Prints,* Arts Council of Great Britain, London, 1978.

Gombrich, Ernst, *The Story of Art*, Phaidon Press, London, 1962.

Gross, Anthony, *Etching, Engraving and Intaglio Printing,* Oxford University Press, London, New York, 1970.

Hamber, Anthony, 'Communicating Colour: Advances in Reprographic Technology 1840–1967', in *Visual Resources*, XV, pp.355–370.

Hansard, Thomas Curson, *Typographica: An Historical Sketch of the Origin and Progress of the Art of Printing*, Baldwin, Cradock and Joy, London, 1825.

Haylock, Bradley, 'Beyond D.I.Y: On Risography and Publishing-as-practice', in *International Journal of the Book*, 8 (4), 2011, pp.119–128.

Hind, Arthur M., *An Introduction to the History of the Woodcut*, Dover Publications, New York, 1963.

Ikeda, M., 'The Fust and Schöffer Office and the Printing of the Two-Colour Initials in the 1457 Mainz Psalter', in Stijnman, Ad and Elizabeth Savage (eds), *Printing Colour 1400–1700*, Brill, Leiden/Boston, 2015, pp.65–75.

Kirsch, Russell A, 'SEAC and the Start of Image Processing at the National Bureau of Standards', in *IEEE Annals of the History of Computing*, 20(2), 1998, pp.7–13.

Lalanne, Maxime, trans. S. R. Koehler, *A Treatise on Etching,* Sampson, Low, Marston, Searle & Rivington, London, 1880.

Le, Hue P., 'Progress and Trends in Inkjet Printing Technology', in *Journal of Imaging Science and Technology*, 42(1), 1998, pp.49–62.

Le Blon, Jakob Christophe, *Coloritto; or the Harmony of Colouring in Painting: Reduced to Mechanical Practice Under Easy Precepts, and Infallible Rules*, London, 1725.

Lengwiler, Guido, *A History of Screen Printing: How an Art Evolved into an Industry,* ST Media Group International, Cincinnati, OH, 2013.

Lewis, Richard J., *Sax's Dangerous Properties of Industrial Materials*, 8th Edition, Van Nostrand Reinhold, New York, 1992.

Mairet, F-A., *Notice sur la lithography, ou l'art d'imprimer sur pierre,* Dijon, 1818.

Mayer, Ralph, *The Artist's Handbook of Materials and Techniques*, 5th Edition, Faber & Faber, London, 1991.

Mitchell, Charles Ainsworth and Thomas Cradock Hepworth, *INKS: Their Composition and Manufacture,* Charles Griffin and Company, London, 1904.

Moran J., *Printing Presses: History and Development from the 15th Century to Modern Times*, University of California Press, Berkeley California, 1973.

Moxon, Joseph, *Mechanick Exercises on the Whole Art of Printing 1683–1684*, Ed Davis. H. and Carter. H., Oxford University Press, London, 1962.

Ostroff, E., 'Etching, Engraving & Photography: History of Photomechanical Reproduction', in *The Journal of Photographic Science*, 17(4), 15 September, 1969, pp.65–80. DOI:10.1080/00223638.1969.11737488

Owen, David, *Copies in Seconds: How a Lone Inventor and an Unknown Company Created the Biggest Communication Breakthrough Since Gutenberg – Chester Carlson and the Birth of the Xerox Machine*, Simon and Schuster, New York, 2008.

Park, Hye Ok, 'The History of Pre-Gutenberg Woodblock and Movable Type Printing in Korea', *International Journal of Humanities and Social Science*, 4(9), 2014.

Pellew, C.E., 'Perkin's Discovery of Aniline Dyes', in *The Art World*, 3(3), December 1917, pp.222–225.

Reissland, Birgit, 'A Practical Guide to the Production of Black Pigments and the Preparation of Black Watercolours, 1350–1700', in J. Boulboullé and S Dupré, *Burgundian Black: Rewording Early Modern Colour Technologies,* EMC Imprint, Santa Barbara, 2022, preface.

Robinson, Stuart, *A History of Printed Textiles*, MIT Press, Cambridge Mass, 1969.

Rodari, Florian, *Anatomie de la couleur: l'invention de l'estampe en coleurs*, Biblioteque Nationale de France/Musee Olympique Lausanne, Paris, 1996.

Roque, Georges, 'Chevreul's Colour Theory and its Consequences for Artists', at www.colour.org.uk/wp-content/uploads/2017/10/Chevreuls-Law-F1-web-good.pdf, p.4.

Savage, William, *A Dictionary of the Art of Printing*, Longman, Brown, Green and Longman, London, 1948.

On the Preparation of Printing Ink; Both Black and Coloured, Longman, Reese, Orme, Brown, Green and Longman, London, 1822.

Practical Hints on Decorative Printing, Longman, Hurst, Rees, Orme and Brown, London, 1822.

Shestack, Alan, *Fifteenth-century Engravings of Northern Europe from the National Gallery of Art, Washington DC,* National Gallery of Art, Washington, DC, 1967.

Simmons, Rosemary and Katie Clemson, *The Complete Manual of Relief Printmaking,* Dorling Kindersley, London, 1988.

Stephens, John, *Screen Process Printing: A Practical Guide,* Blueprint, London, 1987.

Stijnman, Ad and Elizabeth Savage, eds, *Printing Colour 1400–1700: History, Techniques, Functions and Reception*s, Brill, Leiden/Boston, 2015.

Taniguchi, Yoko and Marine Cotte, *The Wall Paintings of Bamiyan, Afghanistan: Technology and Materials,* Archetype Publications, London, 2022.

Wiborg, Frank B., *Printing Ink: A History with a Treatise on Modern Methods of Manufacture and Use*, Harper & Brothers, New York, 1926.

ENDNOTES

Chapter 1

1 Thomas Carter, revised by L. Carrington Goodrich, *Invention of Printing in China and Its Spread Westward*, 2nd Edition, Ronald Press, New York, 1955.

2 Yi Xumei and Lu Xiuwen, 'The Calligraphy and Printing Cultural Heritage of Gansu – The Development of the Engraved Printing Process and Papermaking: An Archaeological Approach', in Susan M. Allen et al, (eds), *The History and Cultural Heritage of Chinese Calligraphy, Printing and Library Work*, K. G Saur, Berlin, New York, 2010, p.64. doi.org/10.1515/9783598441790.45

3 Hye Ok Park, 'The History of Pre-Gutenberg Woodblock and Movable Type Printing in Korea', in *International Journal of Humanities and Social Science*, 4(9), July 2014, p.10.

4 Carter, *Invention of Printing in China*, p.224.

5 Marjorie G. Wynne and A. Hyatt Mayor, 'The Art of the Playing Card', in *The Yale University Library Gazette*, 47(3), January 1973, pp.137–184.

6 Colin Clair, *A Chronology of Printing*, Praeger, New York, 1969, p.7.

7 Wynne and Mayor, 'The Art of the Playing Card', pp.137–184.

8 Yoko Taniguchi and Marine Cotte, *The Wall Paintings of Bamiyan, Afghanistan: Technology and Materials*, Archetype Publications, London, 2022, pp.67–92.

9 Ernst Gombrich, *The Story of Art*, Phaidon Press, London, 1962, p.240.

10 Joseph Moxon, *Mechanick Exercises: or, the Doctrine of Handy-works Applied to the Art of Printing; The Second Volumne*, London, 1683, plate 9.

11 Colin Bloy, *A History of Printing Ink, Balls and Rollers, 1440–1850,* Evelyn Adams and Mackay, London, 1967, p.102.

12 Gawdat Gabra and Hany N. Takla (eds), *Christianity and Monasticism in Upper Egypt: Volume 1: Akhmim and Sohag,* American University in Cairo Press, Cairo, 2008, pp.211–224.

13 *New Rylands Exhibition*, at: sites.manchester.ac.uk/bodies-emotions-material-culture/2022/10/10/new-rylands-exhibition-modern-research-technologies-reveals-stunning-insights-into-the-european-printing-revolution/ Accessed: 10 January, 2024

14 *The Woodpecking Factory: Victorian Illustrations by the Brothers Dalziel*, at: www.sussex.ac.uk/english/dalziel/the-woodpecking-factory-victorian-illustrations-by-the-brothers-dalziel/ Accessed: 10 January, 2024

15 Alan Shestack, *Fifteenth-century Engravings of Northern Europe from the National Gallery of Art, Washington DC*, National Gallery of Art, Washington, DC, 1967, p.260.

16 Arthur Mayger Hind, *Andrea Mantegna and the Italian Pre-Raphaelite Engravers*, W. Heinemann, London, 1911, p.10.

17 Ad Stijnman, 'Experiment and Trial: Technical Developments in 17th-century Intaglio Printmaking, an Overview', in *In Monte Artium, Journal of the Royal Library of Belgium* 3, pp.115–26. doi.org/10.1484/j.ima.1.102082 Accessed: 10 January, 2024.

18 François-Ambroise Mairet, *Notice sur la lithography, ou l'art d'imprimer sur pierre*, Dijon, 1818, p.18.

19 Bloy, *A History of Printing Ink*, pp.111–124.

20 Bloy, *A History of Printing Ink*, p.148.

21 Ana Gomez, *A Historical Essay on the Development of Flexography*, Thesis, Rochester Institute of Technology, 2000. repository.rit.edu/theses/3825 Accessed: 10 January, 2024

22 E. Ostroff, 'Etching, Engraving & Photography: History of Photomechnical Reproduction', in *The Journal of Photographic Science*, 17(4), 15 September, 1969, pp.65–80. DOI:10.1080/00223638.1969.11737488

23 Guido Lengwiler, *A History of Screen Printing: How an Art Evolved Into an Industry*, ST Media Group International, Cincinnati, Ohio, 2013, p.29.

24 Pat Gilmour, *The Mechanised Image: An Historical Perspective on 20th Century Prints*, Arts Council of Great Britain, London, 1978.

25 Zea Mays Printmaking, 'Flocculating Acrylics', at zeamaysprintmaking.podia.com/flocculating-acrylics

26 Jackson's Art, 'Acrylic Painting, Microplastics, and the Environment', at www.jacksonsart.com/blog/2023/09/28/acrylic-painting-rinse-water-microplastics and Golden Artist's Colors, Inc, 'Removing Water-Based Paint Solids from Rinse Water' at justpaint.org/removing-water-based-paint-solids-from-rinse-water

27 Elizabeth Jablonski et al, 'Conservation Concerns for Acrylic Emulsion Paints', in *Studies in Conservation*, 48, June 2003, pp.3–12. DOI: 10.1179/sic.2003.48. Supplement-1.3.

28 David Owen, *Copies in Seconds: How a Lone Inventor and an Unknown Company Created the Biggest Communication Breakthrough Since Gutenberg – Chester Carlson and the Birth of the Xerox Machine*, Simon and Schuster, New York, 2014.

29 Russell A. Kirsch, 'SEAC and the Start of Image Processing at the National Bureau of Standards', in *IEEE Annals of the History of Computing*, 20(2), 1998, pp.7–13.

30 Anthony Hamber, 'Communicating Colour: Advances in Reprographic Technology 1840–1967', in *Visual Resources*, XV, pp.355–370.

31 Hue P. Le, 'Progress and Trends in Inkjet Printing Technology', in *Journal of Imaging Science and Technology*, 42(1), 1998, pp.49–62.

32 Bradley Haylock, 'Beyond D.I.Y: On risography and publishing-as-practice', *in International Journal of the Book*, 8 (4), 2011, pp.119–128.

33 Mayumi Ikeda, 'The Fust and Schöffer Office and the Printing of the Two-Colour Initials in the 1457 Mainz Psalter', in Stijnman, A and E. Savage (eds), *Printing Colour 1400–1700*, Brill, Leiden/Boston, 2015, pp.65–75.

34 Jakob Christophe Le Blon, *Coloritto, London, 1725*.

35 Charles E. Pellew, 'Perkin's Discovery of Aniline Dyes', in *The Art World*, 3(3), December 1917, pp.222–225.

Chapter 2

36 Colin Bloy, *A History of Printing Ink, Balls and Rollers, 1440–1850,* Evelyn Adams and Mackay, London, 1967, pp.101–2.

37 Bloy, *History of Printing Ink*, p.66.

38 Anthony Gross, *Etching, Engraving and Intaglio Printing*, Oxford University Press, London, 1970, p.122.

39 Gross, *Etching*, p.123.

40 Colour Pigments Manufacturers Association at wordpress-600054-4734251.cloudwaysapps.com/news-resources/pigment-faqs

41 *The New York Times*, 'Camden Paint Factory Blows Up', at: www.nytimes.com/1940/07/31/archives/camden-paint-factory-blows-up-10-feared-dead-205-hurt-in-fire.html

Chapter 3

42 Jakob Christoph Le Blon, *Coloritto, or, The Harmony of Colouring in Painting*, London, 1725, p.6.

43 Georges Roque, 'Chevreul's Colour Theory and its Consequences for Artists', at www.colour.org.uk/wp-content/uploads/2017/10/Chevreuls-Law-F1-web-good.pdf, p.4.

44 Stephen Westland, 'The CIE System', in Janglin Chen et al, *Handbook of Visual Display Technology*, Springer International, Cham, 2016, p.1.

Chapter 4

45 Birgit Reissland, 'A Practical Guide to the Production of Black Pigments and the Preparation of Black Watercolours, 1350–1700', in J. Boulboullé and S Dupré, *Burgundian Black: Rewording Early Modern Colour Technologies*, EMC Imprint, Santa Barbara, 2022, p10.

46 Birgit Reissland, 'Charred Vine Lees and Pomace', at burgundianblack.tome.press/chapter/preface/#vinelees

47 Colin Bloy, *A History of Printing Ink, Balls and Rollers, 1440–1850,* Evelyn Adams and Mackay, London, 1967, p.46.

48 IPCS International Programme on Chemical Safety, 'White Spirit (Stoddard Solvent) Health and Safety Guide', at www.inchem.org/documents/hsg/hsg/hsg103.htm

49 Anthony Gross, *Etching, Engraving and Intaglio Printing*, Oxford University Press, London, 1970, p.122.

Chapter 5

50 Colin Bloy, *A History of Printing Ink, Balls and Rollers, 1440–1850*, Evelyn Adams and Mackay, London, 1967, p.110.

Chapter 7

51 John Stephens, *Screen Process Printing: A Practical Guide*, Blueprint, London, 1987, p.116.

52 Irena Zdena Adams, *Exploration of Water-based Inks in Fine Art Screenprinting*, D. Phil Thesis, Faculty of Art and Design, University of Ulster at Belfast, 1998, p.56.

53 Golden Artists Colors, Inc, 'Removing Water-based Paint Solids from Rinse Water', at justpaint.org/removing-water-based-paint-solids-from-rinse-water

54 Catherine Aiello and Lydia Giangregorio (2021) and Margo Temple and Olivia Arau McSweeney (2020), 'Flocculating Acrylics' at zeamaysprintmaking.podia.com/flocculating-acrylics

55 Aiello et al, 'Flocculating Acrylics'.

Chapter 9

56 www.stopdrowningnow.org/drowning-statistics